SUZANNE SIMMONS-LEWIS

WHO AM I?

Swap Your Straight Jacket for a Bespoke Suit

How to unlock your core identity and free yourself to be who you really are

Valery,
Best Wishes,
your best is yet to come!
Suzanne / xxx.

DEDICATION

This book is dedicated to women everywhere who want to swap their straight jacket for a bespoke suit.

WHO AM I?

Swap Your Straight Jacket for a Bespoke Suit

First edition printed in 2023 in the United Kingdom

For permission requests, email the publisher: info@suzannesimmonslewis.com

Names and identifying details have been changed for all client case studies and illustrations contained in this book to protect their identities and preserve the confidentiality of the coaching relationship.

ISBN: 978-1-7394186-2-5 (Hardback)
ISBN: 978-1-7394186-0-1 (Paperback)
ISBN: 978-1-7394186-1-8 (e-Book)

A catalogue record of this book is available from the British Library

Design: Nick McKay
Sub editor: Philippa Batty

WWW.SUZANNESIMMONSLEWIS.COM

ACKNOWLEDGEMENTS

This book would not have been conceived without the wonderful clients I've had the pleasure of working with and the privilege of seeing their transformation first hand. I am grateful for their honesty, openness and willingness to show vulnerability, in addition to trusting in the transformation process and in me as their coach.

My late father, who supported and believed in me was instrumental in enabling this book to be published. He invested in my career as a journalist and coach and was a positive force throughout my adult life. Even after death, I am still learning from his example.

My close friends Chinyere and Melanie for their constant encouragement and belief in me throughout this endeavour. Nick and Philippa for their stellar expertise in design and sub-editing. Soulla and Richard for their review and feedback. And, my wonderful son who continually inspires me.

Most of all, my Heavenly Father who gave me the idea, inspiration, motivation and insight for this book, enabling me to see His heart for women to transform into who they were created to be, uniquely.

Contents

Preface

THIS STRAIGHT JACKET DOESN'T FIT!

WHO AM I?

Who am I beneath the gloss and façade?
Behind the status and the smile
Who am I?
When all is stripped away?
The layers of possessions
The public face

Who am I, if not for a day, a mother, a wife, sister and friend?
Who would I be, without the chorus of worries that plague me?

Who can I be?
If I could break free of childhood demons that paralyse me
From fully moving on to live without the limitations of a childhood long gone

Who would I be?
If healed from the heartache and betrayal, living with the enemy
Who could be, if I fully step outside the box of expectations imposed on me?

Who am I then? I need to know so I can embrace the future road
How I long to break free, and finally see the divine path for my destiny
The hardest thing it seems is to know myself and embrace the gifts that I possess
To break free from the fears and mindless cares
To see my light and live right there
Who am I then?
Lord, help me find ME.

I wrote this poem on a warm summers evening in Cyprus in early September 2009.

It was the first holiday I'd had without my husband since having our son, and I approached it with a sense of adventure, and a bit of apprehension. How would I manage our six-year-old son on my own in another country? I questioned my ability to do this, even though I have always been independently minded and very resourceful.

It would seem becoming a mother had impacted my confidence and belief on a subconscious level. I was only vaguely aware of a feeling of being disconnected with my true self. To be fair, I didn't really know who that was before then, I only thought I did. But in reality, my belief about my identity was tied up with my achievements, career and goals that I had set for myself, along with thoughts about the person I thought *I wanted to become*, and how I would have to change and conform to achieve this.

But there was something bubbling away on the inside of me, something that was curious, dissatisfied and needing to find direction – a NEW and authentic direction.

As I lay on the bed, I was re-evaluating.

You see, I *always* had a plan and set goals for my life and career. After becoming a mother, for the first time, I felt cast adrift for a while, I could no longer define myself through work or outward activities, or my five-year plan. I had a new identity to absorb, which required more flexibility.

I was learning more about myself on this holiday, firstly because I had done something I wasn't sure I'd be able to do which ended up being an adventure, and secondly, I had time to reflect in a different environment on the inner frustrations of my life at the time.

So, on that warm and dusky evening, I wrote this poem to express my need to find new purpose and relevancy, from a deeper more authentic place.

Little did I know this poem, which was really my prayer, set a catalyst of things in motion. God set to work and has not only provided answers to finding myself – but enabled me to guide numerous women through this journey of transformation to discover who they really are and live out of the truest expression of themselves.

"I AM, TWO OF THE MOST POWERFUL WORDS: FOR WHAT YOU PUT AFTER THEM WILL SHAPE YOUR REALITY."

Introduction

MESSAGE TO WOMEN

"YOU FIND PEACE, NOT BY REARRANGING THE CIRCUMSTANCES OF YOUR LIFE, BUT BY REALISING WHO YOU ARE AT THE DEEPEST LEVEL."

ECKHART TOLLE

WHO AM I?

There may be many significant points in the road map of your life, when you have asked yourself this question; whether it's navigating yourself through school and the peer pressures associated with it, finding your way in the pecking order of your family hierarchy, being the *ideal* partner or even assuming a certain demeanour at work.

Knowing who you REALLY are, and being able to answer that question in an informed and honest way is the key to finding your purpose and achieving fulfilment and inner peace.

We live in a society that is constantly clamouring to tell us who we *should be*, what we *should aspire to*, or what stereotype or expectation *we should emulate* that will build our self-esteem and enable us to *fit in*.

There are so many issues – inward and outward – that impact our perceptions of ourselves, it can feel like walking a tightrope over a minefield. In the absence of knowing who you really are, it is easy to get swept away on the tide of expectation, hiding behind the mask of acceptance. It seems almost normal to get sucked into this, believing you should fulfil the expectations of yourself held by trusted people and society at large, in order to cement your belonging to a social group, your family or even to accept yourself.

But this takes a lot of energy without any meaningful result.

These pressures – many of which are self-imposed or have existed under your conscious radar and never been challenged – can pull your around like a puppet. In effect, you are sleepwalking through your own life; feeling restless and unfulfilled, but unable to put your finger on exactly what the problem is.

Until this is challenged and brought under microscopic introspection, you will never be truly happy trying to morph into what you think you should be. It is better to work on discovering who you really are and your unique strengths and natural talents. This will make the biggest difference to your ability to live your best life and positively impact the world around you.

"ONE OF THE GREATEST TRAGEDIES IN LIFE IS TO LOSE YOUR OWN SENSE OF SELF AND ACCEPT THE VERSION OF YOU THAT IS EXPECTED BY EVERYONE ELSE."

K L TOTH

LAYING STRONG FOUNDATIONS

Living behind a false mask is a life of instability that puts you on shaky ground. If your foundation is incomplete, everything that is built on that foundation will fail. In construction it is called groundwork: whenever a new building is to be erected, or even a new house extension, groundwork begins. It is a process of digging new foundations, several feet beneath the surface of the ground to ensure that a firm foundation can be laid before any structure can be erected. Similarly, we all need a period of honest reckoning, excavating through the layers of *persona* to lay a robust and solid foundation from which to build on.

Discovering your true identity is like building your house on the strongest possible foundation.

We are all unique and were not created to fit specific pre-existing moulds. To fulfil your truest expression of yourself, you must be in tune with your real motivations and values and be able to freely express your talents without the fear of rejection. This place is the springboard to achieving genuine success.

This is not a quick fix solution, but it is perfectly doable and even enjoyable! The goal is to uncover your unique identity and release the real person inside – the person you have always been but didn't know it – not give you another, more comfortable mask to put on.

In my experience of coaching women on various issues of personal development and careers, there is a common theme around identity. Some key questions not answered before the coaching journey are significant contributors to personal identity crises:

- Who am I?
- Whose expectations am I fulfilling?
- What DO I really want? (Opposed to "what SHOULD I really want?")
- What's missing?
- What are my unique skills and talents?
- Have I given myself permission to use them?

- Have I even given them recognition or credibility?
- What is stopping me?
- What is my purpose?

Once these questions are addressed, progress is much quicker and more dynamic, my clients usually fly through the coaching process when the foundation has been laid well.

The journey needn't be a difficult one. This book provides a bespoke approach enabling you to dig deeper, helping you to understand what's going on inside, and identify what has led you down your current path. It will guide you to create a personalised road map for your future and help you deal with the road blocks preventing you from being your true self, creating a firm foundation and catalyst for change. And then, unveiling your *unique core identity* and journeying with you to reveal your *authentic purpose.*

Your raison d'être.

> "THERE IS NO GREATER GIFT YOU CAN GIVE OR RECEIVE THAN TO HONOUR YOUR CALLING. IT'S WHY YOU WERE BORN AND HOW YOU BECOME MOST TRULY ALIVE."
>
> **OPRAH WINFREY**

How many times have you put off doing an important thing in your life, or giving birth to that secret passion that has always been drawing you? How many times have you made excuses about why something important (and often challenging) can be disregarded for another time? How often have you put the needs of others who are fulfilling their purpose before your own?

If you are fortunate enough to reach your twilight years, don't be the person spending them in regret, full of "I wish I should haves". We all have a unique purpose inside of us waiting to be realised, something that will make a difference to your life and the lives of others. Your gift to yourself and the world. It all starts with understanding who you really are.

It's time to rewrite your script.

WHAT'S IN IT FOR YOU?

"THE VOYAGE OF DISCOVERY IS NOT IN SEEKING NEW LANDSCAPES BUT IN HAVING NEW EYES."

MARCEL PROUST

If you can relate to one or more of the scenarios below and desire meaningful change, this book is for you.

- Feeling trapped on a treadmill going nowhere
- Feeling like something is missing from your life
- Insecure, seeking validation and acceptance in the wrong places
- Lacking confidence to pursue your dreams
- People pleasing, unable to say "no" for fear of rejection
- In unhealthy relationships
- Suffocated by the apron strings
- Unsure of your worth and value
- Needing a new more fulfilling direction
- Going through a period of change (kids growing up, divorce)
- Needing healing and inner peace
- Paralysed by rejection
- Losing the battle against stress and burnout.

I take women on a journey of transformation to get to the core of who they really are to live a genuine life with passion, clarity and purpose. The process involves breaking free from the mask of acceptance and limiting beliefs to develop confidence, personal growth, impact, healing and inner peace. You will recognise your true value and potential, unlocking your powerful unique strengths and natural talents and give yourself permission to use them.

The prize? Freedom to swap your straight jacket for a bespoke suit, living out of the truest expression of yourself.

Are you ready to embark on your journey of transformation?

You will learn:

- Who you REALLY are and why you act in the way you do
- What truly motivates and inspires you
- How to identify and overcome the stumbling blocks that often enslave you
- How to unlock your unique potential while staying true to who you are
- Your unique purpose and how to take the required steps to live an authentic, intentional life.

Your pledge

"Rome wasn't built in a day" and undoubtably authentic transformation takes time, but it is completely achievable. However, your desire for transformation needs to outweigh your level of satisfaction with your current situation.

Are you willing to challenge yourself, face your fears and ask and answer questions you haven't asked yourself before?

Can you answer yes to the following statements?

- I am fully willing to do the work required to get me where I want to go.
- I am willing to stop or change the self-defeating behaviours that limit my success.
- I am willing to try new things even if I am not 100% convinced they will work.
- I am willing to persevere in taking consistent action towards my goals, regardless of how immediate the results are.
- I am committed to being honest with myself, while treating myself with kindness.
- I am committed to my personal transformation and will make time to invest in myself.

If the answer is yes, then welcome aboard.
Carpe diem.

"THE GREATEST DISCOVERY IN LIFE IS SELF-DISCOVERY. UNTIL YOU FIND YOURSELF YOU WILL ALWAYS BE SOMEONE ELSE. BECOME YOURSELF."

DR MILES MUNROE

HOW TO READ THIS BOOK

This book is written as a carefully integrated whole to be read in its entirety from beginning to end in *chronological* order. The core identity model and related concepts builds knowledge in sequence. Each chapter relying on you the reader to have assimilated learning from the previous chapter.

To benefit from the transformation that is the promise of this book, it is important for you to complete all of the exercises and reflective actions in *each chapter* and integrate what you have learned into your daily life. It is not enough to merely acquire knowledge, for real transformation to take place your new knowledge and insights must be followed by action.

The butterfly symbol to the left indicates where there is a practical exercise or reflective action to complete.

As you travel along this journey, I encourage you to share what you have learned with receptive loved ones and close friends. This helps to embed your learning and can offer new insights as it triggers thought-provoking conversations.

Keep a journal to record your thoughts, feelings and learning. Over time, this reflective practice will prove to be an important tool in helping you to gain clarity and understanding. It will also be tangible evidence of your personal growth.

PDF downloads of the more detailed practical exercises are also available from my website: **www.suzannesimmonslewis.com**

Part One

CORE IDENTITY DEFINITION

"We search for everything we believe we don't have, not knowing that everything we are looking for is already inside us. We are born with it."

MIGUEL RUIZ

Chapter 1

WHO DO YOU THINK YOU ARE?

"IN THE SOCIAL JUNGLE OF HUMAN EXISTENCE, THERE IS NO FEELING OF BEING ALIVE WITHOUT A SENSE OF IDENTITY."

ERIK ERIKSON

IDENTITY CONFUSION

When it comes to understanding who you are or defining your identity, the majority of people will struggle to come up with a unifying concept of what this means.

This is because there is no singular dictionary definition of the word: and herein lies the problem. The word "identity" is used in so many interchangeable ways, it's no wonder there is confusion around an individual's understanding of a concept of their own identity.

Google the "definition of identity" and multiple responses are listed. These range from self-concept, cultural, ethnic and religious identity to professional identity, group expression, national identity and digital identity.

For the purposes of this book, I will list some of the most relevant definitions, although flawed, they will illustrate how understanding who you really are [self-identity] is often interpreted in ways that lead to confusion and take the focus away from a real excavation of your true self.

DEFINITIONS

- The fact of *being* who or what a person or thing is.
- *Characteristics* determining who or what a person or thing is.[1] A *sense of self*, providing sameness and continuity in a personality over time.
- Who someone is: the *qualities* and *beliefs* that make a *person or group* different from others.[2]
- The *set of characteristics* by which a person or thing is definitely recognisable or known.[3]
- The awareness that an *individual or group* has of being a *distinct persisting entity*
- Self-identity: the qualities and beliefs, *personality, looks* and *expressions* that make a *person or a group.*
- One's *self-image* [mental model of oneself] self-esteem and individuality.
- In cognitive psychology: the capacity for *self-reflection* and the awareness of self.
- Social identity: a social category, a set of persons marked by a label and distinguished by rules deciding membership and (alleged) characteristic features or attributes.[4]
- How one views oneself as both a person and in relation to other people, ideas and nature.

Notice, some of the definitions relate to an individual's *personal identity* and to *group identity*, and how the term is used interchangeably.

Although useful, none of these definitions are complete, or give a full picture of what it means to define who you really are as a unique individual. But they do give an indication of ways in which your core identity can become distorted, through the pressure to conform to external standards and expectations of social, cultural, ethnic and professional groups. In many cases, group identity takes preference like a magnetic compass with a subconscious belief that this external method is the true marker to understanding and defining one's identity.

In sociology this is defined as *identity negotiation*. It relates to the learning of social roles through personal experience: how a person negotiates with society at large regarding the meaning of his or her identity. This is a common attempt to define who you are through external influences.

However, there can be a conflict between conforming to the values and behaviours of a particular group and being who you really are.

Peer pressure is a commonly used word, but it encapsulates the intense demands placed on people to conform and be the same to fit in and be accepted. Even if this means being the "square peg in a round hole".

Although appearing neat and tidy, there are problems with group definitions that seek to conform. Society wants to categorise, label, make easily identifiable and understood and promote sameness, often reducing things to their most basic to find synergy. But how many people have done amazing things, conforming and being the same? I can't think of one, because they are not recorded in the annals of history.

THE IMPORTANCE OF BEING UNIQUE

In contrast, there are individuals who have achieved incredible things, changed history or broken world records because they did not subscribe to the limitations placed on them by the contemporary beliefs of their time. They were individuals in tune with who they were and courageous enough to believe and honour their uniqueness. This enabled them to connect with and pursue their purpose regardless of the naysayers around them.

> "THE MAN WHO HAS NO IMAGINATION HAS NO WINGS."
>
> **MOHAMED ALI**

As a young teenager I remember watching The Olympics and being mesmerised by Florence Griffith Joyner, also known as "Flo Jo". This American sprinter was a force of nature. Not only did she dominate her sport, she did it with a panache and individualism I had never witnessed in sprinting before. Flo Jo broke both Olympic and world records with flair. Her inventive bold fashion and colour choices along with her flamboyantly decorated nails and full makeup, ensured she stood out not only for her ground-breaking performances, but her irrepressible personality also shone through.

I had never taken much of an interest in athletics before 1984, but after this, I was hooked. I saw Flo Jo as multi-dimensional; no longer just another talented athlete on the elite conveyor belt competing for their country. Everything became more interesting.

Flo Jo's unique style gave athletes the confidence to express themselves through their sporting attire and personal appearance (hair, nails, makeup) when competing. The impact was such that this practice is commonplace today.

These days, lucrative sponsorship deals await athletes who are successful in their sport and at the very top of the tree are those athletes whose unique personality shines through, such as the charismatic Usain Bolt.

But Flo Jo was a trailblazer; and while many athletes have emulated her style statement in subsequent years, no one has matched her dominance on the track. After more than 30 years she is still considered the fastest woman of all time, with her 200m Olympic record and her 100m World record still standing.

Flo Jo did not follow the pack in neither her training regime nor appearance, and her unique approach set her apart for success. To this day, some naysayers still refuse to accept that her achievements on the track were humanly possible, but when you have the inner confidence to express who you are and the ability to live right there, anything is possible.

At some point in your life and quite possibly more than once, someone will have asked you what you want to be or you would have read advice somewhere about *how you can become* whatever it is you want to be. The implication here is that *you can choose who you want to be* and how you will conform to that to fit into society.

But with *true identity* the focus should be on *who you are,* not *what you do* for a living or what social groups you belong to. The "what" is changeable, and using this as definer for personal identity is a significant contributor to identity crises, which leads to a host of problems that will be covered throughout this book.

> "IF YOU DON'T HAVE AN IDENTITY, YOU DON'T HAVE A CHOICE. YOU'RE LIKE A JUKEBOX IN THE CORNER. SOMEBODY STROLLS OVER, DROPS IN A FEW QUARTERS, PRESSES A BUTTON AND YOU PLAY THEIR TUNE."
>
> **STEADMAN GRAHAM**

We are all unique, and so to help you reach the core of who you really are, I have used my own definition of personal identity, which forms the basis of this book. Knowing this is the key to true freedom, purpose, fulfilment and peace.

Your *core identity* is: your unique personality, strengths and natural talents, passions and motivations, your guiding beliefs and core values. It's what's on the inside, your unique DNA. Through this you will find your true purpose. Your core identity flows from the *inside outwards*. Not as a social construct or through identity negotiation, but as the truest expression of yourself, unencumbered by negative beliefs and the conforms of social groups and wider society.

This may be a hard concept to grasp, particularly if you have spent your entire life up until this point defining yourself through identity negotiation – who you are in relation to various groups you belong or aspire to – but the following illustrations will help you shift your paradigm.[5]

THE CORE OF THE MATTER

Think of your true identity as something you are born with; all the attributes that exist inside of you in *seed* form, before they have been tampered with by external factors.

Envisage an apple with the seeds at its core. The apple gets its DNA from the seed. The seeds are planted, from this inward activity, the core is developed followed by the *apple*, which is the final outward expression of what is situated on the inside.

The characteristics of the apple's core contains the DNA that is expressed through the outer layers of the fruit, growing from the inside outward.

While external influences (soil rain, sun, pollination) will affect how the apple grows and its final appearance and quality, it will not lose its identity as an apple because of these factors. Only its quality will be variable.

Crucially, the apple seed does not develop its identity as an apple AFTER it has grown and is recognisable as an apple, its identity is at its core.

At *your core is your true self,* from which your real identity should grow. The outward expression of your identity should be dominated by the flow from your inner core, not the other way round.

The problem I have found is that many people do not know who they really are, because their identity has been nurtured from external influences and social groups that expect them to conform to be accepted. Therefore, they end up living caricature lives, being inauthentic and pre-occupied with perceptions of who they ought to be to gain acceptance, rather than exploring who they really are and recognising the value, skills and unique talents in which they will flourish.

They develop an *alter ego*[6] that enslaves them. They make up for what they perceive to be their deficits in an exaggerated version of what they think they should be, based on society's perspective. Trying hard to project their "ideal self", when all the while their real self is fading, becoming more lost on the inside.

The result? A huge chasm exists between who they really are and who they *think* they should be. Time and energy are exhausted trying to morph into a distorted version of whoever they think they should be.

NATURE VERSUS NURTURE

Your core identity is also distinct from nurture. The "nature versus nurture" debate concerns whether human identity and behaviour is determined by a person's upbringing and environment (external factors) or by a person's genes (prewiring, DNA).

Core Identity Components

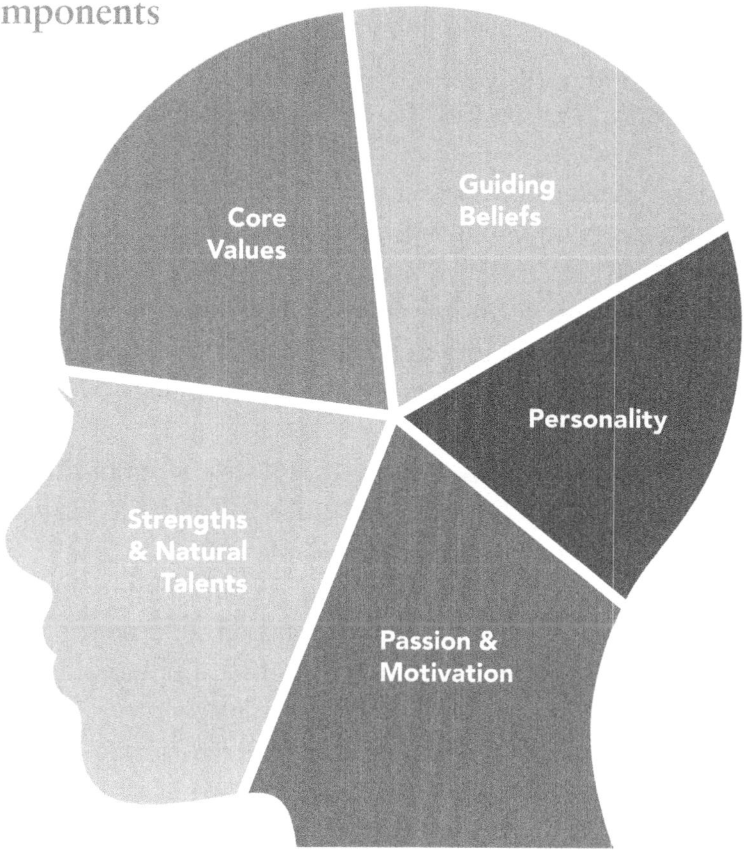

Nature: DNA

- Personality: likes and dislikes, how you engage with the world
- Passion and motivation: what fascinates you and gives you energy
- Strengths and natural talents: the things you do with ease
- Core values: what is most important to you
- Guiding beliefs: your inner filters and view of the world.

DNA is the core of an individual's innate attributes where authentic identity is expressed. Studies confirm that genes/DNA, including psychological traits such as intelligence and personality make a substantial contribution to identity.[7]

These elements weave a rich tapestry of who you are, that you may never get to know, savour or enjoy, because of the pressures to conform to who you think you should be and the intense focus on the external elements that will achieve this to gain the approval of others.

Nurture: influences of upbringing and environment

- Parents, peers, social groups and society
- Occupation and accepted social norms that accompany it
- Childhood positive and negative experiences
- Beliefs we hold about ourselves (true or false)
- Cultural and religious norms and expectations.

While a person's overall behaviour, social and emotional skills and wellbeing are influenced a great deal by nurture, it does not define the innate core identity of a person.

Still sceptical? Think of a baby, they are a blank canvas to be nurtured. The type of nurturing will depend on a number of factors including where they are born, how they are raised and by whom. But there will be many innate characteristics that they display independently from the start that convey their core identity. At this point, nurture will not have had a chance to lead them towards accepted cultural, social and religious standards and expectations.

The seed of their core identity is already there, but how it is able to express itself will depend on a number of factors, to which the nurturing environment plays a key part.

A good way to see the core identity as distinct from the impact of nurture is to look at siblings from the same family. Although each one is born to the same parents and grows up in the same environment, they will not be clones of each other. Each will display their individual personality, likes, dislikes, skills and abilities. I have never seen two siblings with identical abilities and personalities, not even twins!

While nurture plays a key role in how a person develops and improves as an individual, its influence is most beneficial when nurtured from the right foundation. At the very least there is an awareness and understanding of the core identity, which points to the correct direction of travel.

HOW IS OUTWARD NON-AUTHENTIC IDENTITY INFLUENCED?

In the absence of knowing what your core identity is, society provides many substitutes like a pick and mix jar of "who do you want to be?" People wear masks all day like ill-fitting shoes, tantamount to straight jackets in the often-subconscious belief that they must compensate for who they already are because it is not enough.

Social media is the latest powerful vehicle to fuel a movement of insincere portrayals of the "perfect self". Those who subscribe to it either consciously or subconsciously are the recipients of intense pressure for acceptance, validation and conformity. We are presented with edited versions of individuals deemed acceptable to the world. Many people are suffering under the torture of this impossible fantasy like a steam roller threatening to flatten anything in its path.

The following quote from the late Cheslie Corrinne Kryst, an American television correspondent, model, and former Miss USA (2019) highlights this contradiction beautifully:

"My Instagram is my highlights reel and I want to look my best when I share a look at my life, my fun, and the body I am proud of. But that's all it is. A fine-tuned glimpse into a moment in time. Don't allow what you see on here to make you forget that I am incredibly flawed; I simply chose not to share those flaws in a photo.

"And definitely don't compare your own flaws to what you see in this picture, or any others on my page. It's not fair to compare

100% of yourself, your good days, bad days and everything in between, to a highly curated fraction of me on my good days."

There are various explanations to how society has got here, but ultimately the root lies in the absence of having a strong foundation for your core identity. Without this, people are likely to go with whichever way the wind is blowing.

The majority of women I meet before coaching have defined their identities based on outward factors in their social environments [occupation, relationships status, financial assets, popularity, belonging], in addition to their perceptions of their self-image.[8] Combined elements from these, lead to what I call *outward non-authentic identity*, because they don't give the full picture, and in most cases present a distortion of the facts (no reliance on the core identity/DNA). These elements are not a reliable definer of core identity because they are distorted and turbulent, the constant changes in society's trends and standards, "keeping up with the Joneses" can be exhausting.

But, when all is stripped away, what's left?

> "We are each gifted in a unique and important way. It is our privilege and our adventure to discover our own special light."
>
> **MARY DUNBAR**

Before you embark in this journey of transformation, I've added the following story to inspire you. It illustrates the power of what can be achieved when you have the courage to be who you really are.

In 1954, Roger Bannister became the first person to run a four-minute mile, something everyone believed to be an impossible feat. In addition to being a great athlete, Bannister was an innovator and change agent of his time, teaching many that "impossible" really is just a word.

Runners had been chasing the goal seriously since at least 1886. The challenge involved the most brilliant coaches and gifted athletes in North America, Europe, and Australia, but the elusive four minutes had always beaten them. It had become as much a psychological barrier as a physical one.

But Bannister was unconventional. He was an individual freethinker: a full-time student who had little use for coaches, therefore devising his own system for race-preparation. The British press constantly ran stories criticising his "lone wolf" approach and urged him to adopt a more conventional method to training and coaching.

The experts believed they knew the precise conditions the record could be broken; perfect weather, 68 degrees and no wind. On a particular kind of track – hard, dry clay, and in front of a huge boisterous crowd urging the runner on to his best-ever performance. But Bannister did it on a cold day, on a wet track, at a small meet in Oxford, England, before a crowd of just a few thousand people.

Once people saw it could be done, they did it too. Just 46 days after Bannister's feat, John Landy, an Australian runner broke the barrier again. In the following last half-century, more than a thousand runners have conquered a barrier that had once been considered hopelessly out of reach.

The runners of the past had been held back by a mindset that said they could not surpass the four-minute mile. When that limit was broken, the others saw that they could do something they had previously thought "impossible".

Bannister followed his passion and stayed true to who he was, enabling him to achieve the impossible. When you understand who you really are and have the courage to live out of it, you too will be able to venture into unchartered waters and achieve your own impossible dreams.

> "No one can say, 'You must not run faster than this, or jump higher than that.' The human spirit is indomitable."
>
> **ROGER BANNISTER**

Let's Begin!

Practical exercise

CORE INSIGHT ACTION

REFLECTION

- What factors do you recognise have influenced your understanding of your identity to date?
- Which outward influences (nurture/self-image) have you used to define yourself?
- How has this informed your understanding of who you think you are?
- How has this impacted the choices and behaviour you are aware of?
- Make a note of your responses and the subsequent insights you've gained in your journal.

YOUR MASK

We all wear masks at some time in our lives. The problem comes when masks become the norm and you lose yourself in the process. It is important to have self-awareness about the masks you wear and the reasons behind it. Recognising this is one way to make sure that they do not gain control over your true self. It is also a good starting point from which to measure your progress as you work your way through this book.

- Illustrate your **public face** with what you think you project publicly in general (true or false)

- Illustrate **behind the mask** with what you keep hidden (what you really think and feel)
- Use whatever words, images and colours you like to illustrate both masks.

A template of the mask can be downloaded from my website: **www.suzannesimmonslewis.com**

The Mask

Where am I now?

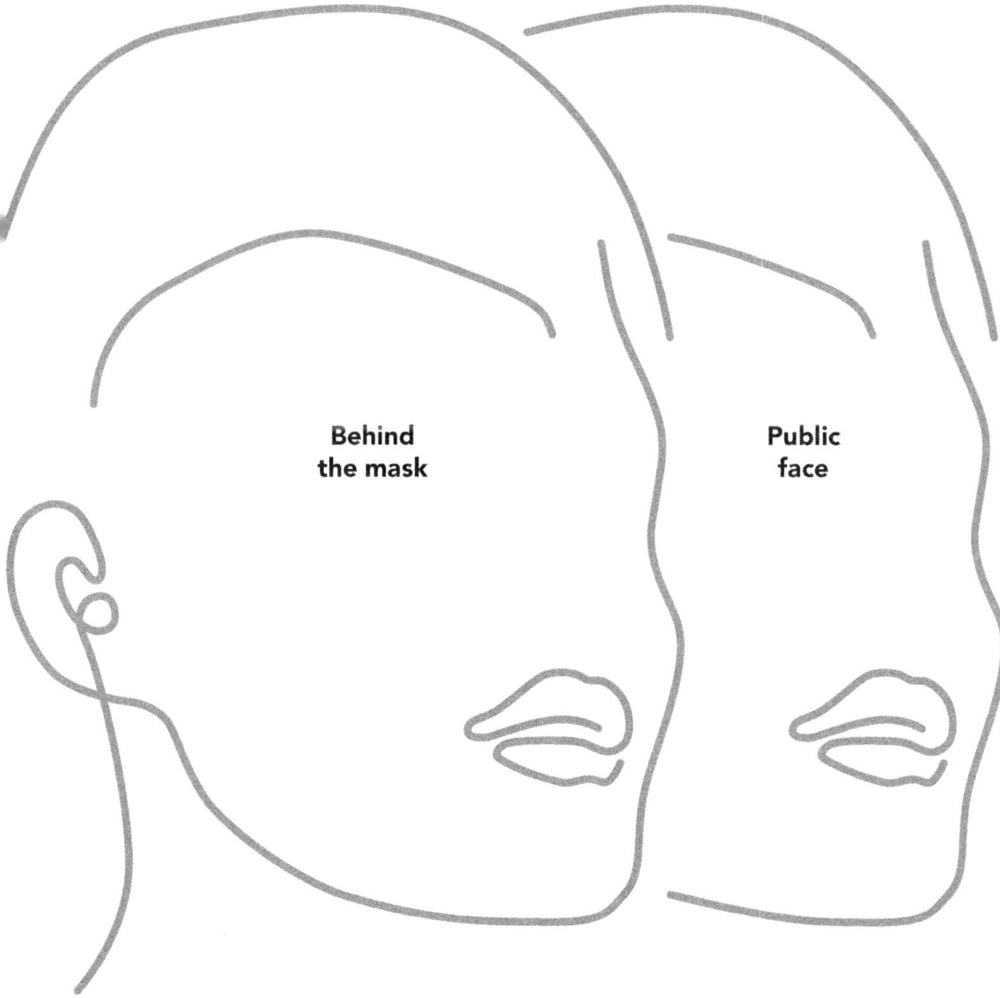

REVIEW

Practical exercise

Compare both masks and answer the following questions:

- Where is the synergy?
- Where are there significant inconsistences?
- What areas need work?
- What do I want to change?
- What is missing?
- What would I like to see *behind the mask* that isn't there now?
- Record your learning in your journal.

THE CORE IDENTITY MODEL

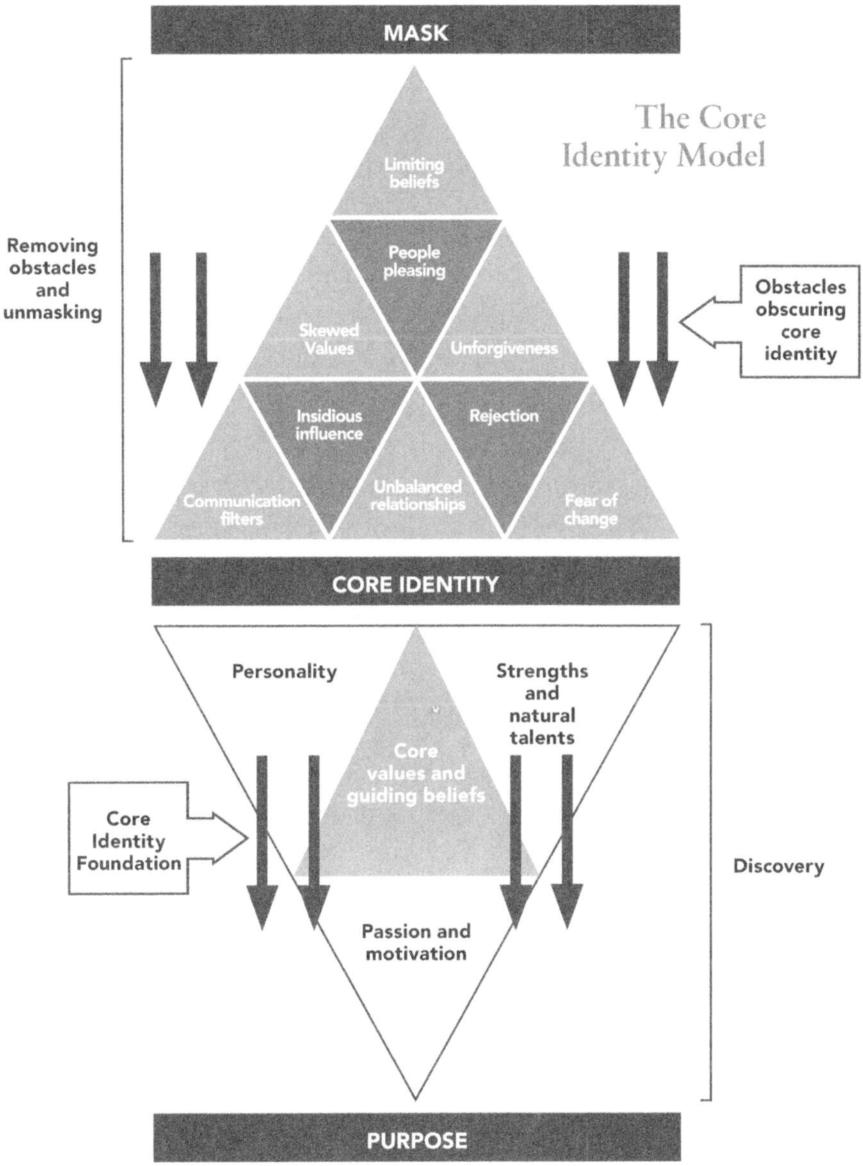

I created this model to illustrate the process of unlocking your core identity, which is the basis of this book.

The mask is the public face that keeps much of the real you hidden.

The mask is propped up by the obstacles that obscure your core identity from its true expression:

- Limiting beliefs
- Skewed values
- People pleasing
- Communication filters
- Unforgiveness
- Insidious influence
- Rejection
- Unbalanced relationships
- Fear of change.

Your core identity sits beneath the obstacles and consists of your:

- Personality
- Core values
- Guiding beliefs
- Strengths and natural talents
- Passion and motivation.

Your *core identity* is unlocked when the obstacles supressing its expression are exposed and dealt with. An unmasking occurs.

The *discovery phase* follows; connecting with the *real you,* free from the obstacles that suppressed your true self.

Your core identity is the foundation that leads you towards your authentic purpose.

Part Two

OBSTACLES

"If you find a path with no obstacles, it probably doesn't lead anywhere."

FRANK A CLARK

THE CORE IDENTITY MODEL: OBSTACLES

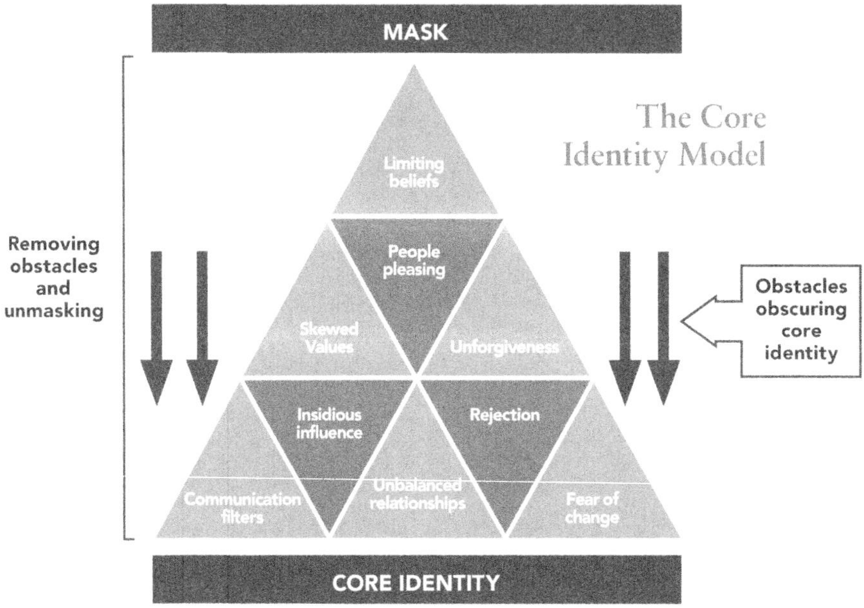

Chapter 2

BELIEFS PART 1: WHAT'S FEEDING YOU?

"BE CAREFUL WHAT YOU THINK, BECAUSE YOUR THOUGHTS RUN YOUR LIFE."

PROVERBS 4:23

The challenge is first won in the mind, before it is visibly a victory or success.

It's currently World Cup season and my teenage son and I enjoy being spectators of penalty shootouts, therefore we envisage the World Cup will provide some more of these. Apart from the gripping finale of luck and chance that a penalty shootout provides, another game emerges for us... We can usually tell if the footballer will land a goal, well before his foot even touches the ball. This is because we analyse his body language, which tells us his level of belief and confidence. We believe the footballer himself knows before he even touches the ball, if he will land the goal; why? Because he has already decided if he believes he can or not, the matter is settled at that moment. Thus far, we have a clean sheet of predictions.

It is impossible to achieve anything without believing you actually can first; and this is why it is crucial to understand and master the realm of beliefs in your own life. Succeeding here will pave the way for you to really take control and break free from obstacles that may have impeded you for years on your path of life. Revealing, examining and challenging your beliefs will help to uncover part of your true identity to live an authentic and purposeful life.

So, what are beliefs and why are they so important?

The dictionary defines a belief as "a principle accepted as true or real, without proof, an opinion, a conviction".

This definition is broader than simply thinking about beliefs in the religious sense. In this context, beliefs are stories we tell ourselves about why we can and can't do certain things in life. They are not based on fact, and often remain unchallenged throughout life.

Beliefs play an important part in forming your identity, self-image, behaviour and habitual ways of thinking. Some beliefs help you to succeed in life while other negative beliefs can keep you shackled. International life coach Anthony Robbins says: "The most important belief a person will ever hold is the belief they hold about themselves."

WHERE DO BELIEFS COME FROM?

Many strongly set beliefs are formed in childhood and teenage years. They can come from any person or thing that has the capacity to exert influence over you.

According to psychiatrist Eric Berne, by 12 years old our core beliefs are formed and lived out daily. Parents, albeit deliberately or unaware, teach their children from birth how to behave, think and perceive. By adulthood, your self-image is a collection of all the *attitudes and opinions* that have been received from others. Your resulting self-image creates the belief of who you are, and liberation from these influences is no easy matter, since they are deeply ingrained.

WHAT ARE LIMITING BELIEFS?

Limiting beliefs are the thoughts and ideas that are no longer challenged that hinder your progress. This is because every thought, expectation and action are a direct result of what you believe. They shape the direction of your life and have the power to create or ruin your progress.

Author Deepak Chopra begins to unpick this with the suggestion that "We each have an estimated 60,000 to 80,000 thoughts a day".

That's a lot of thoughts! Research suggests around 80% of these thoughts are negative. Talk about creatures of habit! But he continues: "Unfortunately, many of them [thoughts] are the same thoughts we had yesterday, last week, and last year. The mind tends to get stuck in repetitive thought loops that squeeze out the possibility for new ideas and inspiration".

If we take an average and then break that down: 70,000 thoughts = 3000 per hour = 50 per minute = just under one per second, with 80% being negative, that's a lot of destructive mind chatter! Is it any wonder we struggle to achieve the things we want out of life, and if we do, then don't enjoy them?

An example of everyday, repetitive (but necessary) thoughts are concepts like how you will plan your day, what you will wear and what you will eat. But there are more sinister thoughts linked to beliefs that impact your outlook, behaviour and ability to succeed.

For instance, a woman has a huge passion to sing and perform in musical theatre. Although she has the ability, she makes a half-hearted attempt at pursuing a career in this area because of a collection of limiting beliefs that exist under the radar that say to her: "It's really only a dream, people like YOU do not make it, it's impossible to earn a good living pursuing your dream, it's not necessary to feel satisfied and love your job, you work to live, work is a sacrifice for your family," and on, and on.

She has accepted these limiting beliefs inherited from her parents and people who have exerted influence over her life since childhood by what was said directly to her and what she observed and experienced growing up. She is not actively aware that these limiting beliefs are holding her back, she has accepted them as FACT, so, the inner conflict flourishes and her frustration grows. She is held back by her limiting beliefs.

To achieve your goals, beliefs must be compatible with your values. But if your values are incompatible with your underlying beliefs, there will be a conflict. While your subconscious mind will undoubtably strive to achieve the goal, your brain reverts back to your belief reference system to ensure that it cannot succeed. It is essential for these beliefs to change for the goal to be achieved.

A Tale of Two Cities

A traveller nearing a great city asked a woman seated by the wayside, "What are the people like in the city?"

"How were the people where you came from?"

"A terrible lot," the traveller responded. "Mean, untrustworthy, detestable in all respects."

"Ah," said the woman, "you will find them the same in the city ahead."

Scarcely was the first traveller gone when another one stopped and also inquired about the people in the city before him. Again, the woman asked about the people in the place the traveller had left.

"They were fine people, honest, industrious and generous to a fault, I was sorry to leave," declared the second traveller.

The wise woman responded: "So you will find them in the city ahead."

Do you see it? The short excerpt above from the book *Chicken Soup for the Woman's Soul* series illustrates how beliefs act as a self-fulfilling prophecy.[9]

The human brain has a cluster of cells that act as a filter to perception, unquestionably accepting information consistent with your beliefs and goals, that fits your picture of the world. At the same time, it filters out any irrelevant information that fails to fit with your picture of life. The perceptions making up your view of life are well-worn and regularly reinforced. When beliefs are entrenched, your expectations become a self-fulfilling prophecy. You interpret life and what happens in light of your beliefs and search around to find alternative evidence to support your stance to the exclusion of all alternative points of view (otherwise known as confirmation bias). Something the wise woman by the wayside understood very well.

HAVE YOU HEARD THE STORY ABOUT THE ELEPHANT AND THE CHAIN?

When an elephant is young, if the keeper puts a chain around its leg to stop it moving too far, at first, it will try to break free. After several attempts the elephant will realise that every time it tries to move away it is painful and will eventually stop trying to escape and give in, spending the rest of its life restricted and restrained.

The elephant never realises that as it grows older and stronger if it tried to break the chain again it could escape, and so never attempts this. Even once its shackles are removed, the elephant will not try to move away. *WHY? Because it doesn't believe it can.*

Unchallenged limiting beliefs can hold you in the same place. Although something that may have been true for you as a child may not be true for you as an adult. If you believe the world is an exciting place, full of abundant opportunities, you are more open to the love and involvement of others and share your life more freely.

But if you are someone who believes the world is a hostile place, where everyone is out for what they can get, you will be less likely to take risks or open up to share your life, gifts and love with others. You're more likely to let the disappointments of the past guide your decisions and actions like an invisible compass. Your subconscious mind – which has filtered and catalogued your subsequent limiting beliefs – is calling the shots. In common terms this is often referred to as "baggage".

I met a young lady at a party who was very vocal about why she believed that all men could not be trusted and why she would stay single. She had been mistreated in a previous relationship and left heartbroken. She said all men were "cheats" and not able to settle down and be faithful. This had become so engrained in her core belief and personality that she had decided to take the extreme measure of becoming sterilised so she would not have any children. She said it was the most sensible thing to do because any man would eventually "leave her holding the baby", and she did not want to be a single parent.

Despite her friends giving her many examples of successful couples and families they knew, there was no moving her position. She was adamant that this was the best way to protect herself from being hurt. I saw someone who was seriously hurting, yet unwilling to do the self-inventory and look at her own decisions regarding the type of choices she had made in past relationships, resistant to learn from them or do something differently. Her limiting belief was like a branding iron on her heart and in her mind.

Conversely, someone else who has experienced similar heartbreak, but who is more open to learning and growing from the experience can have a better outcome.

A friend called Helen who is enjoying a successful fulfilling marriage, shared with me her journey to recognising "Mr Right".

Helen's previous relationship was very turbulent. Her boyfriend was wealthy and forging a successful career in the city. She was living with him for some time and her parents were keen to see them become engaged because they liked his material success. In this relationship she was insecure and constantly in strife. Her boyfriend had serious character flaws; he was manipulative, disrespectful and constantly cheating on her. His arrogance was so immense he was even unfaithful with one of her friends!

This led to Helen being very insecure and constantly stressed. She was regularly having angry stand-offs with other women who her boyfriend had cheated with. Her parents valued her boyfriend's material success and potential for financial security above the happiness and wellbeing of their daughter. As long as things looked good outwardly, their daughter should stick with him.

Things however did not improve and Helen found the courage to leave the relationship, even though it meant disappointing her parents. Helen took time to evaluate the relationship and her part in it. She shared how her values and underlying beliefs were heavily influenced by her parents' values and the need for their approval. As one of six children, she did not feel valued by her parents who were strict disciplinarians and used material success and "keeping up with the Joneses" as their means of validation. They were emotionally unavailable throughout her childhood, so she had no frame of reference for what true affection and a loving healthy relationship looked like.

But the trauma of the relationship taught her what *she did not want* from a future relationship. By evaluating herself and challenging the veracity of her values and underlying beliefs, she was able to break free and reframe the limiting beliefs that led her into such a destructive relationship.

After this, Helen described how she said a prayer to God asking that her future husband would be a devoted, faithful, considerate, honest and trustworthy man of good character; a loving father and good provider and that they would be genuine friends. From that moment, her internal radar began searching for these characteristics. Soon after, she met the man who became her husband. He met all of the characteristics she'd prayed for and they continue to enjoy a fulfilling marriage, very different to her parents.

Helen took responsibility and learned valuable lessons about herself from her experience. Because of this, she was able to take control and use *a different approach to achieve a different outcome*. The lessons learned have served her well throughout her relationships [wife, mother, friend, daughter] as she inevitably comes up against the different challenges of life.

Are you feeding your history or your destiny?

THE COST OF NOT DEALING WITH LIMITING BELIEFS

From the examples above, you can see there is a price to pay in not dealing with limiting beliefs that can govern your life and rob you of your true potential. The impact on your identity, self-image, confidence, relationships, level of success and fulfilment in life are a significant cost. Being stuck in your *comfort zone* is less of a comforting place, as it becomes really a place of stagnation. Such is the power of your beliefs to create or sabotage.

Do you fear or avoid trying because you believe something is beyond your reach? Can you identify the invisible chain around your ankle?

Did you fail at something or have a bad experience in the past and believe that it is not possible for you to ever succeed again in that area? Do you make excuses about why you should maintain a position and stay in your comfort zone?

When you accept limiting beliefs and they remain unchallenged, the real you is hiding from yourself and others. You are cheating yourself! This was certainly the case for Eva, who was suffering under the weight of limiting beliefs linked to childhood trauma. So, if you need more convincing of the damaging impact of limiting beliefs or the motivation to deal with your own limiting beliefs. Eva's story will help you find it.

Chapter 3

BELIEFS PART 2: BURIED ALIVE

"If you continue to carry bricks from your past, you will end up building the same house."

UNKNOWN

CASE STUDY EVA

We cannot underestimate the impact of unresolved trauma in childhood. I have worked with a number of women who have had a significant event or series of on-going traumatic experiences that have left a deep and negative impact on their conscious and more often subconscious mind. These can shape the identity and behaviour of a person in adult life.

Traumas include emotional, physical or sexual abuse, neglect, bullying, major illness/disability and negative sibling rivalry, although this is not an exhaustive list, it is the most common I have come across.

In some instances, adults remember these experiences but choose to bury the feelings and thoughts associated with the painful memories of it, in the belief that because the event happened in childhood and they are now adults, they can move on without ever having to revisit them. In other cases, the event is blocked out completely and there is no active memory. This can happen when the trauma has been so substantial that the brain has shut down to protect itself.

There are clues this can be an issue, when a client has large chunks of childhood that they cannot recall, or a very patchy recollection of large amounts of time from their childhood, in particular significant seasonal or personal events such as birthdays, Christmas or school.

Some clients who do remember, actively seek to suppress any memory or event that they still find emotionally upsetting as an adult. Even if forty-plus years have passed and they recall the event and/or speak about it, they are visibly shaken and distressed, as if the traumatic feelings that had cut through to their very soul were happening all over again. They're re-living the event and feelings attached in real time.

The problem with this scenario is that traumas buried alive are not dead, they just keep eating away at you, manifesting in all kinds of negative behaviours that cause damage to your identity, core values and self-worth. They can blight your potential without you even realising the root cause of the resulting problems in your life. Because these traumas are *buried,* they remain unchallenged and act as an invisible compass dictating the course of your life through negative belief patterns, which leads to negative behaviours, which can lead to broken relationships, unfulfilled potential and physical and mental health issues.

Psychiatrist and trauma expert Bessel van der Kolk explains: "Trauma is not just an event that took place sometime in the past; it is also the imprint left by that experience on the mind, brain and body. This imprint has ongoing consequences for how the human organism manages to survive in the present. Trauma results in a fundamental reorganisation of the way mind and brain manage perceptions. *It changes not only how we think and what we think about, but also our very capacity to think.*"

Eva's case study illustrates how powerful the beliefs stemming from childhood trauma are at shaping identity and self-worth in adult life. Although Eva buried her trauma it did not disappear, instead it constantly turned up, invading every area of her life controlling her subconsciously. A poignant lesson on the importance of *calling the subconscious mind to account*, so you are not blindly led around.

REASON FOR COACHING

Eva came for coaching because she was deeply unhappy, unsettled and angry. She really wanted change in her life and to develop a positive mindset, but was not exactly sure what goals she wanted and how to go about it. Tired of nursing negative thoughts and feeling unworthy – while she put up a good façade to all those around her – Eva was unfulfilled, frustrated and exhausted with the incongruence of her inner thoughts and outward actions.

In addition to this, her deep need for acceptance and acknowledgement from extended family members left her feeling disempowered. This is because she continued to endure negative treatment from them. Despite reducing herself for acceptance, Eva was not in control of the outcome, these family members had no plans to validate her, on the contrary they were exacerbating an already toxic situation. Eva hadn't yet learnt the strength of operating within her circle of influence.[10]

THE MASK

Eva is a well-presented and stylish woman who appears very "together" and controlled with exceptional decorum and manners. She is savvy; her professional life is progressing well. At home she has a loving husband and adult daughter, with whom she shares a good relationship. Her home is hotel pristine in its presentation. *Everything* appears very measured and in order.

Eva has a network of close friends which she values and invests in. She is well travelled. Her friends experience her as someone who is adventurous, kind and knowledgeable with strong views and opinions. She can be the life and soul of the party, and could "drink most people under the table". They also describe someone who has a low tolerance threshold for certain people and situations that do not agree with her view of the world. In short, if you're in, you're IN, but if you're not, it's COLD out there, brrrrrrr!

BEHIND THE MASK

A frightened, unhappy, vulnerable child who has cultivated a tough exterior with a shiny veneer not even those closest to her could crack. Her childhood trauma of exceptional neglect and physical and sexual abuse from close family members set her on a path at war with herself. She was someone working hard to bury and keep buried the trauma of her past while living a "successful" well-ordered life. Working hard in order to not be discovered was a full-time job.

But she was dealing with a number of issues stemming from her trauma of acute childhood rejection, neglect and abuse; and inadvertently Eva had put up a wall around herself limiting the amount of self-exposure she was willing to give. She had major problems with trust and committed to her belief of self-sufficiency. Unable to fully trust even those who could be trusted, even her husband found himself on the wrong side of her well-maintained wall. On more than one occasion he'd said: "Sometimes I feel like I do not know parts of you".

An accumulation of self-talk that protected Eva when she was young to cope with the acute unrelenting attacks, was working against her. Into adulthood these out-dated coping mechanisms were no longer needed and began to hinder some of her key relationships, and her career progression. She often displayed unhelpful behavioural traits such as shutting down and not dealing with certain conflicts. She had difficulties with communication and was weighed down with unforgiveness and holding grudges.

Eva's health was also suffering; recurrent migraines, high blood pressure, low mood, binge drinking alcohol in social settings and poor sleep were some of the side effects she was enduring.

Eva found it exhausting keeping everything "buried in a box" and not dealing with it. This became overwhelming, and led to depression for a number of preceding years before her transformation began through coaching.

The buried items were causing a *depression* of her true personality and uniqueness. She had major difficulty with putting a true and authentic VALUE on herself, instead spending much of the time hiding her true self to the extent that Eva was unaware of who she really was.

The result? Eva was experiencing an *identity crisis*: trapped between who she REALLY was now and the public face she presented to the world. Her real identity had been seriously impacted by these traumas and – more significantly – the subsequent burying of those traumas.

"AS MAN THINKS WITHIN HIMSELF, SO IS HE."

PROVERBS 23:7

PREVIOUS LIMITING BELIEFS

Eva's self-talk can be described as a series of limiting beliefs that governed her thinking and behaviour over time. Up until the start of coaching, most of these beliefs went unchallenged and simply existed predominantly in her subconscious mind, controlling her actions like a puppet on a string. It was like an invisible conductor of a vast orchestra. She never stopped to challenge the legitimacy of these thoughts, but accepted them as fact, a passive bystander in her own destiny and causing great turbulence to her peace of mind to a large extent.

The repetitive soundtrack of these guiding limiting beliefs were:

- I'm not worthy of love and respect
- I need to protect and look after myself. No one is going to do it for me
- This is how it is, I can't change the things inside, so control whatever I can outside
- If I don't control everything I can, I will be exposed!!!!
- BURY EVERYTHING that hurts or causes me discomfort and work diligently to keep it buried
- "Don't argue with stupid"– dismiss people and views that do not fit with my view of the world
- I'll always feel ashamed
- I don't belong here, I'm a fraud
- Showing vulnerability and emotion are weaknesses, man up!

WHERE DID THESE BELIEFS COME FROM?

These beliefs came principally from Eva's mother and siblings in addition to key people in the wider community, some of whom she had previously loved and respected. To them, Eva's "sass" and uniqueness were perceived as negative. By the time she reached adulthood these beliefs were well worn an adopted as her own.

The impact of not dealing with these issues in adulthood:

- High blood pressure
- Poor sleep
- Restlessness
- Protection of real self at all costs means lack of vulnerability [being real]
- Lack of peace and inner fulfilment
- Yearning for acceptance and to be "part of a family" that rejected her
- Frustration with lack of closure from mother
- Fear of being exposed

- Depression and moodiness
- Suicidal episode
- Extreme control in the home: "my way or the highway!"
- Inability to see the positives: viewing life through a negative or glass is half empty lens
- Late bloomer, only recently beginning to recognise her own value and potential
- Feelings of shame and rejection, "I won't be accepted if they know the truth", building a wall around herself.

By compartmentalising, Eva had unwittingly become a FRAUD working diligently to not be found out.

THE JOURNEY TO TRANSFORMATION

> "When I come to these sessions (coaching) and sit in this chair I am a child re-learning what I need to know to grow up. But when I leave, I'm an adult."
>
> **EVA**

When Eva first began her coaching, she was still apprehensive and scared of "being found out". Although the inner person wanted change very much, she was quite prepared to pay me to *fake* her way through coaching because the fear of being exposed prevailed everything: *vulnerability* = *weakness*.

She described an analogy of dirty and clean clothes. All the "dirty clothes were buried in the box, never to be seen again". Her clean clothes were the carefully manicured image she presented to the world. The thought of unpacking dirty smelly rotten clothes and all that this represented was so horrifying for Eva, she was like a deer caught in the headlights.

This was a genuine concern, because Eva had worked hard to block out the trauma, thus not truly confronting or dealing with it as an adult, and the fear of revisiting these events and the potential emotions attached became overwhelming.

What she hadn't realised was that she'd simply put on her clean clothes on top of her dirty clothes, working hard to finesse the smell. Part of Eva, was also buried alive along with those dirty clothes. She would never know who she really was [discover her true identity] and experience the real freedom and peace that comes with living authentically, until she unburied the contents of that box and dealt with each item.

Thankfully, Eva took what she describes as a "leap of faith" and embarked on her path to transformation. Her journey was incremental over a period of months, which broadly comprised of the following:

STEPS TO FREEDOM

1 Exposure, letting go: no more burials

"I feel exposed to the bare bone!" Digging up and unpacking the box, dealing with the contents and letting go of the buried items *up and out.*

2 Revelation

Understanding the real impact and cost on her present life of not previously dealing with the buried items and trauma fuelled an urgency to embrace change. Becoming aware of how she was subconsciously entertaining negative thoughts and behaviours, and understanding the root cause for the first time. Using this newfound truth to begin the walk to freedom.

3 Reframing beliefs starts the journey to self-discovery

Calling her subconscious mind to account and no longer being led around by previously unchallenged negative thoughts and patterns of behaviour. For the first time she was able to recognise the root of her limiting beliefs, accept how they were acquired and from whom, and able to assess their veracity. Reframing beliefs based on truth, including personal positive affirmations as the basis for embedding new more helpful guiding beliefs.

4 Paradigm shifting behaviours

Eva went from seeing the world in black and white to seeing the world in technicolour, gaining a wider and more balanced viewpoint. More open to seeing and understanding other people's perspectives that varied from her own. More open to people that did not share her values and seeing the same people differently, discovering their valuable qualities.

For example: *vulnerability was seen as weakness*. Eva didn't like that word and always fought against it, because when she was a child, she had to be strong and resilient to survive. But through the level of vulnerability and openness needed to get to the root of her issues in coaching, she could see the benefits and freedom that came from it. Eva preferred the words "self-exposure" and could now equate a number of positive benefits to these words because of her transformation experienced through coaching. This enabled her to reduce the size of her wall, and be open to new people and experiences.

5 Discovering real identity and value

With the shedding of baggage and limiting beliefs, the true and authentic personality of Eva began to emerge, unchained from the remnants of past traumas.

Now, almost autonomously, she was closing the gap between her public and private face to live a congruent life, with more peace and fulfilment. Eva was taking off her mask.

6 Unlocking unique gifts and talents

Embracing her real value and self-worth to unapologetically pursue her dreams, develop her talents, with awareness and the self-belief and inward resources to make it happen. Instead of using her energy running away from unresolved issues of the past, she can now run free to fulfil her goals and dreams.

7 Freedom and vision for the future

In Eva's own words:

I'm really beginning to know and accept who I really am.
I'd taken on other people's beliefs an made them my own. I now realise how beliefs have affected me, my brain is now "unlocked" and I have reprogrammed my thoughts. What a difference positive thought based on truth can make!
My new-found self-esteem enables me to now be solution focused, before I would shut down and ignore difficult situations, even though it did not make sense.
I've been in this relationship [husband] and wouldn't allow him to experience the best of me.
I've been in a relationship with myself!
Now I have the confidence to stand out in a crowd, I'm going on a new bus with a new driver. I'm learning new ways to deal with situations that are empowering me.
I respect and admire my husband in a new way instead of focusing on what he was not, I can see more clearly his qualities.
Mistakes are just setbacks, stepping stones: I am capable, confident, energetic and powerful.
I feel good about being unique, I now trust myself and my inner wisdom now I recognise it.
My suffering never allowed me to take life for granted and I finally gave faith a chance by believing.

In addition, Eva experienced results in the following areas:

- Peace: restlessness decreased by 100%
- Now able to reframe limiting beliefs, focus on and live by personal positive affirmations, based on truth
- Health significantly improved: migraines gone, stopped drinking alcohol
- Blood pressure down to normal, sleeping well
- In control and empowered, able to operate within her circle of influence to remain powerful and stable regardless of circumstances
- More able to let go of grudges: being more open
- Positive self-belief, value and self-worth is opening up new opportunities
- Awakening of new level of ambition
- A shift from not believing and being in faith to trusting and taking steps towards God
- Being kinder and not quick to judge
- Feeling "joyful, it comes from within".

Eva completed a life priorities wheel at the beginning of her coaching journey, looking at key aspects of her life: partner, family, health, career, personal growth, environment and friends. She rated her level of satisfaction in each area. The wheel was jagged and uneven, but after just a few months of work, she repeated the exercise. This time the wheel was smooth. It's amazing the difference excavating burials can make to well-being!

"I've finally stopped running away from myself. Who else is there better to be?"

GOLDIE HAWN

Eva's story demonstrates how working on your limiting beliefs:

- Unlocks your subconscious mind and reveals the ways your limiting beliefs have been most damaging to you
- Challenges the origins of those beliefs
- Reframes your beliefs to be consistent with *who you really are* creating alignment with your values and goals
- Achieves greater control over your life and desired direction =TRUE EMPOWERMENT!

Chapter 4

BELIEFS PART 3: DIVIDING FACT FROM FICTION

Who you think you are *on the inside* is *who you are*, even if you try to overcompensate *on the outside*, the limiting beliefs you hold will show up everywhere. When you conquer the obstacles blocking your core identity, you will be free to be who you really, truly are, inside and out.

Like Eva, you too can address and change the beliefs that are holding you back. The path to change is a route less travelled, but numerous rewards are reserved for those who venture out into unchartered waters to reach the other side.

ARE YOU READY?

Muhammed Ali said: "Impossible is just a big word thrown around by small men who find it easier to live in the world they've been given than to explore the power they have to change it. Impossible is not a fact. *It's an opinion.* Impossible is not a declaration. It's a dare. Impossible is potential. Impossible is temporary. Impossible is nothing."

This inspirational quote by the famous African American professional boxer, activist and philanthropist, widely regarded as one of the most significant and celebrated sports figures of the

20th century, encapsulates the power of beliefs. Ali understood the word "impossible" was just a belief; and lived out this principle in his own life, as have many others who have pressed through to achieve things previously deemed impossible.

The truth is, everything is impossible before it has been achieved. Records are broken regularly by people who do not accept the status quo and push beyond accepted boundaries. Impossible really is just a *belief*, and those who do not subscribe to it are at the forefront of innovation throughout history. When your mind is free from the limiting beliefs holding you back, the possibilities for you to achieve your full potential are endless.

Citizen Kane is considered to be one of the greatest films of all time. Orson Welles co-wrote, produced, directed and starred in the 1941 movie which broke new ground, changing cinematography forever with its pioneering filming techniques. He was just 26.

In an episode of *Talking Pictures*, Welles explains how he was able to create a ground-breaking movie and negotiate a contract guaranteeing him total artistic freedom to make the film of his choice, something which was unheard of at the time.

The interviewer asks: "Where did you get the confidence from?"

Welles explains: "Sheer ignorance. There is nothing equal to it. It's only when you know something about the profession that you are timid and careful. I thought you could do anything with a camera that the eye could do or that the imagination could do. If you come up from the bottom in the business, you are taught all of the things the camera man doesn't want to attempt for fear he will be criticised for having failed.

"I had a cameraman who didn't care if he was criticised if he'd failed and I didn't know there were things you couldn't do. So, anything I could think of in my dreams I attempted to photograph. Enormous technological advances were achieved simply by not knowing they were *theoretically* impossible," he concludes.

All this from someone who had never created a film before and had no experience of the Hollywood movie industry. However, what Welles did have was a vision and belief which he turned into action. Impossible was not a FACT.

Many successful people, past and present understand this principle.

Jim Hines was the first person to run 100m under 10 seconds in 1968, something that was previously an *impossible* feat! Hines *believed* that he could, despite the majority of people saying it was impossible.

The UK suffragette movement's hard-fought campaign that earned women the right to vote achieved what was deemed impossible, to the extent that many young women in the UK today cannot imagine ever being deprived of their democratic rights.

In recent history, young African American gymnast Simone Biles created a signature move that was entered into the International Federation of Gymnastics Code of Points in 2013. The unprecedented gravity defying *double layout with a half twist out* known as *The Biles* deemed impossible to execute, even had physicists mystified.

What about the late bloomers, who were written off but kept their belief?

KFC's Colonel Sanders followed an unlikely path to creating a multibillion-dollar international company. He was an entrepreneur who didn't become a professional chef until he was 40, didn't franchise *Kentucky Fried Chicken* (now KFC) until he was 62, and didn't become an icon until after he sold his company at 75.

Biles and The Colonel had something in common, they had a *vision* and a *belief* in that vision, in spite of the naysayers and conventional wisdom that said: "It's never been done before, that's impossible". They took action.

Belief is the ingredient [in the sandwich] that enables your vision to turn into *action*, but it is also the place where people flounder when they listen too much to the obstacle of limiting beliefs.

The well-known 80-20 rule (Pareto Principle), applied to human potential says most people, operate on just 20% of their potential. So, there's a whole 80% of potential waiting to be untapped that can lead you to greater personal and professional fulfilment.

With most people having 80% of negative repetitive thoughts, it's easy to see the link: when you have fewer limiting beliefs, you will operate on more of your potential, gaining more positivity and peace. Your mind is freed to nurture your vision to achieve more of your genuine desires, without unnecessary interference.

Dealing with limiting beliefs gives you a more purposeful life, with less stress and negativity. As you peel away the layers of limiting beliefs, more of the authentic person emerges, with confidence. But this requires a microscopic introspection to assess the authenticity of each limiting belief holding you back.

When you commit to changing limiting beliefs you enter into the realm of change, empowerment and action!

Envisage relatives coming to stay at your home. Suddenly you view your home through new eyes; the clutter, the dirty skirting boards, things that were invisible are now glaring out at you. As you move through the exercises in this chapter, you will gain similar insights as your subconscious mind is called to account.

CORE INSIGHT ACTION

RENEW YOUR MIND, TRANSFORM YOUR WORLD

Practical exercise

Think of these exercises as the beginning of a deep spring clean, an excavation of items no longer needed or wanted that are cluttering up your head space.

Complete the exercises in your journal. Alternatively, you can download the corresponding worksheets from the website: **www.suzannesimmonslewis.com**

The following two exercises will help to uncover your triggers to the negative self-talk that occurs most often in your mind. It will begin the process of shaking you out of passively accepting the barrage of negative thoughts that occupy your mind most of the time and often control your behaviour subconsciously.

RECOGNISE AND CHALLENGE YOUR NEGATIVE THOUGHTS

Complete the following sentence SIX times. Do not think too deeply about the sentence, write the first things that come to mind, these are your most prevalent thoughts.

I must...........

For each of the six answers, ask yourself '**What would happen if I didn't?**' Write it down.

For each consequence, ask yourself:

- What is important to me about this?
- What am I trying to avoid?
- What is the worst that could happen if I didn't?

REVIEW

- What have you learned from your responses?
- Now you can examine the consequences of various actions as you become aware of the automatic responses you give.

Practical exercise

This exercise will help you look at how your beliefs have a bearing on what you think you cannot do. **Complete the following sentence SIX times** with the first thing that comes to mind.

I can't...

For each of your six answers, ask yourself '**What stops me?**'

Look at each of your responses and ask yourself the following questions:

- What am I trying to avoid?
- What is important to me about this?
- What have you learned from your responses? Write it down.

Now ask yourself:

- If I knew I could not fail? What would I do?
- If I had the resources to do it, what would I do?
- If I didn't have to live with the consequences, what would I do?
- If there were no obstacles, what would I do?

If you completed the exercises fully, you will have also gained new insight into what gets in your way most of the time and experienced "suspending" negative beliefs to enter the energising realm of possibility.

What needs to change as a result of your powerful new insights?

LOCATE YOUR INNER VOICE

The first step to transformation is diagnosis! Now you are becoming more aware of the negative voice in your head. It is important to be able to distinguish it from your other more kind and positive voice that may not shout as loudly. The former is the voice that you have entertained that feeds you excuses about reasons why you can't achieve what you want to do, or even allow yourself to believe you are worthy of your true desires.

Locate your inner voice: pay attention to how that negative voice sounds; how you feel, hear, see or experience it. For example, a close friend of Greek Cypriot descent says her inner (negative) voice "shouts at her in Greek!" This will enable you to recognise more easily what triggers it and take action to actively eliminate it, one thought at a time.

Now, let's go a little deeper...

Practical exercise

IDENTIFY YOUR LIMITING BELIEFS

PART 1

Write **FIVE** answers to **EACH** of the following questions:

- Something I learned about myself from my mother was...
- Something I learned about myself from my father was...
- Something I learned about myself from school was...
- Something I learned about myself from my friends was...
- Something I learned about myself from (college, work, or another authority figure was...

Do some answers appear more than once? Do you instantly recognise the familiar ones? Can you see clearly which statements are the chief culprits in restricting you and holding you back?

Write down your insights.

PART 2

From the insights you have gained make a list of the **10** most prevalent limiting beliefs you hold about yourself.

For EACH response ask yourself; what happened to lead me to hold this belief? List each one in relation to the corresponding answer.

Now complete the following statement:

The **FIVE** limiting beliefs that hold me back most of the time are...

With your responses to these statements, you have all the information you need about the most damaging and restrictive ways in which you see yourself.

These five key beliefs, in particular have a powerful influence over the way you shape your life. When you choose to change these beliefs, then you are no longer at the mercy of your conditioning.

"HEALING MAY NOT BE SO MUCH ABOUT GETTING BETTER, AS ABOUT LETTING GO OF EVERYTHING THAT ISN'T YOU – ALL OF THE EXPECTATIONS, ALL OF THE BELIEFS – AND BECOMING WHO YOU REALLY ARE."

RACHEL NAOMI REMEN

Practical exercise

CHALLENGE YOUR LIMITING BELIEFS

For the top five limiting beliefs you have identified in part 2 of the previous exercise ask yourself the following questions and write down your responses for EACH one:

- What are the personal consequences of holding this belief?
- How does it cause me to behave?
- What evidence supports this belief?
- In what way is it irrational or senseless?
- Do other successful people I know hold this belief?
- What caused me to have this belief in the first place (who gave it to me) and do these assumptions still apply?
- How do I feel about the person that gave me this belief? Do I respect them? Are they always right? What is their history?
- What is this belief costing me on a daily basis?
- What will holding this belief cost me in the long term?
- How will my life be different if I let go of this belief?
- Do I want to change this belief?

HARNESS A POSITIVE MENTAL ATTITUDE

"WATCH YOUR THOUGHTS, FOR THEY BECOME WORDS. WATCH YOUR WORDS, FOR THEY BECOME ACTIONS. WATCH YOUR ACTIONS, FOR THEY BECOME HABITS. WATCH YOUR HABITS, FOR THEY BECOME CHARACTER. WATCH YOUR CHARACTER, FOR IT BECOMES YOUR DESTINY."

UNKNOWN

To make any meaningful transformation to your beliefs, it's important to have a positive mental attitude. This is the fuel that fires and energises you to believe and achieve the things you desire in life. It also contributes to a positive identity and sense of self.

Have you ever heard a successful person or someone you admire talk in a negative self-defeating way? It's virtually impossible to entertain negative thoughts and words about something and be successful in that area. And if by some miracle you do succeed, you won't have the mental strength to enjoy that success.

Negative thoughts are very draining. Repetitive words like "never," "should" and "can't," complaining and "woe is me" thoughts diminish your sense of self-worth and deplete the body by producing corresponding chemicals that weaken your physiology.

Conversely, positive thoughts and self-talk leads to action rather than stagnation, galvanising and propelling you forward to achieve your goals.

Your attitude is a habit. When you recognise a negative or limiting thought, you can consciously choose to change it. Enduring transformation comes when you tackle the underlying limiting beliefs that fuel your negative thoughts and emotions and hinder you from operating out of your core identity.

"IF A FELLOW ISN'T THANKFUL FOR WHAT HE'S GOT, HE ISN'T LIKELY TO BE THANKFUL FOR WHAT HE'S GOING TO GET."

FRANK A. CLARK

AN ATTITUDE OF GRATITUDE

A key element of maintaining a positive mental attitude is gratitude. Harvard Medical School defines gratitude as: "A thankful appreciation for what an individual receives, whether tangible or intangible." With gratitude, people acknowledge the goodness in their lives and it helps them connect to something larger than themselves.

Gratitude is *recognising* and being *appreciative* and thankful for everything that is good in your life. Having a deeper appreciation for someone or something produces lasting positivity that goes beyond a fleeting thank you. Gratitude helps you to become a greater participant in your own life, creating feelings of wellbeing, peace and joy. All these elements are a direct counter balance to negative thinking.

Self-help author Melody Beattie says: "Gratitude makes sense of our past, brings peace for today, and creates a vision for tomorrow."

One of the most humbling times in my career was working in a communications consultancy role for company that owned a private rehabilitation hospital for brain injury, spinal cord injury and other debilitating neurological conditions. I was personally challenged and inspired in equal measure by the various patients fighting to improve the quality of their lives. Huge mountains were overcome on a daily basis.

It was a vivid reminder that in an instant a life could be changed completely. For example, a patient involved in a car crash was paralysed from the neck down. He was a young man in his early thirties with primary school aged children. In an instant, the trajectory of his and his family's life were altered forever. Yet, his attitude and belief enabled him to overcome many "impossible" challenges to greatly improve the quality of his life.

For me, the importance of being grateful significantly intensified from this time onwards. I began to give thanks on a regular basis for many things I had previously taken for granted such as the fact that I could see, hear, speak, walk, write and so on. The more thankful I was, the more I could see there was to be thankful for. The more I gave thanks, the more my attitude remained positive. I became more aware and grateful for the many blessings in my life.

To develop an attitude of gratitude, **try documenting the things you are thankful for in your journal** each day. Start your day thinking about what you are grateful for and then saying them out loud to yourself. Developing this habit will assist you in reframing your limiting beliefs.

CHANGE YOUR LIMITING BELIEFS

Mobilisation starts in the mind; and when your mind is going in the right direction, your life will follow.

By now you will have probably identified the key limiting beliefs that have held you back. This exercise will enable you to eliminate these by developing *positive beliefs based on FACT.* A positive mental attitude is an important part of this transformation because it illuminates the positive aspects of your life and your environment and generates positive energy, through empowering self-talk, based on the truth.

Before you begin to reframe the limiting beliefs you've identified, complete the following task, using positive language written in *the first person and the present tense.* For example:

Positive belief: "I am a gifted musician with a particular talent for playing the piano".

Evidence based on fact: "I can play the piano by ear, and read music to grade five level.

List 10 positive beliefs you have about yourself

For EACH positive belief ask yourself: What happened to lead me to hold this belief? Write down your responses.

Once you replace limiting beliefs with empowering ones, you'll start having positive results.

Make it your endeavour to commit to positive thinking.

Now you have generated some positive energy from the former exercise, go back and review the *top five limiting beliefs* you identified **from the exercise on page 47**. What would be a better belief? Write an **opposite belief** to the one you now hold and frame it positively. Write all of these in the PRESENT TENSE.

- My first new belief is......
- My next new belief is......
- My next new belief is......
- My next new belief is......
- My next new belief is......

Practical exercise

For EACH reframed belief answer the following questions:

- What evidence supports this belief?
- When have I known it to be true?
- Who do I know that has this belief?
- What will happen when I hold this belief?

Actively look for evidence to support your new beliefs. As you locate that evidence, you will develop empowering beliefs.

When you actively practice the learning from these exercises your kinder inner voice will become more distinct and the negative self-talk will diminish over time. After all, it's no longer being fed the three-course meals and treats the limiting beliefs were providing! For some of you it may even have been a banquet. And be kind to yourself, lasting change takes time.

Record your successes in your journal. Notice how your behaviour changes and how other people's behaviour changes in your interactions.

Feed your destiny, not your history.

Chapter 5

VALUES PART 1: THE COMPASS THAT GUIDES YOU

"LIVE YOUR DAYS ON THE POSITIVE SIDE OF LIFE, IN TUNE WITH YOUR MOST TREASURED VALUES. AND IN EACH MOMENT YOU'LL HAVE MUCH TO LIVE FOR."

RALPH MARSTON

What is most important to you? What would you do almost anything to avoid?

Have you ever asked yourself what really guides the decisions and choices you make in your life? Why you select one situation over another? For instance, choosing to be a stay-at-home mother over pursuing a full-time career? Getting married instead of co-habiting? Staying in a job you detest? Or, why it is that some choices you make do not sit well with you, even though on the surface they would appear to give you an easier life? For example, observing your manager bullying a junior member of the team, but you choose to "stay out of it", even though it makes you uncomfortable.

The answer is your *values*. These shape your character and reside in the core of your identity; they are a significant part of what defines you as a person. Values have a primary influence on your behaviour and attitude. They provide the motivation to change or remain stagnant. Your *personal values* furnish you with broad guidelines for all aspects of your life.

WHAT ARE VALUES?

In its broadest sense, values are basic and fundamental beliefs that guide or motivate your attitudes or actions, helping you to determine what is important, like an "evaluation filter". Values provide the principles that help you to decide what is right and wrong and how to act in various situations. They also help you decide how you *feel* about your actions.

Values are used in cultural (group) and personal (individual) contexts. *Cultural values* are the norms accepted by members of religions or societies and reflect what is important, good or bad in each situation. *Personal values* are reflections of your needs, desires and what you care about most in life. You can think of them as categories for all your preferences in life i.e. work, family, relationships, health and finances.

Both types of values operate in the background and influence everything that you do, it mostly happens on autopilot. You just know instinctively what sits well with you and what doesn't, what motivates you and what doesn't.

There are some universal moral values like honesty, kindness and service that are generally accepted around the world. But these are not to be confused with the prescribed specific cultural values of a group (society, organisation, tribe) or personal values that are specific and unique to an individual. These are much wider in scope and go deeper than a general set of universal moral guidelines. According to leadership guru John C. Maxwell: "Your core values are the deeply held beliefs that authentically describe your soul."

WHY IT'S IMPORTANT TO KNOW YOUR PERSONAL VALUE SYSTEM

Personal values are a component of your identity. They represent your unique and individual essence, your ultimate and most fulfilling form of expressing and relating.[11]

They are part of an internal compass that directs and motivates your thoughts and actions, pointing out what it means to be true to yourself.

When you understand your own personal values, they act as a great cohesive force assisting you to unlock your core identity. This is because the values you hold tell you about who you are and what is most important to you in life, reflecting your needs and desires, enabling you to live in alignment with your values.

You may be thinking "this sounds great! Define what my values are and I'll know who I am". The trouble is, most of us are not *consciously* aware of our personal value system so we don't understand what is *most* important to us. Even though it's subconsciously directing us, sending messages to our mind, body and emotions about what we want, think and feel. We often override this and instead, focus on what our society, culture and media values, idealising about what we should value and then we try to fit in.

But this creates a huge inconsistency between *who you really are*, what you really want and what is externally deemed to be *accepted*. This is because values are part of who you are in your life RIGHT NOW, not a future oriented version of what you would *like to be*, or who you think you *should be*. When you operate outside of your innate set of guidelines, you experience dissatisfaction, restlessness, internal condemnation and lack of authentic purpose and effectiveness. Part of you is missing and unfulfilled and you may not even recognise the root cause.

For example, Azura a pastor's wife is striving to fit in and support her husband's work while bowing to perceived cultural and church members' expectations of being dutiful and always helping others to a sacrificial level. Submerging herself into meeting the needs of others (husband, children, church members) left a highly intelligent and talented lady unfulfilled. She was unable to say "no", or even identify how to fix the void, unease and dissatisfaction growing within her. Part of Azura was lost. When she identified and honoured her personal values and the beliefs that were limiting her potential, she was able to get in touch with her core identity to gain congruence and carve out a purposeful and fulfilling life. You'll learn more about Azura in a later chapter.

Psychologist Carl Rogers coined the phrase *incongruence* to explain the conflict of having feelings that are not aligned or inconsistent with your actions. In effect, wearing a mask in an attempt to hide your true feelings, whether consciously, or subconsciously.

The most unfulfilled people are those who are attempting to live incongruently with what they truly value and believe because they are in conflict with their core identity.

Conversely, when you become aware of your core personal values and honour them consistently you experience fulfilment, peace, confidence, purpose and effectiveness. When you are living out your truest values as an expression of yourself you are benefiting from a form of healthy self-love and care. Some of the most contented people in the world today are those whose lives are lived in harmony with their innermost convictions and values.

WHERE DO VALUES COME FROM?

Your values mostly come from the principal influencers in your life, such as your family and peers. Your environment is also an important contributor. For example, a person who grew up during the Second World War may have strongly embedded values around thrift, community and helping others.

However, there is another influencer of your core values which resides inside of your core identity. This is not so dependent on your primary influencers, but your DNA; (remember chapter one?) Your unique personality, strengths and natural talents, passions and motivations that guide you towards valuing a particular thing – your inner-bent.

The career of Dolly Parton – the hugely successful American singer-songwriter, actress, philanthropist and businesswoman – spans over seven decades, and her distinctively overdone, flashy style has become legendary.

Despite being berated and discouraged for her "trashy look" over the decades, Parton refused to change. In the documentary *Dolly Parton: The Queen of Country*, she explains: "I patterned my look after what they called 'the town tramp'. I thought this woman was beautiful; she had peroxide hair piled on her head, red nails and high-heeled shoes. I thought she was the prettiest thing I'd ever seen, but my mom said 'oh she ain't nothing but trash' and I thought 'that's what I wanna be, momma!'"

Parton, who was from a conservative and religious family, had to deal with the disapproval and criticism over her image from her relatives and industry peers. Early in her career, music industry bosses tried to "trim her down". Another musician Parton idolised disparaged her and advised her to tone down the "cheap-looking hair and makeup to be taken seriously". She described the embarrassment and pain that such a comment made, but despite the hurt she felt, it didn't change anything.

"This was my idea of glamour; it came from a sincere and honest place of a country girl who wanted to be beautiful and wanted to have everything so I could shine," she says. "Inside, I was shining, but outside I looked drab and plain. I wanted my hair to be big and light, I wanted my make up to be radiant and a lot of it. It made me feel good, like a star.

"I'm really impressed with pretty things and beautiful clothes and I really enjoy it, it's something playful for me and my personality. I'm so outgoing and when I perform, I seem to project better if I feel I have got on all of the glitter and glamour. I hate flat hair and natural make up."

Parton's iconic style has transported through the generations and has become part of her unique selling point. She has composed more than 5,000 songs, received nearly 200 industry awards and sold more than 100 million records around the world; all while remaining true to her flamboyant look that we've come to love and forever associate with Parton. These days, an internet search will turn up many articles from on how to re-create Parton's outfits to why she's now considered a style icon.

Parton has always unabashedly been herself, which has enabled her to sustain decades of success in a still growing and multi-faceted career. By not denying who she was at her core, her talents could freely grow and flow outward in their truest expression. From this place, creativity is limitless. Her true self could breathe. This is the power of remaining true to your values, no matter if they seem out of step with the cultural norms and expectations of those around you.

ARE VALUES FIXED OR CAN I CHANGE THEM?

Unlike beliefs that can change all the time, your personal value system is quite stable. Key values are formed and consolidated early in life and become engrained in your character. But as you move through life, single values can change, for instance, when something big happens in your life, or when you are consciously re-evaluating your life and make a decision, based on your experiences to change your values hierarchy (more about values hierarchy later in this chapter).

For example, before I became a mother, my focus was on career and advancement, which honoured some of my top values of freedom, learning and achievement. I always had a plan! After my son was born, my values hierarchy changed. Because I'd experienced a fairly lonely early childhood with both parents working long hours, I'd promised myself I'd prioritise being present for my son and honour my values of nurture, love and belonging over my desire to progress in my career. So, when I was on maternity leave, I resigned from my job as a full-time journalist (with all the benefits of travel, variety, connection, learning and finance), to prioritise nurturing my son so he would not experience the loneliness and related issues I'd faced.

YOUR VALUES GUIDE YOU IN ACHIEVING YOUR GOALS

I mentioned earlier how values have a primary influence on your behaviour and attitude, providing the *motivation* to change or remain stagnant. Values also have a fundamental role in your ability to be effective, because how much you want something and its importance to you, impacts your ability to succeed in it. Values, along with beliefs play a key part in determining the success of your goals. If your goals do not mirror your personal values, they will not be successfully achieved.

Think of a driver who wants to get to a certain destination in their car. The driver is present, the car is present, but there is no fuel in the tank. Values provide the motivation, represented as the fuel needed to get to the desired destination.

Your life is lived from the *inside out*, because it flows from the core. At the core of your identity is your values. Your values help make you the person that you are, so the greater clarity or self-awareness you have regarding your values, the more precise and effective your actions will be.

Personal development guru Brian Tracy uses the following example to illustrate the foundational impact your values have on your ability to achieve your goals in life:

Imagine your personality by thinking of a target with five concentric rings. Starting from the centre, with your values radiating outward to the next circle.

1 Your VALUES determine

2 Your BELIEFS about yourself and the world around you

3 Your beliefs determine your EXPECTATIONS (positive values promote a positive mental attitude)
4 Your expectations determine your ATTITUDE (an outward manifestation of your values and beliefs – a positive mental attitude goes hand in hand with success)
5 Your attitude determines your ACTIONS – that are a reflection of your inner most values, beliefs and expectations on the inside. This is why what you achieve in life and work will be determined more by what is going on inside of you than by any other factor.[12]

According to Tracy, someone who is confused about their values, goals and beliefs will accomplish very little. But someone who has clarity and lives in alignment with their values may have fewer resources and capabilities, but can go on to accomplish very much because they are clear about what they stand for, what they want and what they believe in.

But knowing and accepting what you truly value takes effort and sincere introspection. The value exercises in the next chapter will help you uncover your personal values, revealing more of your core identity and providing the basis for authentic and effective decision making.

But before this, it is necessary to understand *different types of personal values* to appreciate how your values hierarchy can help you set and achieve genuine and intentional goals that reflect the real priorities in your life.

VALUES HIERARCHY

Your values are unconsciously arranged in your mind in a hierarchy, where the value at the top is the most important. As you evaluate your actions, the top values are the ones you subconsciously seek to honour first. When your more important values are found and satisfied, then the next most important one becomes important.

Being aware of your highest values can act like a guide for you, helping you to gain clarity and take more control of your life.

Conversely, knowing your negative values, those you try to keep away from, are also very helpful.

Why is this important? The brain is focused on what we want most and what we fear most and there can be some real conflict between the two.

For example, the values of *creativity* versus *security* when deciding to embark on full-time study for a dream career, over the security of a steady but mundane and unfulfilling job. Or, staying in a relationship that you know is not right for you and stifling your personal growth because you are afraid of being alone. The conflict? The values of *growth* and *achievement* versus *belonging* and the fear of being alone.

When you are clear about your values hierarchy you can consciously check your decisions against which values you are honouring which leads to better decisions and results. You can be more pro-active by creating positive experiences that express the top values in your life and decrease experiences that are aligned with the opposite negative value in your life.

DIFFERENT TYPES OF VALUES

So far, we've discussed values and how they influence you. Now it's time to dig a little deeper. There are different categories of personal values, that have varying degrees of impact: idealistic, means, operational and core values.

At the very heart of your identity are the most important values you prioritise over everything else: your **core values**. These are part of the central compass flowing from the inside out; sitting right at the top of your values hierarchy.

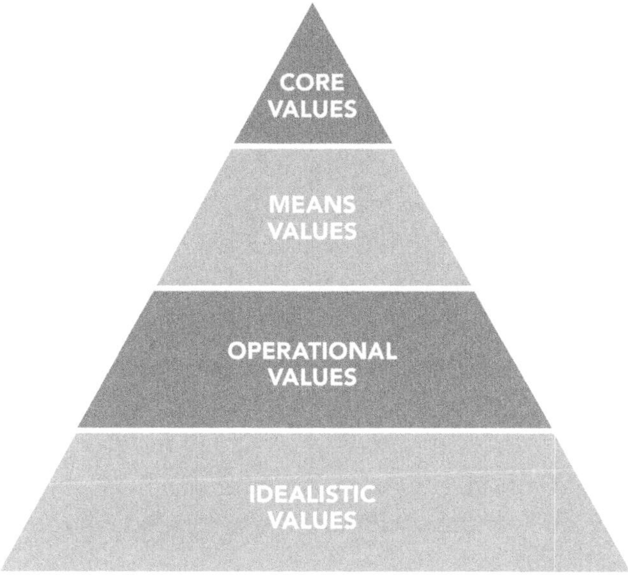

Idealistic values are your GOALS, *how* you would like your life to be in your chosen area of life, such as your ideal career, house, relationship or car.

Operational values represent how you currently *spend your time* in that area (career, house, relationship, car) doing 'this' in order to get 'that'. For example, working a 60-hour week to pay the bills and take care of your family.

Means values are the *things* you value (family, money, career, relationships). You need them to get somewhere else or to obtain or achieve something else which is closely linked to the end *core value*. For instance, we don't want money just for money's sake. We want it because of what it can give us. Earning enough money to pay off a mortgage 10 years early, could provide greater freedom, peace, security and choice that could transform your life.

Core values are single abstract words linked to emotions i.e., respect, peace, adventure, security, freedom, connection, love, belonging. They are the traits or qualities that you consider to be not only worthwhile; they represent your highest priorities and deeply held beliefs, and are the driving force to your attitude, motivation and actions. They represent what you stand for – your guiding principles – and form part of the solid core of who you are and what you believe.

When you uncover the core values residing in the purest form of your identity, you will better understand yourself and your motives, and be enabled to make decisions that will positively impact your life. You will have more control over your life and be able to measure your choices against what really matters to you, and not what society and cultural standards expect of you. This, in turn, will help you prioritise moving towards your goals, rather than moving away from (or avoiding) particular situations.

When you honour your true values, you flex the muscles of authenticity and create a dynamic foundation for personal and professional success.

> "CORE VALUES SERVE AS A LIGHTHOUSE WHEN THE FOG OF LIFE SEEMS TO LEAVE YOU WANDERING IN CIRCLES."
>
> **J LOREN NORRIS**

Chapter 6

VALUES PART 2: WHAT ARE YOUR VALUES?

"THE SECRET TO ACHIEVING INNER PEACE LIES IN UNDERSTANDING OUR INNER CORE VALUES – THOSE THINGS IN OUR LIVES THAT ARE MOST IMPORTANT TO US – AND THEN SEEING THAT THEY ARE REFLECTED IN THE DAILY EVENTS OF OUR LIVES."

HYRUM W. SMITH

CORE INSIGHT ACTION

1. IDENTIFY YOUR VALUES

Practical exercise

Step 1

From the list below select the values that you feel are most important to you and also add any that are not included in this list.

Achievement	Adventure	Art	Awareness
Balance	Challenge	Community	Creativity
Connection	Cooperation	Curiosity	Diligence
Effectiveness	Empowerment	Fairness	Fame
Health	Helping others	Honesty	Independence
Family	Freedom	Friendships	Fun
Generosity	Growth	Knowledge	Laughter
Love	Loyalty	Legacy	Money
Nature	Openness	Order	Patience
Peace	Pleasure	Power	Recognition
Relationships	Religion	Responsibility	Reward
Risk taking	Security	Self-respect	Spirituality
Spontaneity	Stability	Status	Success
Time	Truth	Understanding	Unity
Vision	Wisdom	Learning	

Step 2

After you have chosen your values arrange them in order of importance.

Step 3

Narrow down your list to the **10 most important values in order of importance**, number one being the most important.

You may find prioritising may take some time. Don't be too hard on yourself: without some considered reflection, it can be hard to know the importance of each of your values. This is especially true if you have been living your life out of alignment with your values, experiencing the discomfort or frustration but not understanding why.

Don't worry, the sequence of exercises in this section will help you identify and prioritise your core values and enable you to make changes that honour them in your everyday life. Ultimately it will help you gain a clearer understanding of your core identity.

Step 4: Find the meaning

The emotion that speaks to your heart through your **core values**.

For each of your *top 10* values listed (in step 3), ask yourself the following questions.

1 What is most important to me in/about [insert value]? (idealistic value)

2 What does it give me? .... (means value)

3 What is most important about this.............. (core value)

For example:

1 What is most important to me about being **fit and healthy** (idealistic value)

Not being a burden to my family

2 What does it give me?

Independence, respect and choice (means value)

3 What is most important to be about independence, respect and choice?

It will give me a sense of **security and peace,** I wouldn't be worried about the future and I have more control over my life. (core value)

Core values = **Security and Peace**

Step 5

List the core values that have emerged from step 4.

You may find some of your core values have appeared more than once.

For example, **security** could be a core value of family, health and money.

Prioritise them in order of importance. You will have between 6-10 core values.

Practical exercise

This is now your *working list*, BUT not the final list of your core values.

Reflection

How are these values currently expressed in your life? Take some time to reflect on your answers before completing the remaining exercises.

The following exercises will help you to test, explore further, evaluate and refine your list.

2: USE PEAK EXPERIENCES TO ELICIT CORE VALUES

This exercise will help you to dig deeper into your core values by analysing some rewarding times in your life when you've been at your best.

Step 1

Think of some positive memorable times in your life when you were deeply inspired. Everything is going well; you are in the zone and its easy and effortless. No self-doubt is present and there is a freedom and joyousness about what you're experiencing. Just thinking about it now creates a warm feeling. It can apply to a moment in time (a few hours) or to a whole period or project.

Identify at least four examples from your personal and working life.

Step 2

For EACH of the four examples listed, ask yourself the following questions and write down your answers.

- What made that experience special to me?
- What values were being honoured in that experience? List in order of priority.
- What did that give me?
- What do those specific values mean to me?
- What is most important to me about this?

Remember to repeat this sequence of questions for ALL four of the rewarding experiences you have identified.

Step 3: Review

- Which of the values come to the fore? Note them down.
- Do they match your current top 10 core values?
- Make a note of how many are already listed in your current top ten.
- Now, edit your existing list of core values to include any new core values that have emerged.
- Remember, your *core values* are single abstract words with feelings attached.

Step 4

Review the priority of your core values based on the new insights you have gained.

Consider your values hierarchy and whether the order needs to change, following the insights you've gained from this exercise.

Reflection

What have you learned about how your core values shape your identity? What values require your constant attention?

3: RATE YOUR CORE VALUES

Practical exercise

Core Values Wheel

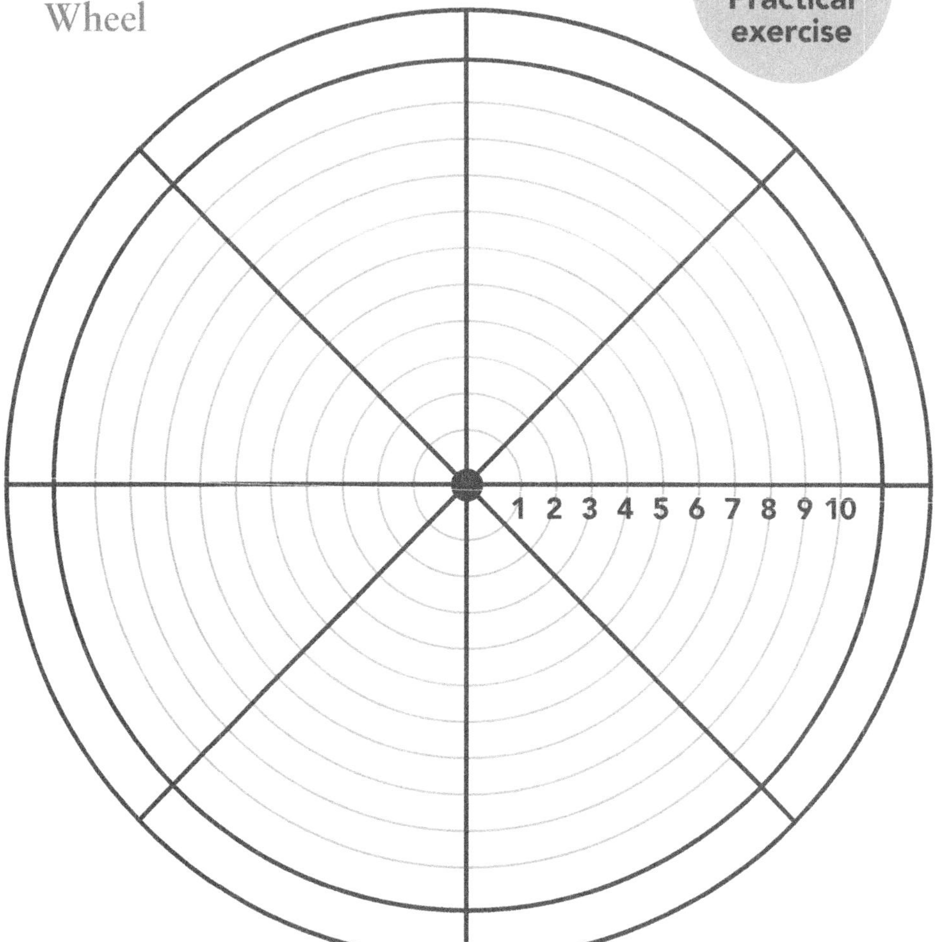

Step 1

Where are you in relation to your core values? Rate your core values against what is going on in your life right now.

- Write a core value in each segment of the wheel.
- Take the centre or hub of the wheel as 0 (totally dissatisfied) and the outer edge as 10 (totally satisfied). Rank your level of satisfaction with each core value by putting a cross on the relevant spoke.
- Draw a line to join the crosses. How balanced does the perimeter of your wheel look?
- How bumpy would the ride be if this were a real wheel?

Step 2

For **EACH** of the core values you have scored, think about what is happening that has caused you to give it this score and ask yourself the following questions:

- Where am I in relation to this value?
- What is currently missing?
- How am I honouring this value in my life right now?
- How do I think, feel and behave when I'm honouring this value?
- What is the benefit of this?
- How am I dishonouring this value in my life?
- How do I think, feel and behave when I am dishonouring this value?
- What is the cost and impact of this to me?
- What insights have you gained? Take some time to reflect before moving on.

Step 3

Review

- Highlight the core values where you want to improve your level of satisfaction score and think about what you can do to accomplish this.

Practical exercise

- What would increase your score by 1-2 points in EACH area?
- Write down your answers.
- If you increased that score by 1-2 points, what would this give you?
- What would it look and feel like?

Step 4
Take action

Think of ways you can consistently honour and embed your core values. Find inspirational quotes that reflect your core values. Write an *action plan or mission statement* on how you will honour these values and increase your satisfaction score.

The following table (also available as a worksheet) may assist you.

Core Value	Current Score	Target Score	Action to be taken to increase score	Timeframe
1				
2				
3				
4				
5				
6				

If you completed these exercises *fully* you will have a set of authentic core values. You will know what values represent your primary way of being and what values are essential to expressing your core identity, enabling you to exhale and experience more fulfilment.

> "A highly developed values system is like a compass. It serves as a guide to point you in the right direction when you are lost."
>
> **IDOWU KOYENIKA**

Chapter 7

PEOPLE PLEASERS PART 1: DON'T SET YOURSELF ON FIRE TO KEEP OTHERS WARM

"I CAN'T TELL YOU THE KEY TO SUCCESS, BUT THE KEY TO FAILURE IS TRYING TO PLEASE EVERYONE."

ED SHEERAN

Are you concerned about what other people think of you? Do you often make decisions based on what you think will please others? Does your sense of self-worth come from the approval of others? Do you often withhold from sharing what you truly want, think or feel because of fear it may upset someone? Are you often last on your list of priorities? Do you prefer that everyone else gets their needs met, even if it's at your expense?

Alas, I see you nodding your head in recognition. These are just some of the traits of a people pleaser. A quick search on the internet and you will find a vast array of advice on how to assert yourself and not be a "doormat". But if the solution were that simple, why are so many people still burdened by this affliction?

Most online advice to counter people pleasing only looks at the problem on a superficial basis, so it's highly unlikely to produce lasting results. A little like a 12-week crash diet, that doesn't take a holistic look at the root of a person's eating habits; or trying to lose 60lbs without diet or exercise and instead taking a diet pill as a short cut. It feels good to get quick results, but in the long run it's likely that you will be worse off.

The issue of people pleasing runs much deeper and a fragmented identity, a disconnection from who you really are, is at the heart of people-pleasing behaviour. While it gives short-term relief, there can be long-term, dire consequences of such behaviour primarily to the individual and their valued relationships.

People pleasing has a direct impact on your identity, self-esteem and overall health and wellbeing. As a people pleaser you are no longer in control of your own life and are in danger of missing the boat in relation to fulfilling your authentic purpose.

WHAT IS A PEOPLE PLEASER?

According to the *Urban Dictionary*, "People pleasers are door-mats who let high expectations, resentment, and saying yes when they mean no, run their lives. They are set on being perfect and nice."

I have added the term "*syndrome*" to this definition because of the seriousness I equate to it. *Merriam-Webster Dictionary* defines syndrome as "a group of signs and symptoms that occur together and characterise a particular abnormality or condition."

Many women are affected: "Women have been raised to be care givers and nurturers, which is why the problem is more prevalent for us than men," says psychologist Dr Susan Newman, author of *The Book of No*. "We want to please because we think it will make us better people. For some women this becomes a habit, or even an addiction."

For years Michaela was a "yes" woman. She did everything for everyone, even when it went against her best interests and made her unhappy. Her parents both died when she was young and she was raised in the care system and by foster parents. Michaela desperately craved unconditional love and approval which she felt was missing throughout much of her childhood. This need manifested in people-pleasing behaviour, in the hope that someone would accept and love her like her parents did, before their passing.

She was overly helpful to her friends' mothers, taking on a "goody two shoes" surrogate daughter façade. She pretended to like whatever her boyfriend of the time was into and even slept with men just because they were nice to her, whether she liked them or not.

Michaela's deep need for approval and her eagerness to do almost anything to get it was draining the life out of her. She was totally disconnected with who she really was and exhausted trying to meet the expectations of everyone around her.

The penny finally dropped when Michaela loaned a friend the money she had saved up to pay for her own much-needed holiday. Unable to pay the outstanding balance she lost the booking. At that point, Michaela realised, no matter what she did for others it would never be enough, she would still be left feeling empty. In fact, people pleasing had taken much more from her than she had gained. This was not the way to receive the love and validation she was craving. Michaela would have to start with accepting herself, which meant honestly getting to know and value who she really was.

Do you relate to any of Michaela's story?

People pleasing behaviour propels you into an inner war. Supressing your true feelings, thoughts and desires leads to a disconnect with who you really are (your core identity). When you don't know who you are, or understand your value and worth, it's like having no anchor, you're just drifting with every tide that comes in, acting out of insecurities, trying to overcompensate for the "perceived" deficits in your identity.

SIGNS AND SYMPTOMS

One of the greatest signs of being a people pleaser is not being completely truthful with others about who you are. You say you like things you really don't like. You go places and say you are enjoying it, when in reality it's the last place on earth you want to be. You agree to things you don't feel right about in your heart. Instead of telling people the truth about your desires, feelings and thoughts, you develop a pattern of telling others what you think they want to hear in order to remain accepted or keep someone else happy.

You may appear on the surface to be a giver and only portray positive qualities; accommodating, kind, generous and thoughtful. But people pleasing can also be a way to influence others to win approval, acceptance, safety, stability and love. You go to great lengths to avoid conflict or any type of emotional discomfort. You avoid it at all costs, usually at a high cost to your self-esteem and psychological health.

There's nothing wrong with doing good deeds for others, but there is a big difference between doing good and people pleasing. Doing good is part of being human and part of what you do for the people you care about and those who need you. It's a benevolent desire linked to your values and purpose. But losing perspective about how much and how often you give of yourself may take you into the territory of people pleasing. This is where your motives are unhealthy and linked to a misguided sense of duty and obligation that serves your perceived emotional and psychological deficits.

Common signs of people pleasing syndrome behaviour:

- You struggle to say "no"
- You find it hard to be assertive and voice your opinions, afraid of being judged
- You pretend to agree with everyone, going against your own values to be liked and accepted
- You're hyper-vigilant about perceived rejection from others (always on the lookout)
- You feel responsible for how other people feel
- You're excessively altruistic, people use you

- You often suffer at the expense of doing a favour for others, feeling burdened by the things you have agreed to do
- You have a weak sense of self and poor interpersonal boundaries
- You become emotionally dependent/co-dependent when in relationships or friendships, usually partnering with an over-controlling person
- You're addicted to approval from others, you need praise to feel good, your self-worth rests on what people think about you
- You apologise often, over-explaining or over-justifying your behaviours
- You have a irrational desire to be liked no matter what
- You feel shattered for days or weeks when someone criticises you
- You have low self-worth
- You act based on what *other people think of you*
- You always put yourself in other's shoes, but you rarely show compassion towards yourself
- You blindly believe in other people's goodness even if they are clearly abusive towards you
- You fear losing control of yourself because you repress so much of what you want, think and feel
- You go to great lengths to avoid conflict and struggle to stand up for the things and the people you really believe in
- You don't admit when your feelings are hurt
- You feel under extreme pressure to keep up appearances
- You have lost touch with the true you! NO one knows the true you
- You're afraid of failure or rejection, or both
- You're passive-aggressive and harbour a lot of resentment
- You have a false concept of perfectionism
- You're easily embarrassed
- You make decisions based on your assumptions and rarely seek clarification
- You're indecisive and have difficulty in making decisions.

The long list shows the multiple facets of people pleasing behaviour, common among many individuals who are well versed in these actions. A people pleaser may not demonstrate every one of these behaviours but will be able to identify with a good portion of them. It can be chronically debilitating over time fuelling the constant deception and subsequent anxiety of living this façade.

While you may be fully aware that you display some of these traits, the full weight of their impact often dwells under the radar of your conscious mind. Therefore, you have never really scrutinised your thoughts or behaviours or their consequences in any meaningful way, but resigned yourself to believing you are not in control so nothing can change. You have unwittingly disempowered yourself.

THE SLIDING SCALE

There are also stages to people pleasing, moderate to severe but all lead to the same place if left unchecked. For example, a mother may have a strong desire to look after her family and prioritise their needs. But people-pleasing syndrome kicks in if the mother doesn't see her own needs as valid and neglects her own health and wellbeing, martyring herself for her family in the misguided belief that she is not important enough to figure in the pecking order of her family.

Over time resentment builds and key relationships are fractured as burnout takes hold. Some call this "perfectionism", aspiring to following an ideal that is impossible. However, the mother is not *challenging* these subconscious thoughts and beliefs that are controlling her actions and causing her to feel out of control and powerless to change her situation.

PEOPLE PLEASERS PAY A PRICE

People pleasing does offer you short-term relief, because pleasing others can be self-serving and mask feelings of low self-worth and insecurity among other things. You may enjoy impressing people and feel good about being needed by others.

But those benefits are outweighed by the far-reaching, long-term negative impact on your identity, self-esteem, psychological and physical health and purpose in life. Saying "yes" all of the time obliterates your boundaries, making it almost impossible to protect yourself. You are in danger of becoming a doormat without personality who is insincere. Overriding your core values to please others will always come at a cost to you: and the personal price is undoubtably expensive.

If you identify strongly with the people-pleasing behaviour I've outlined, perhaps you've already arrived at this point.

THE COST OF PEOPLE PLEASING

No one really knows the *true* you

Keeping so much locked inside of you for fear of being disapproved of makes you extremely guarded; and when you're a people-pleaser no one really knows the *true* and *authent*ic you, only the façade that you present. While you desire to be loved and accepted, over time you feel lonelier and more disconnected from yourself and others. Entire parts of your personality that are incompatible with your façade, such as anger, disagreeing with others and setting boundaries will always alienate you from your true self.

Neglect self

People Pleasers devote very little time to taking care of their own health. Your efforts towards taking care of others steals away the time you need to de-stress, exercise, nurture hobbies and interests and so on. As a result, you may be more prone to health problems.

Unexpressed anger causes resentment

Over time you can become silently angry at the people in your life. The desire to be kind will suppress that anger, but unexpressed anger often turns into passive aggression. Mounting resentment is the biggest destroyer of relationships.

Ruins relationships

You can't form authentic relationships with people unless you're willing to speak up sometimes and say that your feelings are hurt. Denying that you're angry, sad, embarrassed or disappointed – even when you're emotionally wounded – keeps a relationship superficial. You may not even realise difficult conversations need to happen.

Easily exploited

People pleasing doesn't gain love and respect. By always saying "yes" to requests for favours, people will take advantage of your kindness by asking for more than what is reasonable. Even people who are generally not exploitive may take advantage because they don't realise that you are overextending yourself and have difficulty understanding where your boundaries are because you have set none. Requests from other people will become overwhelming, leading to stress and burnout.

Stress and burnout

Stress is having more demands than you can handle. You feel burdened by the things you must do and are constantly overcommitted. Your schedule is full of activities that other people want (both real and assumed) because you don't realise that you're in charge of how you spend your time. People pleasing can turn into a vicious cycle of chronic stress and unhealthy behaviours.

Loss of self-respect

When you pretend to agree with everyone, you lose your integrity and self-respect; engaging in behaviours that go against your core values (if you are still aware of what they are). Your efforts to be "all things to all people", changing with each tide that comes in makes you a "double minded person, unstable in all your ways".

Co-dependent intimate relationships

You live in denial about the true state of your relationship. You give much more than you receive and let your partner have their way, yet feel overwhelmed with hurt and resentment. You tolerate irresponsible and hurtful behaviours from your partner and repress your true thoughts and feelings. You feel disempowered to improve your situation, reassuring yourself that you are a nice and giving person, but all the while you feel like a failure.

I have outlined just a few of the most common ways people pleasers pay dearly for this destructive behaviour, but there are many more casualties and losses.

I have seen many examples where people crash and burn before their epiphany, while others break free before they reach the precipice. Sooner or later though they wake up to count the cost and decide whether to face head on the personal consequences of their behaviour and empower themselves.

Former British popstar Louise Redknapp caused a media stir in 2017 when she left her football-hero husband after 19 years of marriage, after a stint on *Strictly Come Dancing*, a British competitive ballroom dancing show.

Media coverage had a distinct air of "Louise has let us all down by throwing away every woman's supposed happy-ever-after" when she moved out of her beautiful multimillion-pound Surrey home, leaving her husband and impacting their two young sons.

After years of standing in the shadow of her husband's fame, Louise gained the courage to say she no longer wanted to simply remain the "good wife".

She is quoted in The Telegraph as saying: "I think this happens to a lot of women when they get married and have children. You have this feeling deep inside you, 'Where did I go?' But I pushed those thoughts away. I'd think of my past life as a popstar as being *not reality*. Looking after the house and my family was my reality.

"I became a sort of Stepford Wife, wanting to be perfect at it. It was only when I agreed to do Strictly Come Dancing that I realised I couldn't just go back to that."

Louise realised how controlled she'd been about the way she thought about herself for so long: "The thing was, I was always overly conscious of being judged. I cared too much about what people thought of me. But I wasn't always like this. Something happened that made me stop being me.

"People might look at me and think I've got everything, but a sweeping staircase and designer handbag doesn't really do it for me. Being fulfilled, being true to yourself, following your passion, they are the things that make you happy. I have no idea what is going to happen, all I know is that I fought for this, it's taken everything, but this is something I need to do for me."

Take a moment to reflect:

- What are your needs (and values)? Can you identify them?
- Have you lost touch with what is important to you?
- Do people close to you know your real likes and dislikes?
- How often do you truly express what you think and want?

WHAT LIES BENEATH?

We've seen the cost; people pleasers lose more than they gain so why is the behaviour so prolific? There is a deeper need, linked to an attempt to gain or avoid a significant feeling or circumstance in your life.

In coaching terms this is described as a *motivation towards* some gain. But most people pleasing behaviour is governed by a *motivation away from* a perceived fear, something you do not want and seek to avoid.

For example, you may enjoy being the go-to person that everyone relies on, you feel significant, needed, popular, valued and accepted. However, you are overwhelmed and overcommitted and you live in fear that you will be rejected if you don't comply with every request. Your people pleasing behaviour is motivated by the *fear of rejection*, losing the "superficial" love, attention and acceptance you've come to rely on to feel validated.

UNEARTHING THE ROOT

People pleasing has deep roots. This is a key reason why many people are not able to detect and identify it for what it really is. They just think it's part of who they are and don't connect the behaviour with the inner conflict it creates, so they don't perceive it as something they can change.

Remember the nurture debate from chapter one? I illustrated how your *perceived* identity is influenced by upbringing and environment (nurture) and the pressure to conform to *who you think you should be* where there is an intense focus on the external elements to gain the approval of others.

Everyone starts out in life wanting to be safe, loved and accepted. Much of the time, people pleasers gain an early start being parent pleasers.

Parents are usually our very first influencers that provide a window through which to view the world. One of the first things we learn from our upbringing is that receiving love is "conditional" and depends on a prescribed set of standards and behaviours.

Many of our behaviours are learned from the family systems of our childhood. Unhealthy family systems tend to be closed and rigid, featuring multiple unspoken rules about how family members should interact with each other and with the rest of the world. Some of these rules may be about hiding negative feelings, keeping problems within the family, and putting others' feelings first. In families like this, it is often unacceptable to say "no" to someone, to openly disagree, or to make choices based on your needs rather than those of others.

Author and family therapist Darlene Lancer explains, "Some children decide that accommodating their parents' wishes is the safest way to survive in a world of powerful adults and the best way to win their parents acceptance and love. They try to be good and not make waves. "Good" means what parents want. Their parents may have had high expectations, been critical, had rigid rules, withheld love or approval, or punished them for mistakes, dissent, or showing anger.

"Some children learn to acquiesce merely by observing their parents' actions with each other or another sibling. When parental discipline is unfair or unpredictable, children learn to be careful and cooperative to avoid it."

In families like this, authentic emotions and behaviours are discouraged. Instead, the family focuses on looking normal and okay to outsiders. A child in this type of family is often told to "put a smile on your face" regardless of how the child is actually feeling. The message to children in these families is that they are valued for their ability to keep up appearances, rather than for their actual value as individuals with unique needs and desires.

Conditional love and acceptance are often the basis for learning about value and self-worth.

In these instances, the belief pattern that is established subconsciously goes like this: Love is conditional and based on my performance, I have to earn love by people pleasing (doing what others want) when I do this, I feel loved and when I do not please people I feel rejected. If love is conditional, how can I believe that I am basically a loveable and valuable person? I look to people to give me self-worth. I do not love who I am, so I do not expect others will love me either (if they knew the real me). I try to earn love and acceptance by what I do. I am trying to avoid rejection and fear of failure is always there.

Fear of rejection is the underlying feeling that, *if I don't do everything I can to make this person happy they might leave or stop caring for me*. This often stems from early relationships where you were rejected or abandoned by an important person in your life.

Fear of failure is the underlying feeling that, *if I make a mistake, I will disappoint people and/or be punished*. Fear of failure can arise from early experiences where there was severe punishment for even small mistakes.

Early experiences with harsh criticism or punishment can lead to significant anxiety. Even though the parent or other important person in your life who was critical may no longer be in your life, anxiety is an emotion that can live on for a very long time.

Dr. Sherry Pagoto, a licensed clinical psychologist and Associate Professor of Medicine at the University of Massachusetts Medical School, confirms the need to please is an underlying fear of failure or rejection and adds that people-pleasing habits are a form of perfectionism, which studies show is closely associated with anxiety.

Pagoto explains that in dealing with anxiety to do things perfectly to avoid or lower the risk of failure and rejection, people pleasers "do everything we can to get things right, finish the job, and make sure everybody is happy. Emotionally, this means that instead of living our life in a place of self-acceptance, we're constantly chasing the feeling of everything in our life being 'right' – which is ultimately unrealistic and unhealthy".

George Hartwell was over 30 before he recognised that he was a people pleaser. An excerpt from an article on his website www.healmylife.com describes beautifully the cost of people pleasing to his true identity, his faith and his relationships.

We lived by mom's motto of 'peace at any price'. Although it was unspoken, mum also enforced a code of behaviour of not sharing personal issues, of not expressing anger and non-contact among siblings.

When I sacrificed being real, open, direct, personal, passionate, aggressive and expressive in order to gain my mum's approval, what happened to me? I lost some things that are priceless to me and that make it difficult for me to be a loving man and a courageous man of God.

My people pleasing trained me to behave by a set of rules of right and wrong. This put me out of touch with my feelings and my inner self.

While I was a people pleaser, I gradually ruined my ability to think clearly for myself; my judgment became impaired; I became a slow and plodding decision maker. In part this is because, as a people pleaser, I was committed to conflict avoidance. My subconscious mind automatically screened and suppressed all information that might be controversial or lead to conflict. Procrasti-

nation was fuelled by my need to be perfect. People pleasers don't want to make a mistake.

Putting on a phony role of 'good boy who follows the rules and does what is expected' resulted in a gradual but profound loss of my true identity. Being out of touch with my inner core, I failed to develop my own tastes, speak with my own voice or take the risk of expressiveness, love and being creative.

I've now entered a process of reclaiming my identity as a spontaneous, creative, clear thinking (and sometimes angry) child of God. Gradually I have reclaimed a sense of who I am and what I like. I am learning to love, to be creative, to express myself and think for myself. It is hard to believe and to explain that being a people pleaser had ruined my love life, damaged my career and fuelled an unconscious rebellion against God.

For some people, summoning up the courage to jump off the people pleasing treadmill may seem like a step too far out into the unknown. But like any successful change of behaviour, results are most effective when you focus not on what you want to move away from, *but what you seek to gain and move towards.*

As you uncover, own and live from your core identity, the transition will become attainable. When you gain awareness and diligently do the work contained in this book to reveal who you really are, the layers of deception will fall away, some parts without you even realising at first.

"THE RACE IS NOT GIVEN TO THE SWIFT OR TO THE STRONG BUT TO THE ONE WHO ENDURES TO THE END."

ECCLESIASTES 9:11

CORE INSIGHT ACTION

Practical exercise

REFLECTION

- What parts of you have you been suppressing?
- What are you seeking to avoid?
- What are you moving towards?
- If there were no fear of rejection, loss, or whatever else you're moving away from, how would you express yourself?
- What parts of you would no longer remain hidden?

THE EMOTIONAL BANK ACCOUNT

The emotional bank account, made popular by personal development guru Stephen Covey, helps you to gain a clear picture of the quality and health of your relationships. Just as a financial bank account is comprised of deposits and withdrawals; the emotional bank account enables you to see if your relationships are in balance. For example, if someone is making numerous withdrawals and very few deposits into your account, it would quickly be in deficit.

It can be a useful tool for you to gain a clear picture of which relationships are taking up most of your time, energy and resources and highlight people-pleasing behaviour in action.

Examples of deposits include being trustworthy, sharing quality time, keeping your commitments and being considerate. Examples of withdrawals include letting someone down without an acknowledgement or apology, being disrespectful and breaking trust.

Get **three** sheets of blank paper and on each one, make two columns: **deposits** and **withdrawals**.

Pick three people where you most display some of the people pleasing traits that you have identified from this chapter.

- How many deposits has the person made? Write them in the deposits' column.
- How many withdrawals has the person made? Write them in the withdrawals' column.

- Section off your responses and repeat the exercise on the same sheet of paper for yourself.
- How many deposits have **you** made? Write them in the deposits' column.
- How many withdrawals have **you** made? Write them in the deposits' column.

Repeat this exercise for the three people you have identified.

Review

- How even or uneven are your columns?
- What have you learned?
- What needs to change as a result of what you are now aware of?
- Make a note of this in your journal.

Tip: You can do this exercise or variations of it for more than three people and at any time in your life to check your behaviour and whether a relationship is out of balance.

Do not be afraid to set healthy boundaries. When you say "yes" to others make sure you are not saying "no" to yourself.

Chapter 8

PEOPLE PLEASERS PART 2: IT'S NOT YOUR JOB TO LIKE ME, IT'S MINE

"SOMETIMES YOU DON'T REALISE YOU ARE ACTUALLY DROWNING WHEN YOU ARE TRYING TO BE EVERYONE ELSE'S ANCHOR."

CASE STUDY
FARIDA

People pleasing has far-reaching consequences on identity, self-esteem and self-worth, to the point that you may no longer be in control of your own life. A fragmented and distorted identity is at the heart of people pleasing, and the roots can often be found in childhood, as highlighted in the previous chapter.

This case study is a first-hand powerful illustration of how childhood trauma, early nurture and subsequent limiting beliefs shaped my client's identity and behaviour in adult life. She spent the next 30 years battling an inner war with herself, fuelling subconscious people-pleasing behaviour to her detriment.

This is a sobering lesson on the importance of understanding who you are, and not compromising your core values and beliefs in the misguided view there will not be a personal price to pay.

REASON FOR COACHING

Farida came for coaching because she wanted a career change that incorporated satisfaction and happiness, something that had alluded her for the majority of her professional life. She had notable success as an economic analyst and was about to be promoted again, a concept which filled her with dread.

Since leaving university she had always worked in her field. She'd worked as an analyst for 20 years and during this time her enthusiasm for her work ranged from dislike to outright hatred. If she could just "change her career" her major problems would be solved, or so she thought.

In addition to this, Farida wanted to achieve more balance in her life and prioritise the right things, gaining confidence the to say "no" more of the time and she wanted to look after herself better emotionally, physically, spiritually and mentally.

While aware of her issues on a surface level, she was unaware of the subconscious drivers that that had got her to this point.

THE MASK

Farida is a smart, kind, thoughtful person who is very altruistic and amiable. She is married with three young children and a nanny helping to hold the fort at home. Her husband a successful businessman is often away with his work. Outwardly she appears organised and in control.

At work she *aspires to appear* "composed, professional, confident, presentable, commanding respect, intelligent and decisive". For the most part she achieves these things, but also displays less-helpful behaviours, such as being over-accommodating (at her own expense) in the misguided belief that if she says "yes" to every request, she will feel accepted and liked. But inwardly Farida resents her inability to say "no" more often.

Because she is able to come across as confident and in control – even when she is struggling to meet excessive work demands – Farida will soldier on to her detriment, rather than ask for assistance.

There is a witty, playful and creative side to Farida, but she increasingly finds fewer outlets for this expression. She is a little less guarded around her friends and family whom she loves. Her friends describe her as fun, having a great sense of humour, clever and creative, a good listener, insightful and resilient. They also highlight her lack of confidence and self-doubt which can manifest as indecisiveness. Close friends describe someone who is slowly losing her spark and zeal for life.

Like most people who lack self-awareness of their core identity, Farida is actively seeking to fit a mould of who *she thinks she should* be, from value systems deeply embedded in nurture and childhood experiences. Forcing the external to shape the internal person instead of the other way around.

BEHIND THE MASK

Farida is thoroughly exhausted, burning the candle at both ends. Even though she is keeping everything together at work and at home, her life feels as though it is spinning out of control. Like a row of spinning plates, if just one fails, the rest will come crashing down.

In sharp contrast to her professional persona, Farida was feeling an array of negative emotions that she fought hard to supress, and these were weighing heavily on her. Before the coaching began, she did not have the tools to deal with them.

Behind the mask she felt defeated, lacking confidence, full of self-doubt, indecisive, anxious, disillusioned, unfulfilled and completely disinterested in her job. She was craving fun with like-minded people [who shared her values and interests]. Her strong desire to put family first had pushed her over the edge to the sacrificial, and she was paying for it with her mental and physical health. High blood pressure, exhaustion, anxiety, low self-esteem: sound familiar? These are some of the traits and behaviours of people-pleasing syndrome and the casualties that result.

Being risk averse and reluctant to change meant Farida had to be pushed to the very edge before she would make a decision where she would be the primary beneficiary. Her marriage was also suffering, with a significant shift in the dynamics over a period of time; there was a growing distance between her husband and herself, and she was finding fewer opportunities for real communication, joy and self-expression within the marriage.

PREVIOUS LIMITING BELIEFS

The following is a list of the prevailing limiting beliefs that held Farida back most of the time, the top three being the most significant. These beliefs played on repeat in her subconscious thoughts and had a powerful influence over the direction of her life:

1 I can't do it – it's too hard

2 I always try to put everyone else first even at my own expense

3 I'm not worthy

4 I don't deserve…

5 I'm responsible for the happiness and well-being of everyone around me

6 I can't show my true self/feelings, if I expose who I really am, I won't be accepted

7 I need to be liked by everyone; I must have approval from all the significant people in my life

8 I shouldn't be boastful but should instead let others shine

9 People like me don't do 'that'

10 I have to pay the bills and so I can't pursue my interests as a career.

WHERE DID THESE BELIEFS COME FROM?

It was not obvious to Farida where some of the most destructive limiting beliefs came from. She had thought them for so long that she accepted them as FACT. Through the coaching process, she was only just becoming aware of how much these beliefs had impacted her life negatively and how she had been at the mercy of their conditioning. Values and beliefs that she'd learned early on from her family and peers had shaped her world view, her choices, her life.

Through a range of coaching exercises on beliefs and focused probing, we began to unpick the key drivers to her problems. In one exercise Farida completed the following sentence as follows:

Something I learned about myself from my parents was:

1 The importance of obeying rules
2 Family comes first
3 How to remain loyal and dutiful
4 Which values are important to me
5 Respect for authority
6 I hate injustice.

Coming from a close-knit family with a strong extended family and cultural influence, this first set of nurture beliefs ensured Farida remained compliant and towed the family line. There was no question of not living up to family expectations, even well into her professional life when she was living independently.

Assertiveness felt harsh, setting limits seemed rude and requesting that her needs be met felt demanding and selfish. It was hard to believe she had any rights at all because she felt guilty expressing real needs on the rare occasions that she was brave enough to attempt to act in her own self-interest.

But even this didn't explain fully the deep-rooted destructive behaviours that left Farida feeling like she like she could not put her own needs first within her relationship, within her work environment and often within her family.

As mentioned in Chapter Four (*Buried Alive*) the impact of unresolved childhood trauma can have a negative impact on the conscious and more often subconscious mind. These can shape the identity and behaviour of a person in adult life.

This was certainly Farida's case and I became increasingly curious about the root of some of the limiting beliefs she had gained from school:

Farida completed the following sentence:

Something I learned about myself from school was:

1 I don't like being different or drawing attention to myself
2 I like to belong
3 I can adapt to difficult situations when forced to
4 How to internalise my feelings
5 I hate injustice.

Farida mentioned that she had been bullied at school. But by delving deeper, to her surprise, we uprooted the keys to her guiding compass that had been leading her around subconsciously for 30 years.

Shortly before becoming a teenager, Farida's parents uprooted the family and moved abroad to a new country with a new language and culture completely foreign to Farida. She says: "The move was extremely traumatic for me and I found the first three years there incredibly difficult. I was bullied and put on a lot of weight." Farida did not fit in and was bullied mercilessly. She had to learn a new language, new customs and find her feet very quickly.

This left a deep and enduring imprint on her identity and in particular, the way her personality became distorted. Although she talked of the experience easily and as something she managed to overcome positively, I sensed there was more to it. Farida could remember very little about herself before this traumatic move and not a great deal of detail about many of her teenage years abroad.

After challenging Farida about this, she resolved to speak to her mother to find out what she could tell her about that time.

Farida was dumfounded by what she heard. Her mother said she'd been waiting many years for her to broach the subject. Before the move abroad, she described a daughter who was happy, confident, outgoing and very sociable with leadership qualities. Someone who would organise the neighbourhood children in games and events, a bright young girl that was happy to express her thoughts and ideas. There was no self-doubt or indecisiveness. Farida could hardly believe what she was hearing, and if it hadn't come from her mother, whom she loved and respected, she may not have been able to believe it!

During those teenage years, Farida lost her confidence and drive, she learned to withdraw, not show her true feelings and not draw attention to herself. By fitting in she was moulding herself into what her peers expected of her in order to gain approval; thus avoiding the isolation of hurtful, humiliating experiences she was frequently subjected to. Through this lens, unique things about her personality that were deemed as being different were rejected in the endeavour to fit in. This was the beginning of the disconnect with her *core identity*.

Much of this happened on a subconscious level, as Farida couldn't remember who she was before this traumatic event. She was just doing what she needed to do to survive, rather than thrive.

Into adulthood, her core identity continued to be suppressed. Behaviours which had helped her make the transition to a new country, school, and be accepted in a new peer group were still operating even though they were not required into adulthood. This learned behaviour created a perpetual "survival mode" mentality that entrenched itself into her personality. But now it was more of a hindrance than a help.

You see, we cannot run away from ourselves. Eventually we will run out of steam and have to face the consequences.

Farida was bent out of shape being the "square peg in the round hole" striving to fit in, be accepted and not make any waves. She was significantly out of touch with who she really was and as a result, no one got the best of her and neither did Farida.

The result? Farida was experiencing an *identity crisis*, there was a significant gulf between the public face she presented to the world and her true authentic self.

She had major difficulty with putting a true and authentic value on herself and as a result of these factors she cultivated the perfect soil for people-pleasing syndrome to grow and flourish, unchallenged.

According to author and family therapist Darlene Lancer, people pleasers are not aware that each time they hide who they are to please someone else, they give up a little self-respect. In the process, their true self; (what they really feel, think, need, and want) retreats a bit more. They become accustomed to sacrificing their needs and wants for so long that they may not know what they are. Decades of conveniently accommodating whittles away at the connection to their true self, and their lives and relationships begin to feel empty of joy and passion.

Because the need to preserve relationships is so strong, in the striving to be lovable and charitable, they reject character traits that won't serve that goal. But they can end up squelching entire chunks of their personality that are incompatible. Like showing anger, winning competitions, exercising power, getting attention, setting boundaries, or disagreeing with others.

THE COST OF PEOPLE PLEASING

Farida was very far from living her best life. The loss of connection with her core identity meant she'd also lost significant aspects of the things that fuelled her passion, energy and creativity. Entire chunks of herself were lost, buried under the mound of people pleasing. And so the perpetual conflict continued; fuelling anxiety, stress, high blood pressure, frustration, exhaustion, poor health, unfulfilled in work and relationships. In short, an emptiness where the light once was. She was in danger of living a completely empty life of servitude to those around her.

The excerpt below from a coaching exercise on beliefs illustrates just *one dimension* of the cost of Farida's belief that everyone's needs came before her own.

CHALLENGING LIMITING BELIEFS

Limiting belief: "I should always try to put everyone else first even at my own expense."

Q What are the consequences of holding this belief?
A The cost to me is that I am not able to feel comfortable doing anything that will bring me joy or pleasure if I have not made sure everyone else's needs are met first. My needs are always last.
Q How does it cause me to behave?
A Like I don't deserve anything good and that I find it difficult to be in a situation where I am the only one who benefits.
Q What evidence supports this belief?
A My everyday life!
Q Do other successful people hold this belief?
A No. Not to the same sacrificial extent.
Q What is this belief costing me on a daily basis?
A It is exhausting. It means anything that is not essential for me, I feel is frivolous or indulgent and will not feature on my list of my priorities e.g., pass times, hobbies, relaxation.
Q What will this belief cost me in the long term?
A Happiness, fulfilment, joy, recreation, relaxation…
Q How will my life be different if I let go of this belief?
A I should be able to benefit from all the things I'm missing out on.
Q Do I want to change this belief?
A Yes, but it's not easy to do so.

Empowering belief: "My needs matter"

Q What evidence supports this belief?
A The fact that if other people are able to ensure their needs are met, then the same should apply to me.

Q Who do I know that has this belief?
A Many of the people I come across who are confident and dynamic hold this belief. Also, those who have self-belief and determination.
Q What will happen when I hold this belief?
A I will be able to strike the right balance between being caring and altruistic with looking after myself and my own needs.

When Farida decided to first challenge then change these beliefs, she was no longer at the mercy of her conditioning.

This was no easy task for Farida because through a close inspection of her true personality through personality assessments, we uncovered key traits like being altruistic, supportive, reliable, patient, imaginative, observant, enthusiastic, loyal and hardworking, good practical skills with a strong desire to take care of her family.

All looking good so far... but conversely, these same traits when exposed to people-pleasing syndrome, acted like a battering ram. It took real work for Farida to distinguish the dividing line between what was authentic and what was flawed.

Imagine a seamstress sewing a garment on a machine, but the hem is skewed. They have to go back and unpick by hand the faulty hem, before it can be stitched back correctly. This was the case with Farida. Only a close inspection and unpicking could separate the fact from fiction.

THE JOURNEY TO TRANSFORMATION

Change was not an overnight thing. Every day Farida had to make choices to actively embrace behaviours that would either move her forward toward her goals or choose to be passive and remain stagnant, which over time would essentially drag her backward.

Farida's journey to transformation was incremental over a period of time, which broadly comprised of the following steps:

STEPS TO FREEDOM

1 Revelation

Finding the root cause of the most harmful self-talk/limiting beliefs that were directing her life. Waking up from sleep walking: gaining self-awareness and an understanding of the true cost of the damaging behaviours that were robbing her of peace, fulfilment and true happiness.

When the *arrested development* of the teenage Farida was revealed, it smoothed the path to finding her core identity and the subsequent beliefs that needed to be reframed for true progress and transformation.

2 Reframing beliefs begins the journey to self-discovery

By learning how to *call her subconscious mind to account*, Farida was no longer being led around by negative thoughts and patterns of behaviour that went previously unchallenged.

For the first time, she was able to recognise the root of her limiting beliefs, how they were acquired and from whom, assessing their veracity. Then she was able to reframe those beliefs based on the truth, including personal positive affirmations as the basis for embedding new more helpful guiding beliefs. With each success, she was rebuilding parts of her core identity, free from the trauma related inhibitors that had held her captive for so long.

3 Paradigm shifting behaviours

Viewing the same situation from more empowered and different perspectives based on genuine revelations helped free Farida to take steps towards making permanent changes away from her people pleasing behaviour, while simultaneously increasing her self-worth and value.

4 Incremental changes

Farida started with taking steps to achieve small wins and then increasing them, such as learning how to say "no" and understanding her triggers, or not over-explaining herself and apologising for everything.

She then moved on to bigger wins. For example, Farida valued traditions and respected those learned from her parents. This coupled with her risk averse nature and difficulty embracing change meant situations would often have to reach breaking point before she could be persuaded by circumstance, or the strong personality of a loved one to alter her course. Combined with her excessive altruism she was reluctant to burden anyone else, while her troubles mounted unassisted.

At work Farida was doing the work of a minimum of three employees but didn't believe she could get any help from the company to employ additional staff. Through coaching Farida stepped out of her comfort zone and we worked on negotiating a proposal for the CEO to invest more resources into her team. This was a huge step for Farida, who had to firstly see and believe the immense value of her department and her work to the company and then believe that by putting forward the business case, her request would not be rejected out of hand. Before this, her attitude would have been to soldier on to the point of exhaustion.

5 Discovering real identity and value

Dealing with the limiting beliefs that had fuelled Farida's distorted identity and people pleasing behaviour led to uncovering her true personality [part of her core identity] that had been supressed from her early teens. By learning who she really was, she gave herself permission to exist in that space.

This began a joyful journey of discovery to recognise, celebrate and focus on her strengths and natural talents, which included being creative, intelligent, articulate, funny, imaginative, perceptive and empathic.

6 Unlocking strengths and natural talents

A series of exercises to raise self-awareness helped Farida to unearth the real person, along with all its suppressed passions that had been obscured for so long.

Unlocking her core identity, reawakened Farida's creative expressive side, her dreams and passions and the things that motivated her and gave her energy. Among these were her desire to perform. Farida was learning to stop shelving her dreams and was finding outlets to begin exercising them again. This began with a commitment to attend spoken word events and join a local performing arts company. Achievable goals that also required Farida to reframe her belief to understand that doing something for herself would bring a benefit not just to her, but her family also because she was happier, more relaxed and energised.

I hope you were inspired by Farida's story. However, it does end with a word of caution. It is never too early to free yourself from the ravages of people-pleasing syndrome. Don't put off what you may now recognise as a significant issue in your life. Farida's health was seriously impacted with the years and intensity of people pleasing. Although the realisation which came through coaching provided a way out, there was also a personal cost for Farida, who through intense stress and burnout suffered a significant blow to her health that has taken months of rehabilitation.

> "Your need for acceptance can make you invisible in this world. Don't let anything stand in the way of the light that shines through this form. Risk being seen in all of your glory."
>
> **JIM CARREY**

Chapter 9

GETTING PERSONAL: MY IDENTITY CRISIS

"A DIAMOND'S CREATION REQUIRES IMMENSE PRESSURE AND INTENSE TEMPERATURES TO REACH ITS HIGHEST POTENTIAL. WITHOUT ENDURING THE ADVERSITY AND PRESSURE OF ITS ENVIRONMENT, THE DIAMOND WOULD NEVER BECOME THE TREASURE IT WAS MEANT TO BE. MAY THE CHANGES YOU GROW THROUGH BRING INCREDIBLE VALUE IN HELPING YOU FORGE A REMARKABLE AND MULTI-FACETED LIFE."

SUSAN C. YOUNG

According to the Urban Dictionary, a *diamond in the rough* relates to "someone (or something) that has hidden exceptional characteristics and/or future potential, but currently lacks the final touches that would make them (or it) truly stand out from the crowd".

But diamonds can be mistaken for worthless pebbles, and that's where my story begins.

My identity crisis began the moment I was born. Stories I heard as a child was that I was supposed to be a boy. I was the youngest of four siblings; one boy and two girls. My parents wanted a boy who was going to be called Patrick.

Unfortunately for them, I was another girl. Although my first name was Suzanne, I was called Patricia (as a consolation) instead of "Patrick" which was abbreviated to "Pat". One of the very first messages I got from this was that my name was insignificant. It rhymed with everything from *cat, fat, bat* and was like a phonic sound, not an actual name, which all my siblings had. No one abbreviated their names to a mere connective sound. An insignificant name for an insignificant child. My position on the pecking order was the last of four children. Far from being the "parents' pet", I felt overlooked and ignored.

I was the reluctant recipient of "*hand me down*" clothes, that passed from not one but two sisters. By the time they reached me they were typically three to five years old, so being in fashion in my early years was out of the question. I often remember resentfully looking on as my two siblings (sisters, two-and-a-half and five-years older than me) received fashionable new clothes. I rarely had anything that was purchased just for me. The subconscious message I heard was *you're not important*, *you're not worth the expense of anything new, you're insignificant in this family.*

Family life was turbulent with regular arguments between my parents. My mother had a sharp tongue and dished out insults and putdowns to my father in quick-fire succession. I was consistently told by her "you're just like your father" – with whom I felt she held such vitriol – another subconscious attack on my identity.

My father's method of encouraging me was constant criticism, lack of praise and making comparisons with other people. In particular a good school friend "why can't you be more like her?" My grades at school were never good enough if I got a 'B' why didn't you get an 'A'? If I got an 'A' why didn't you get an 'A+'? and the subconscious message: "you're not good enough, nothing you do will ever be good enough".

Being the youngest, I always felt that when my older siblings became teenagers, much of the basic parenting stopped, particularly from my mother. Although there was six years between me and my oldest sibling, I felt neglected as a child in many ways, because I was expected to or left to do the things that they could do, even though I still needed nurturing and assistance. For example, I was hand washing and ironing much of my own clothes from a very young age. When I was eight years, my brother was 14 and my older sister was 13. Yet *I felt* some of the same practical responsibility.

Although I was the youngest sibling of four, I always felt a little different and apart from my siblings. I didn't attend the same schools that they did.[13] They all went to the same primary school together. I went to a different primary school on my own. Similarly, I went to a different secondary school too, and therefore didn't have many of the same shared experiences they had.

I also looked very different to my siblings. I was lighter skinned in complexion and the only one who looked like my father. All three of my siblings would often make fun of me, claiming I wasn't really their sister. "Go and put a red dot on your head like the Indians", "you're not one of us", "go and find your real family", "the stork bought you here, not our mum."

In a family of six, I felt very alone.

When I was around nine years old, I discovered the pop group Adam & The Ants. I was a massive fan and I got the album. This horrified my siblings, who said it was "too white!" and "I was not black enough". I was only allowed to play the record before 9am on the family HiFi system because it wasn't black music and frequently told that was what I *should* be listening to instead. Undeterred, I played my album under their curfew and never stopped being a fan.

Message that was reinforced: "You're different, you don't fit in."

I had a very close friend at primary school who lived nearby. But unbeknown to me, my friend's mother did not like me spending too much time with her. When we were around 10 years old, she told my father I was distracting her daughter from her studies. My father told me "I was not wanted there." And the message that became embedded was: "You're not good enough!".

This is in no way a criticism of my parents or siblings' actions, but rather to highlight how just a few key events impacted on how the flaws in my identity were developed in my formative years. These individual events alone would not be significant, but together they formed a powerful tapestry for my subconscious mind to draw on as an ever-ready resource, sending a stream of messages to my *conscious* mind about my identity, value and worth.

In my early years I was not very fond of my parents and I do not believe they were particularly fond of me. I do not remember receiving emotional love and affection from my parents, particularly my dad, after the age of about five or six, so I didn't feel especially loving towards them. I viewed home merely as territory I had to navigate until I could gain my freedom. I didn't know it then, but I had learned to live with a constant stream of anxiety, anger and resentment. It was me against the world!

But depending on whether you believe the proverbial glass is half-full or half-empty, there were many upsides to my experience, which I didn't always appreciate at the time. I was that diamond being refined; I just didn't know it then!

I had an independent streak from a very young age. For my voice to be heard and my needs to be met within my family I had to make a lot of noise, assert a strong will and strategize constantly.

When I was about five or six years old, I had already learned that could not rely on my mother's promises, because she often did not follow-through on things (she juggled a great many responsibilities: four children, a full-time job, husband and numerous entrepreneurial ventures). I had already figured out that I was responsible for ensuring I got what was important to me, rather than leave this to fate or the mercy of others.

I really wanted a new kilt skirt that I had seen in a clothes shop in Bruce Grove, Tottenham, about two miles from our home. A russet plaid skirt complete with a jumbo pin, which was all the rage in the mid-1970s. I had already been given the money (five pounds) and was waiting for my mother to get home from work on Saturday afternoon to take me. Time was ticking, I thought she was going to let me down, so I decided to get on the bus and go to Bruce Grove myself. I told my older siblings I was going, and set off. I was nervous, wondering if I would remember exactly where to get off the bus, but this didn't perturb me. I had my eyes on the prize. A brand-new kilt skirt. I did it! I got there and got back safely: my first-round trip alone on the bus!

Well, my mother nearly passed out when she got home, ready to take me, only to find I'd already gone without her. She charged down to the shop on the first bus to find me, convinced that I would be lost somewhere, only to be advised by the sales assistant that I'd been and gone.

On a week-long school trip to Pendarren House in Wales when I was 10 years old, my classmates and I were presented with a range of physical pursuits, one of these activities being caving. The night before I had slipped on soap and fell badly in the shower bruising my legs and arms. A few hundred yards inside the cave we were told to go single file crawling on our stomachs through a tunnel as big as a tree trunk. Now for a child who did a "risk assessment" to even use the school's playground jungle gym, I was very apprehensive about attempting this. As I saw my classmates proceed single file through this narrow tunnel on their stomachs (I couldn't determine how many metres long it was) with low-level water flowing through at the same time, my anxiety levels grew.

As I approached to proceed, I could feel the bruises on my legs rubbing against the hard rock surface and resolutely decided that was it: I was not going through that tunnel! I made such a commotion about being in pain with my bruises, that an adult worker had to personally escort me out of the cave and wait with me for the expedition to finish. The adult was clearly disappointed she couldn't complete the activity, but I was very happy to be waiting at the top of the hill for my classmates to emerge.

It wasn't until many years later recounting this story that a friend pointed out how single-minded I was. I hadn't cared what my classmates thought of me "chickening out", or the annoyance of the adult worker who was forced to chaperone me until the expedition was complete. I realised that my friend was right, and the relief of not going through that tunnel on my stomach had been more than enough for me.

I never did get used to the phonic sound my name was abbreviated to, so I bided my time, and at the age of 10, I decided to change my name and be called by my first name "Suzanne". I thought this would be a good time to make the change as I would soon be leaving to attend secondary school and it would be a fresh start. At first my family were not fully respectful of this and I didn't feel they took me seriously. They would try and call me Suzanne, but as soon as my back was turned, they would still refer to me as "Pat" to one another. But after many years of perseverance, my first name finally stuck.

These were glimmers of the abundance of resilience, determination and single-mindedness embedded in my identity. Key attributes that spurred me on through many challenges and adventures through life, granting me the ability to be my own person: but who was that person?

Up until the age of five when I started school, I was at home. I didn't go to a nursery, and during the day I spent many hours in my own company entertaining myself, as my siblings were all at school. This is where my love of reading and imaginative play really took hold. I would spend hours transporting myself into different worlds through books, imagining how the lives of characters I'd become engrossed in would develop long after the book had come to an end. I displayed great talent and ability for reading, writing and poetry.

However, I was poorly socialised with children my age and lacked the social skills needed to make a smooth transition to infant school. At playtime, I learned quickly that I wasn't comfortable in large groups. I preferred making meaningful friendships with only a handful of friends at a time.

For many years I believed I was an introvert because I was often told by my family that I was shy, a cry baby and a coward. I was given some of these labels before I even understood what they were. In my very early years, I do remember crying often and not being amiable to certain people. The truth was that even at a young age, I refused to pretend I liked people that I didn't, I cried out of frustration of my circumstances and to get my voice heard, and my poor socialisation in early years meant I had a steeper hill to climb. The question was, did I believe what they said, or did I know better?

The messages transported directly to the subconscious mind are powerful. I was too young to articulate the feelings of rejection, loneliness and being misunderstood, but they were imprinted on my subconscious mind, making destructive inroads and advancing on my core identity. They were showing up in my behaviour without me realising it and I was hiding in plain sight. What you seek to project isn't always what people see.

Even though I believed many things were wrong with me, I was determined to push through in spite of those strikes on my identity. As a result, I subconsciously sought to overcompensate for my perceived deficits.

MASK

- I thought I was shy (I just hadn't socialised in early years)
- I thought I could hide (what I thought was wrong with me)

- I thought I could work out who I SHOULD be and be that person
- I thought I could be whoever I wanted to be (something outside of myself)
- I thought I could rely on outward things, possessions, looks, career and achievements to determine who I was (my identity)
- I had to work hard for anything that was of any value located outside of myself (didn't see the diamond already inside of myself).

It didn't for a second cross my mind that I would have to deal with the limiting beliefs always bubbling under the surface – that had interwoven with my very being – to the extent that I didn't question whether they even belonged there.

I used talent and determination to push through in spite of these underlying beliefs, but on reflection, this path was a much tougher journey. I had *bravado and resilience,* but not the inner confidence that comes with the peace of knowing who you really are; and dealing with the limiting beliefs that place a cap on your ability to achieve your full potential or enjoy the serenity and harmony that come with it.

NOT DEALING WITH LIMITING BELIEFS AND TRYING TO OVERCOMPENSATE

Passive acceptance of the negative beliefs around my identity gained from childhood meant I didn't recognise or put value on all of my *strengths and natural talents* that came as easily as breathing. I knew I had talent and ability, but didn't recognise the *depth* of what I already had, or the potential positive impact I could make in the lives of others. I was only halfway there. I needed to uncover and remove the *obstacles* blocking the full expression of my core identity. Until then, the cost to myself can be summarised as follows:

- I could not fully enjoy the successes in my life, I didn't have full rest and enjoyment in them because I felt like I was always striving (never good enough)
- Not being satisfied or content with my achievements – being too hard on myself and judging myself too harshly
- Always feeling like something was wrong (anxiousness)
- Didn't use my innate skills as adeptly as I could have (I didn't yet know the value and impact they had)
- I didn't value the unique traits in my personality and understand how they could benefit my goals and my passions
- I didn't see (at the time) how some of my lessons were gifts: I only saw the struggle
- A ring of steel – rarely showing true vulnerability around people I loved or cared about – to keep up the bravado
- An expectation that I would be harshly judged and rejected by the handful of people I loved or felt devotion towards.

The result for myself and those around me was a distorted picture of Suzanne. To some extent we are all walking around with a mask, carefully assembled from the experiences and subsequent limiting beliefs that help shape a distorted picture of who we really are. Picture trying to walk around with a foot in plaster on a pair of crutches, with one of your arms in a sling. For more deep-rooted cases, add a pair of blindfolds. That's basically how we navigate life before we deal with the limiting beliefs that have helped shape our thoughts about who we are; our value and how willing we are to find and fulfil our authentic purpose.

Removing my mask was going to require the truthful introspection of everything I was hiding behind. When all was stripped away, I had to be naked and vulnerable, stepping out of my comfort zone to take the leaps of faith required one stride at a time.

This book and the insights and exercises within it takes you on a comprehensive journey to discovering your core identity and authentic purpose, while dealing with the obstacles holding you back. I have also had to embark on the same journey to find out who I really am, so I know it works! But I'd like to highlight below just a few pivotal moments that helped me on my journey to discovery and surmounting the obstacles that were holding me back.

FORGIVENESS

One of the biggest obstacles for me was unforgiveness. I had anger and resentment towards my parents about the way I grew up, that I didn't even realise was there. I'd grown up in a family that were not big on forgiving and forgetting, so being in this state seemed very normal.

However, it was fuelling a distorted filter to my life and the world. When I recognised this and forgave my parents from my heart, my relationship towards them transformed. I understood them better, I even felt genuine love for them and more appreciation for the things they did that had benefited me, *which were many*. I accepted them as they were warts-and-all. I felt like a huge weight had been lifted from my shoulders. An inner-healing took place. I was beginning to understand what *unconditional love* meant in practice and also learning to forgive myself.

Unforgiveness and all the negativity associated with it acts as a deceptive barricade that blocks anything good from coming in, while trapping the junk inside which needs to be disposed of.

UNDERSTANDING MY STRENGTHS AND NATURAL TALENTS

Around 2010, I had a lightbulb moment. I really understood for the first time the value and impact of my strengths and natural talents. At the time my former editor Richard was mentoring me through career transition and asked me what my skills and motivations were. He said: "It's one thing thinking you know, but you determine this by the impact that you have on others." This prompted me to seek feedback and assess results from other people's perspectives more keenly.

As part of my coach training, I completed a simple 360-degree feedback exercise, which asked key people, (close friends and colleagues) a series of simple questions related to what they thought about me; my skills, value, impact, etc. At the time I was quite cocky and thought I knew the majority of what they would say.

But when the responses came in, I gained so much valuable insight. Many of the things my colleagues and friends found most valuable about me were things that came most naturally to me that I hadn't put a value on. I thought they would value the things I'd strived hard to achieve more, so it truly was a revelation. Until that time I had been viewing things through my limiting belief filter of "everything of value has to be earned" such as my Bachelor's degree; while in fact what my close friends and colleagues had told me they valued was my spirituality, wisdom, honesty, openness, straightforwardness, humour, ability to get people to open up and tell me things they thought they never would and my genuine interest in people and their lives.

This was the impetus I needed to discover parts of my core identity that had been obscured, overlooked and not fully understood and set me on the path to discovering my purpose. The personality traits and gifts I had to get me there were always present.

What an amazing time of revelation and freedom it was when I began the active journey of discovery. Recognising and dealing with the limiting beliefs that had impacted me for so long.

LEARNING TO LISTEN, *REALLY* LISTEN

I was a good listener when helping and assisting others, but my inner filters kept blocking and bouncing off many valuable messages *to me* that would have been like golden nuggets, had I had the focus to receive them at the time.

Think of a game of squash; two players are facing the front wall. Player one hits the ball [the message] to the wall and it rebounds straight back to the same player. If the second player gets a handle on the ball [the message] they will also slam it again to the front wall, but it will keep rebounding.

Like the wall in a squash court, my inner filters were blocking and then rebounding numerous messages that could have made many positive differences to my life. When I identified and dealt with those filters [limiting beliefs, distorted identity], *my ability to listen, hear and really benefit* from valuable insight and guidance supercharged my progress to understanding who I am and fulfilling my purpose.

YOUR PURPOSE

All things are guiding you to your destiny. We all have messages – *golden opportunities* around us all of the time which are often missed because our focus has been obscured by unhelpful filters – that hinder us from recognising these opportunities and taking subsequent action.

But if you recognise and respond in the right way, before your very eyes the elements come together like an ornate tapestry.

The peace that comes with knowing who you really are is priceless and more valuable than any monetary wealth. All things can really work together for good; nothing is wasted if you will learn from it and keep moving forward.

Now I can happily say that I am a passionate, emotional and fiercely loyal encourager, explorer of the psyche who operates with integrity, compassion and vigour to transform lives out of straight jackets into bespoke suits.

Remember diamonds are created under pressure so hold on, allow the refining process to do its work, then it will be your time to shine.

Chapter 10

INFLUENCE: DON'T WALK IN MY HEAD WITH YOUR DIRTY FEET

"To live is to influence."

Influence is the capacity to have an effect on the character, development or behaviour of someone or something. Every interaction, conversation, attitude and action have the potential to influence. We are like sponges. We take in various stimuli from whatever is around us, filtered by our values, beliefs and experiences.

I used to believe I was pretty much immune from negative influence or control by others because I have such a strong sense of myself and I'm a determined and decisive person. I was wrong.

What I didn't realise is that influence – powerful influence – is insidious in nature and no one is immune. This is because for the most part, you are not consciously aware of how you are influenced, and therefore simply accept its impact or effect without a fight or a challenge. Subtle influence is powerful. And it works both ways; you influence others and others influence you.

The *Merriam-Webster dictionary* defines influence as "the power or capacity of causing an effect in indirect or intangible ways: *sway*." Think about how you sway, it is subtle and not a deliberate action, more like a drifting or leaning. If you've ever ridden home on a train, tired after a long day at work, no doubt the rocking motion of the train can cause you to drift in and out of consciousness in a sleepy stupor, swaying from side-to-side without noticing, until a sudden jolt wakes you up.

That's how subtle influence works. You don't see it coming, it catches you off-guard, but if you don't wake up, you'll miss your destination.

This is why it is important to shine a light on what influences you, to eliminate unhelpful and negative sources and actively promote positive sources of influence more aligned to your core identity and your authentic purpose.

A crucial aspect of influence is the emotional connection you make with people; when there is relationship and trust, it is easy for people to align their views and values with your own.

Influence involves the process of two emotional states coming together.

This emotional connection can also be applied to objects and ideas. Marketing is heavily reliant on making an emotional connection with the consumer to influence their decision to purchase their products. We shop with the heart much more than the head. Marketing and advertising campaigns failing to evoke consumer feelings are largely unsuccessful.

We know there are some obvious positive and negative influences, for instance, a friend encouraging you to try illegal drugs or commit a crime is an obvious bad influence. A friend who encourages and supports you to succeed in your new business venture is a good influence.

This chapter is concerned with uncovering the influences not obvious to the naked eye, but play a big part in distorting your true identity and scuppering your authentic success by steering you off course.

THE POWER OF ASSOCIATION

"Show me your friends and I'll show you your future" is a biblical concept taken from the Proverbs of King Solomon: "He who walks with wise men will be wise: but a companion of fools shall be destroyed."

The influence of those you spend time with is going to have a profound effect on your success or failure in life and even how you view yourself.

Think about it... When you spend a lot of time with someone, you start speaking in the way they speak, use phrases they use, think like them and emulate them without even realising it. Similarly, if you watch a lot of a particular television series, you may well start to use terminology you have picked up from it or fashioning yourself like the characters. Two emotional states have come together. Wakanda Forever anyone?

Have you noticed that when someone moves to another country, even if that country speaks the same language they do, their accent changes and reflects the country they are living in, whether in obvious inflections, or a full-blown transformation?

On social media, different communities pop up and form a type of herd mentality. They go along with the majority to fit in, and agree to remain accepted as opposed to what they really feel but are too afraid to say. This is *peer pressure*; people or groups that you associate with, applying their influence to move you toward their way of thinking. In your need to be popular and accepted within the group you may not even realise you have given up your individual thoughts and opinions. Part of your identity is becoming warped right under your nose.

We are either limited or we excel by the type of company we keep. Research and salient advice from successful people back this up. Research by social psychologist Dr. David McClelland found the people you habitually associate with [your reference group] determine as much as 95% of your success or failure in life. Entrepreneur and motivational speaker Jim Rohn said: "You are the average of the five people you spend the most time with."

This is why your friends and associates are a reflection of you. Colin Powell, the late former United States general and statesman said: "A mirror reflects a man's face, but what he is really like is shown by the kind of friends he chooses. The simple but true fact of life is that you become like those with whom you closely associate for the good and the bad."

Our friends provide us with a certain comfort level. It can be a calming feeling having like-minded people around us. Unfortunately, that degree of security doesn't do much to push us to expand our horizon or to challenge our thoughts.

If everyone in your network shares the same opinion, what do you learn? If everyone in your network is afraid to step a toe into uncharted waters because they cling tightly to their comfort zone, how likely are they to push you to break out of your self-imposed barriers?

So how does this work in practice? If you spend time with people who spend more than they make, the chances are high that you will spend more money than you make. If you socialise with people who go to the pub five nights a week, the chances are excellent that you will be there too. If your friends don't like to travel and try out new destinations, the chances are you won't either. If most of your close friends don't read many books, the chances are excellent that you won't either. If people around you have a negative and cynical attitude, its practically a sure thing that you will become negative and cynical too.

If this were not so, you wouldn't spend as much time with them as you do. You would be uncomfortable, maybe restless or frustrated in their company because alignment is no longer there. The ambitions and dreams inside of you would be at odds with your environment and calling out for change.

When you hear the phrase "we don't have a lot in common", that's exactly what it means, there is no alignment, but friction. The dream in your heart may be bigger than the environment in which you find yourself.

Sometimes you have to change that environment and the people within it to see that dream fulfilled. Powell advised: "The less you associate with some people, the more your life will improve. Any time you tolerate mediocrity in others, it increases your mediocrity.

An important attribute in successful people is their impatience with negative thinking and negative acting people. As you grow, your associates will change. Some of your friends will not want you to go on. They will want you to stay where they are. Friends that don't help you climb will want you to crawl. Your friends will stretch your vision or choke your dream. Those that don't increase you will eventually decrease you."

A common theme I see with my coaching clients who work with me to transform and achieve their goals is that they often do not have support from friends and sometimes family for their ambitions or personal growth. As they begin to grow and excel, one of the first things to change is their circle of friends and acquaintances, which enables the metamorphosis to take hold and work. It's like the shedding of excess skin, like a caterpillar. I've noticed that shedding is an evolutionary thing because revelation which brings awareness precedes change, *two cannot walk together unless they agree.*[14]

This isn't necessarily because friends are intentionally causing obstacles. They are just content where they are and do not share the client's vision and are often afraid of change.

But staying the same is not staying in neutral, rather it implies losing ground. It's a fact of life that some people hold us back, while others propel us forward. There is no middle ground. Do not be deceived and compare yourself to the lowest common denominator in your group and tell yourself that you are alright. These are excuses and justifications for why people remain stagnant and do not fulfil their potential.

For example, if you are part of the close group of friends that consume alcohol regularly at the pub five nights a week while you only go four times; you can convince yourself that you do not have a drinking problem. Despite the impact on your health and family life, you reason that your partner should not complain because you do better than your other friends in the group that you compare yourself to. Just because they drink more often than you, it doesn't mean that you don't have a problem.

SUBCONSCIOUS INFLUENCE

"THE SUBCONSCIOUS IS CEASELESSLY MURMURING, AND IT IS BY LISTENING TO THESE MURMURS THAT ONE HEARS THE TRUTH."

GASTON BACHELARD

The subconscious nature of insidious influence is what makes it much more powerful than your ability to simply control your actions, which would require a conscious intention. We are always exerting influence simply by being who we are, saying what we say and doing what we do. Being aware is the only real choice you have in deliberately filtering out the unhelpful influences and promoting positive influences.

For example, Naomi started coaching sessions a few weeks ago. She has a great idea for a business venture born out of the current global outpouring of consciousness around the *Black Lives Matter Movement*. She shared her idea with her best friend Natasha and asked for her support. Natasha proceeded to tell her all the reasons why the idea would not work and discouraged her from continuing with it. Natasha meant well, but she was reflecting her own insecurities and hopelessness onto Naomi. Before, Naomi would have agreed with Natasha and not pursued it any further. She may even have added more reasons for why she shouldn't bring her idea to life.

This is a familiar scenario for Naomi and Natasha, they are very close friends, having both connected through similar experiences of difficult childhoods. Both are unsatisfied with life and feel stagnant in their progress. But because of this mutual respect and connection, neither is able to sufficiently challenge the other. They are both in the "*same boat*" rowing around in circles.

But something is awakening in Naomi, she has a burning desire for change and fulfilment, and is gaining awareness of the subconscious negative influences that have held her back. This time, instead of giving up, she realises the impact of Natasha's influence and is consciously able to reject it and move forward with her plans, seeking out the support of like-minded people.

Without challenge, your subconscious mind will always revert to familiar patterns [of your associations] and easily override your conscious intentions, leading you down unhelpful paths without you realising it.

Simon was in his late thirties and constantly talked about wanting more out of life and settling down to start a family. His current lifestyle was "rolling with the boys", who were all grown men with children of their own, but with no particular focus and were not really settled. I met him at a wedding and we talked about the desires that he had for his life and what he thought was missing. He was eager for change and to get more meaning out of his life. He wanted some life coaching sessions to set things in motion.

After our conversation he was very excited and intrigued at the fact I had so much insight into his predicament. He told me that it was as though he had a chance to exhale for the first time in years. In this excited fervour he shared his intentions with his close friends. They all laughed at him and said coaching would be a waste of time, telling him that there was nothing wrong with him, and besides, I might put some kind of spell on him.

Simon had seen a window of light, but this ridicule and discouragement from people he loved and respected was enough for him to back down and put his dreams on hold.

It took another seven years for Simon to put his head up above the parapet and make the desired changes to his life, as the inner conflict had only grown stronger and his dissatisfaction deeper in what he described as "those empty years". After making a *conscious decision* to settle down, he met his special lady and they started a family. He also made a conscious decision to pursue business interests not associated with his close friends, instead of being the "third wheel" in some of their previous business deals.

Why did it take so long for Simon to pursue his authentic goals? He was heavily influenced by his friends. Although his desires were changing and his life was increasingly becoming incongruent, he didn't yet have a clear picture of who he was and his core identity. Instead, he got swept along on a "boys about town lifestyle" to fit in with his close circle of friends, none of whom had the desire to change.

When he finally broke away and was able to make his own authentic choices, it cost him the majority of his close friendships because those friends would not accept his choices, despite the obvious happiness and fulfilment it was giving to him. But Simon has no regrets, only that he wasted seven good years, playing a role and maintaining a lifestyle that no longer suited him.

Remember, we don't normally let people yank us off course and wreck our lives completely because we would notice and wake up; but they do unconsciously nudge us off course like the swaying action of a train, bumping us off course a little at a time. Then many years later you may well wake up and wonder how did I get here? What was I doing with my life?

Being aware gives you the power to do something about it.

So far, I have highlighted how the people closest to you can influence your mood, how you spend your time and your perspective on the world. They can even change your view of yourself. I have also highlighted how much of this influence does not happen on a conscious level. Casting light on these influences enables you to take control and make conscious choices that are positively aligned to your core identity and authentic purpose.

"IF YOU ARE NOT IN THE PROCESS OF GROWING INTO THE PERSON YOU WERE CREATED TO BE, YOU ARE AUTOMATICALLY ENGAGED IN BECOMING THE PERSON YOU DON'T WANT TO BE."

DALE CARNEGIE

Practical exercise

CORE INSIGHT ACTION

WHAT INFLUENCES ME?

Part 1: The time ratio

Take a look at your friendships/network:

- Who do you spend the most time with? List the top 5 people.
- How do you feel when you are with them?
- Do they help to elevate you or diminish you?

Answer the following questions for EACH of the five people you have listed:

- What does this have me listening to?
- What does this have me reading?
- What does this have me thinking?
- How does this have me feeling?
- What does this have me saying?
- What does this have me settling for?
- What does this have me becoming?
- What do I have to show for it?
- What have I learned?

Part 2: Make an inventory

- Take a sheet of paper and divide it into two columns with headings **Positive Influences** and **Negative Influences**.

Practical exercise

- Look at your responses from part one and put them into the positive or negative influences column. Think about why you have judged each response to be positive or negative. i.e., did you learn something, feel empowered, focused and inspired, or did you get side tracked, were you left feeling ineffective, stagnant or drained?
- How long is each column?
- How much of the influence you uncovered was *subconscious influence*; things that you hadn't noticed before?
- Add a third column (on a new page) called **Subconscious Influence / New Awareness** and write down your responses.
- Pay attention to how many of the answers in this column are **positive** and **negative.**
- What did you learn?

"YOUR SUBCONSCIOUS IS A POWERFUL AND MYSTERIOUS FORCE WHICH CAN EITHER HOLD YOU BACK OR HELP YOU MOVE FORWARD. WITHOUT ITS COOPERATION, YOUR BEST GOALS WILL BE UNREALISED; WITH ITS HELP YOU ARE UNBEATABLE."

JENNY DAVIDOW

Part 3: Take responsibility and action

Now you are more aware of what is influencing you for the better or worse, you can put the brakes on and change direction. You have control over what influences you and what influence you will allow to continue in your life. The following steps will guide you:

1 Be clear about your values and beliefs and let them guide your direction
Set mental boundaries: take time to consciously plan which activities, opinions, attitudes and life-philosophies you *will and will not allow* in your life. Refer to your guiding beliefs from Chapter Four.

2 Take responsibility and set clear boundaries
Look at the positive influences in your life that align with your values, beliefs and goals and increase the time ratio you spend with these people (and related activities). Minimise the time spent with people who influence you negatively and the time spent on redundant activities.

3 Set a vision for your future so you don't get side-tracked
Have a vision for your life; be clear about the goals and milestones that will take you there. Keep your eyes on the prize. Be clear about the characteristics of people that will enable you to thrive. There will be more on discerning and shaping your vision in part three of this book.

At the very least, the people you spend the most time with should:

- Motivate you to be your best
- Support you
- Push you to meet your goals
- Inspire you
- Help you transform.

4 Take control: actively create and nurture your network
Birds of a feather flock together, therefore you cannot soar like an eagle with a pigeon mentality. In other words, it is unrealistic to hang out with negative people and expect to have a positive life.

Actively construct your social environment. Don't let it depend on proximity or chance or on how it has always been. Now your radar is switched on, you will actively seek out new friendships or develop exciting acquaintances that are aligned to you. Be persistent with surrounding yourself with those who bring out the best in you. Be relentless in having a network who constantly challenges you as much as you challenge yourself.

Taking responsibility for what you allow to influence you will help you to:

- Live authentically and be your true self (one less obstacle)
- Perform at a higher level, be more productive
- Find solutions more readily
- Get along better with others
- Reconcile conflict more quickly
- Come up with great ideas
- Reduce stress
- Give your best
- Positively inspire and motivate others, just being who you are!

"With some people you spend an evening: with others you invest it. Be careful where you stop to inquire for directions along the road of life. Wise is the person who fortifies his life with the right friendships. If you run with wolves, you will learn how to howl. But, if you associate with eagles, you will learn how to soar to great heights."

COLIN POWELL

Chapter 11

COMMUNICATION PART 1: WHAT DO YOU SEE?

"THE WAY WE COMMUNICATE WITH OTHERS AND WITH OURSELVES ULTIMATELY DETERMINES THE QUALITY OF OUR LIVES."

ANTHONY ROBBINS

We all share a fundamental drive to communicate. Communication can be defined as the process of understanding and sharing meaning.[15] We communicate to express ourselves and connect with others. If you could not communicate, what would life be like? A series of never-ending frustrations; not being able to ask for what you need or even to understand the needs of others.

Good communication helps you understand yourself and others, solve problems, learn new things and build your career. It helps you to get the best out of relationships that will enable you to grow, thrive and experience fulfilment.

Whether you are aware of it or not, you are always communicating with your family, friends, colleagues and even strangers; both verbally and in many other non-direct ways. However, only a small percentage of what you communicate during each of these conversations is verbal.

A widely accepted study by Dr Mehrabian, devised a formula to describe how the mind determines meaning. It found that in the interpretation of a message, just seven percent of meaning is verbal, 38% is in the tone and pitch of the voice and 55% is visual in the body language.

So, the vast majority of what we convey through our interactions with others is innate and instinctive and is commonly described as nonverbal communication. Think about it. If 93% of all communication is *non-verbal,* what are you REALLY communicating?

Take a look at your clothes; what brands you are wearing? What do you think they say about you? What about your hairstyle; what message is it communicating about you? Do you have a signature style or certain types of shoes, jewellery or tattoos that express who you are? Think about your home and the way you have furnished it, does it express who you are, your interests and tastes?

Have you ever tried on an outfit and felt so uncomfortable you said: "This isn't me"?

Communication is an important part of expressing your core identity. When you express yourself, you distinguish yourself from others; you reflect your own beliefs and needs and validate your own self-concept. Your self-concept is made up of your self-image, self-esteem and belief in your own abilities. It plays a major part in the way you communicate with others.

Being unable to communicate authentically is like losing a part of yourself because you are not communicating your true self: your genuine needs, beliefs, values, likes, dislikes and personality. This robs you of making genuine choices and disempowers you.

Monique is married to Benjamin who has a stronger more dominant personality. Monique's opinions, ideas, interests, choices are not validated in the relationship. Instead of the relationship being a meeting of equals, Monique struggles to express herself and have her voice heard and it begins to erode parts of her identity.

Benjamin's views, needs and wants take preference. He believes everything is okay in the relationship because he is happy having all his needs met. He assumes these needs and desires are jointly preferred, because Monique has not directly communicated anything different to him. On the surface, Monique appears quiet and agreeable, but there is a wealth of frustration building under the surface. Slowly, Benjamin is seeing the woman he loves disappear and is clueless about why this is happening.

Monique's communication style is influenced by her self-concept, because she believes Benjamin is smarter and more attractive than she is and that she is lucky to have him; she defers to his choices and doesn't feel worthy enough to express any needs and desires that do not mesh with her husband's.

You see there is an internal part to our communication with others which is based on the way that we see ourselves. *How you see yourself* and what type of feelings and thoughts you hold about your strengths and weaknesses, your emotional states, talents, likes, dislikes, values and roles shape your communication habits. Those habits are also influenced by *how you want others to see* you.

For Monique, her self-concept did not match the elevated value she placed on her husband, and her unhelpful communication habits in the relationship developed as a result. This will inevitably lead to conflict. Where there is an inner conflict taking place, there is also an outer conflict bubbling on the surface waiting to erupt.

When your self-concept is flawed and not based on your true self you lose the benefits of real connection that only comes with honest communication.

"A LOVING PERSON LIVES IN A LOVING WORLD; A HOSTILE PERSON LIVES IN A HOSTILE WORLD. EVERYONE YOU MEET IS YOUR MIRROR."

KEN KEYES

WHAT ABOUT YOUR BODY LANGUAGE?

Body language includes your posture, tone of voice, eye contact, facial expressions, hand gestures and even the pace of your breathing. We unconsciously pick up on subtle nuances of position, gesture and expression in our interactions with others.

The ability to understand and interpret body language can help you to pick up on unspoken issues, problems or negative feelings that other people might have (and vice versa). When you make your self-expression more congruent, it contributes to how well you can communicate with and understand others.

Even if you don't realise it, you are constantly picking up on and responding to people's non-verbal cues. This is often *habitual* and *unconscious* behaviour, until you pay attention to it.

For instance, how can you tell someone's mood, openness and attitude without them saying a word? If they were sitting quietly on their own, in just a few seconds you would have a distinct impression about them. Even silence can be interpreted as having meaning.

> "WHO YOU ARE IS SPEAKING SO LOUDLY THAT I CAN'T HEAR WHAT YOU'RE SAYING."
>
> **RALPH WALDO EMERSON**

You can't hide. When you are being inauthentic it shows, when you are carrying around negativity it shows. You project outward through communication your inward self, with all its flaws. When your self-concept is flawed and not based on your true self, but a distorted version of you, problems emerge that alter and misinterpret the true message from your soul. So, because you cannot *not* communicate, it's essential that you communicate as accurately and clearly as possible, reflecting your true self, rather than leaving it to chance.

Rebecca is constantly interrupting and talking over her partner and friends. She is not listening or validating the other person's experience. She appears rude and domineering. Rebecca's inner self-talk is saying: "I'm insecure and I need to control this situation, I've been hurt in the past, I am still hurting. I don't care about your needs or your opinion, I am the victim here so it's all about me, it's my way or the highway. I am emotionally unavailable for real connection that requires vulnerability. I need to protect myself." But Rebecca's external non-verbal messaging is conveying, I'm rude and I don't have the patience to listen to you, it's all about me. Rebecca lacks self-awareness of how she is perceived.

Outward appearance can also be a smokescreen. There was a friend I knew very well; whenever her makeup was perfectly applied and her outfit looked pristine, I knew she was depressed and avoiding any attention that would highlight her true emotional state. Instead, she would increase the volume and become a caricature version of her usual bubbly self. Her inner self-talk would play on repeat "pretend it's not happening; hide don't deal with the issue".

Don't mistake loudness or brashness for confidence. It can just be a personality trait or even a fake persona the person has adopted to hide who they really are and how they really see themselves. Whatever you say and do is a projection of *your own* reality.

So, the question is then not whether you communicate, but is what you are communicating congruent – is it moving you towards or away from your core identity?

"BETTER KEEP YOURSELF CLEAN AND BRIGHT; YOU ARE THE WINDOW THROUGH WHICH YOU MUST SEE THE WORLD."

GEORGE BERNARD SHAW

Practical exercise

Non-verbal communication pyramid

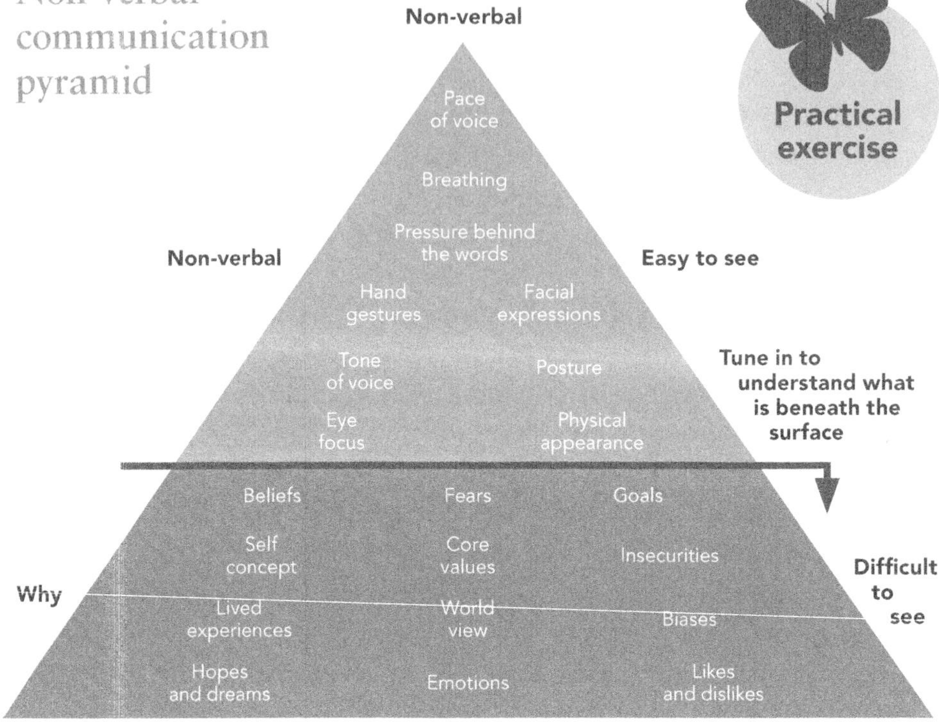

CORE INSIGHT ACTION

Your mind and body are part of the same system, so the thoughts you have affect your physiology and it shows up in your non-verbal interactions. The non-verbal communication pyramid above illustrates what lies beneath the non-verbal cues. When you tune in, listening to understand; you can get to the true meaning of what is *really* being communicated: the "what" and the "why".

NON-VERBAL CUES

- Pick five interactions. It could be in person or over the phone.
- Pay attention to non-verbal cues such as the tone and pace of their voice, their breathing, include their body language (if you are meeting in person).

- What has this information told you about them and their interaction with you?
- Did what they said match with the other non-verbal cues you detected?
- What about their mood, were they happy, relaxed, nervous, angry? How could you tell?
- Could you detect any of the *difficult to see* aspects from their non-verbal messaging?
- Now think of *a recent meaningful* or *importan*t interaction: how much did *you reveal* about what was really happening on the inside, based on your non-verbal communication?
- How will you apply what you have learned to communicate better in future interactions?

In this chapter, I've illustrated how the quality of your communication is a good marker to see how connected you are to your core identity and how well you are expressing your genuine self. Good communication can be learned, particularly when you deal with the obstacles that fuel the bad communication habits often picked up from our families, associations and friendship groups.

I've found two of the biggest barriers to good communication that can hinder your progress are not handling conflict well, or not at all and not knowing how to really listen.

Chapter 12

COMMUNICATION PART 2: WHAT GETS IN THE WAY?

"UNTIL YOU HAVE LEARNED TO BE TOLERANT WITH THOSE WHO DO NOT ALWAYS AGREE WITH YOU, YOU WILL NEITHER BE SUCCESSFUL NOR HAPPY."

NAPOLEON HILL

CONFLICT

In simple terms, conflict begins when one person perceives that another person has negatively affected or is about to negatively affect something that the first person cares about.

I was working in a busy newsroom as a Features Editor for a political magazine. Deadlines were very tight and the workload was easily more than my contracted hours. I was working well into the night most days to fulfil my responsibilities. There was a new head sub-editor who I came into conflict with. I really didn't like this person as I felt his demands were unrealistic. In my view he was highly strung, always seemed to be in a state of panic and his expectations were on the cosmic scale. He was an irritant and didn't understand how the features desk worked. This was in sharp contrast to his predecessor, whose people skills and working style were more to my liking.

I was reaching boiling point with his repetitive requests and close to telling him just what he could do with them. My line manager and Deputy Editor Emma sensed the situation was about to blow and called a meeting between us where she mediated.

I remember going into the meeting with a fixed and combative mindset. We were going into the trenches and only one of us was coming out. There was no way I would give him what he wanted because his expectations were "pie in the sky". This would be a win/lose[16] outcome or stalemate.

During the meeting Emma asked us both what the issues were and we both had a chance to express our grievances without interruption. Emma summarised and clarified she had the correct meaning when each of us spoke. We were not rushed or misinterpreted.

This meeting wasn't going as I expected. I was surprised at my own responses. It felt strange to have been listened to and understood – without compromise – which made me willing to do the same. Instead of digging my heels in, I felt myself becoming more open. I suspended judgment of the preconceived outcome I was expecting and was genuinely able to discuss solutions for win/win[17] scenarios. Something less than an hour before, I didn't conceive was possible.

What happened in that room was a watershed moment for me. Emma was so skilful in listening and mediation it totally transformed my understanding of the power of skilled communication to achieve a resolution beyond my limited expectations.

Because I was heard and understood and my position was validated, I was able to suspend my defensiveness (didn't feel like a battle) and be open to hearing the other side's perspective.

This allowed me to be open to moving from my position of no compromise to somewhere in the middle. From this new standpoint, solutions to solve both of our issues that I didn't even envisage were possible before the meeting were discussed and agreed. Win/win.

Why was this such a big deal for me? Well, this wasn't the way conflict was dealt with at home. Growing up, there only seemed to be win/lose or lose/lose[18] resolutions when conflict arose. I was not accustomed to being listened to without judgement, or even listened to at all. Because of this I'd developed a form of defensiveness that I wasn't *consciously* aware of.

"CHILDREN HAVE NEVER BEEN VERY GOOD AT LISTENING TO THEIR ELDERS, BUT THEY HAVE NEVER FAILED TO IMITATE THEM."

JAMES BALDWIN

WHAT DID YOU LEARN AS A CHILD ABOUT CONFLICT?

How you were taught to deal with uncomfortable situations can determine your responses, actions and how willing and able you are to stay connected to one another until a peaceful resolution is found.

It may be that you learnt to walk away from conflict and uncomfortable situations. Perhaps you came from a family that solved differences with physical actions like fighting. Maybe as a child, you froze with fear and didn't know what to do, or you witnessed a barrage of verbal abuse until the other-side gave in.

Being poorly equipped to deal with conflict can lead to unresolved inner fears and narrow perceptions as adults. It can damage relationships that would have been perfectly good if conflicts were not allowed to grow and fester.

Unresolved conflict is like a jack-knifed lorry in the road that blocks your path and takes you off course. It disempowers you from continuing on your journey because you can't see the road ahead, let alone journey on it. Picture the lorry's cargo piled high and then strewn along the road, that's the baggage of unresolved conflict.

While you diminish yourself by not dealing with conflict, you can gain so much by learning how to face important issues head on to express what truly matters to you. Author Shannon L. Alder says: "When you give yourself permission to communicate what matters to you in every situation you will have peace despite rejection or disapproval. Putting a voice to your soul helps you to let go of the negative energy of fear and regret."

REFLECTION

Practical exercise

- Think about the last conflict you had.
- What was your part in it?
- How was it resolved?
- What was the benefit or cost to you?

PERCEPTION

"PERCEPTION IS MERELY REALITY FILTERED THROUGH THE PRISM OF YOUR SOUL."

CHRISTOPHER A RAY

From time to time an optical illusion will go viral on social media and make it onto the television news and magazine programmes as a discussion point. In 2015, *The Dress That Broke the Internet* was one such case. The world was divided on whether the image of a dress was blue and black or white and gold. The dress caused such a stir after being posted on Tumblr that several peer-reviewed articles were published to explain why people's brains processed the colours differently.

An optical illusion is popular because it can be both challenging and fascinating to decipher an image while accepting that someone else looking at the same image may see something completely different from you. It's a matter of perception. Similarly, not being able to understand that people's perceptions vary widely will often lead to conflict. Most people fall into conflicts unwittingly because they do not understand the power of perception. It's not enough to just focus on your intentions [how you plan to come across] as people have a vast diversity of values, beliefs, thoughts, attitudes, likes and dislikes. The chances are your own views and beliefs are not universal among your friends, family or colleagues, even if you think they are.

Communication becomes a battle-ground when you only see things from your own perspective and do not acknowledge the other person may have different values and even the interpretation of words mean different things. Covey points out that each person has lived with their perspective and viewpoints for years thinking they are "facts" and question the character or mental competence of anyone who cannot see "the facts".

There are times when national or even international events radically divide opinion. At the 94th Academy Awards, Actor Will Smith unceremoniously stormed onto the stage and backhanded comedian Chris Rock for "disrespecting his wife Jada" following a joke about her GI Jane look. In the weeks that followed, households across the world were divided on whether they supported Will Smith or Chris Rock. My own household was divided on the verdict along with friends, colleagues and public commentary. Such is the power of perception.

Our perception is as unique as our lives. The way we perceive all that happens inside and outside is individual. Even though we may both be speaking the same language, we may not mean the same thing when we use words to express ourselves. But when it comes to feelings, emotions and getting our needs met it can be even more complex.

How we perceive our world will result in attaching different meanings to our experiences. Individual filters of the world are often shaped from childhood, we use these to make sense of current experiences in a way that works for us personally.

For example, five friends watch the same movie and all come away with different meanings or emphasis based on their own perception and filtering of the information.

Each person has a different viewpoint. They will notice things that you have missed and vice versa. Their view of "reality" is as valid to them as yours is to you. If you believe everyone sees the world in the same way you will be constantly perplexed and you will be constantly disappointed if you believe that others *should* see the world the same way you do.

When you learn to deal with conflict with an objective eye and willingness to understand the other persons point of view, conflicts can achieve win/win solutions.

However, being defensive and steadfastly denying any wrongdoing without even entertaining the possibility that you could be contributing to a problem, is a recipe for disaster. This approach leaves no room for personal growth. Denying responsibility may seem to alleviate stress in the short term, but creates long-term problems when others don't feel listened to and unresolved conflicts continue to grow.

When you fear conflict and you perceive it as a negative experience you harm your chances of dealing with it effectively. But it doesn't have to be this way. There are pro-active positive approaches to dealing with conflict, but to really grasp this you may have to revisit some of your beliefs about conflict and challenge the effectiveness of how you have dealt with it in the past.

NON-VIOLENT COMMUNICATION

Psychologist and author Marshall B Rosenburg identified a specific approach to communication, speaking and listening which he called *Non-violent Communication.* A process for supporting partnership and resolving conflict with people, in relationships and in society. This approach enables you to give from the heart. It connects you with others and yourself in a way that allows natural compassion to flourish.

The method provides tools for authentic communication and expression. It causes you to become present in the situation instead of acting from habitual automatic reactions.

When you are present with yourself, you are more tuned into how you are feeling and what you are thinking. From this empowered place, you are more likely to know what your needs are and be able to articulate them in a way that is more likely to be heard by others. You are also more able to hear and have empathy for other people's feelings and needs.

The four components of non-violent communication:

1 Observation: noticing what is happening in a situation without judgment or evaluation.

2 Feeling: expressing how you feel when you observe the situation i.e. are you hurt, sad, joyful…?

3 Needs: communicating what your needs and values are with regard to the situation.

4 Request: making a specific request to meet your needs.

According to communication expert Tracy Seed, nonviolent communication is relevant to all situations in life from family and friends to work colleagues. The four components provide a container to help you to express yourself clearly, efficiently and effectively whilst nurturing much needed empathy, compassion, and connection.

I encourage you to try this method and connect with me to share your results.

LISTENING: LEAN IN

"Listening is a magnetic and strange thing, a creative force. The friends who listen to us are the ones we move toward. When we are listened to, it creates us, makes us unfold and expand."

KARL A. MENNINGER

Listening is defined as the ability to accurately receive and interpret messages in the communication process. Listening is key to all effective communication. Without the ability to listen effectively, messages are easily misunderstood. Effective listening is a skill that underpins all positive human relationships.

Listening is not the same as hearing. Hearing is the sound that enters your ears, it happens automatically. But listening requires more, it requires a focused and concentrated effort that is mental and physical.

Can you remember a time you were listened to... *really* listened to? Where you felt heard, known and understood without judgment; you grew, you expanded, you had more presence, you felt safe and more secure, you could EXHALE.

To be listened to is a striking experience, partly because it is so rare. When another person is totally with you, leaning in, interested in every word, eager to empathise, you feel known and understood. People open up when they know they're really being listened to; they expand, they have more presence. They feel safer and more secure, and trust grows.

Sadly, for most of us this is not a common experience. People are rarely ever listened to this deeply which is probably why talking therapy services are at a premium.

When people speak, they are more likely to experience misunderstanding, they fear judgment and rejection, so only share small portions of what they really want to express in the hope that the listener will offer a net of safety to encourage them to reach out and share more of themselves.

Nia's parents have high expectations and standards for her. They have mapped out her future, her school, the types of friends she should have, what she should study. Even her choice of career. There are rewards when Nia lives up to her parent's expectations, she is loved, accepted and valued. But Nia is living a double life. She doesn't aspire to the goals of her parents. She has secret friendships and boyfriends and lies to her parents about where she goes and what she wants. She takes drugs and engages in reckless activities to get respite from her domineering parents. She confides in her friends about her real thoughts and desires as her peers are the only ones who really know her.

Nia gives her parents just enough information or lies to keep them happy and preserve a level of acceptance that will get her through to adulthood, where she is planning her escape. She feels suffocated and duplicitous. She has learned that true self-expression is of no value to her parents, yet she feels this freedom when she is among her peers because there is no judgment, she can just be. She is conflicted. Her self-esteem is impacted negatively because she wants to be her true self around her parents and be accepted for who she is.

Nia's parents have not given her the space to be listened to and understood. She is not able to express who she really is through her communication with them because they are closed and *only listen to what reflects their own needs*. They do not know who their daughter really is; they only see the caricature version they have created in their own minds. She is overpowered by their values and expectations. They assume their values and goals are universally accepted.

HOW COULD NIA'S EXPERIENCE BE DIFFERENT?

The key to good listening lies with Steven Covey's 5th Habit: seek first to understand, and then be understood. How often do you seek a solution for someone before you have taken the time to really listen to first understand, only seeing things from your viewpoint? According to Covey, we have a tendency to rush in and try and fix things with good advice, but we don't take the time to listen and really understand what the issue is from the speaker's perspective.

Even a partner will be more open and authentic with their spouse if they feel they are being listened to and understood. It becomes a safe place for honest self-expression. The partner doesn't have to agree with their perspective, they just need to try and understand it and be mindful of it.

"TO TOUCH THE SOUL OF ANOTHER PERSON IS TO WALK ON HOLY GROUND."

STEPHEN COVEY

Covey encourages "empathic listening" which inspires openness and trust. This is where "you see the world as the other person sees the world, you understand how they really feel. You listen not just with your ears. You listen with your eyes and your heart. You *listen for feeling and meaning*".

Good listening benefits your core identity.

Have you noticed that when you say something out loud, it becomes more meaningful, and you gain clarity? Something is released that energises you, positively or negatively.

When you pay attention to what people are saying in your interactions, you learn more about yourself and it can even help you deal with your blind spots. Valuable feedback is golden. You can understand more about how you are perceived and assess how this matches up to your core identity. There is always a gap between the two, but being aware of it and closing the gap has numerous benefits for you to live authentically and improve the quality of your life.

Unhelpful inner filters may seek to block valuable messages. But as your blind spots are revealed, treat them as precious gems of information that will enable you to better connect with and understand yourself.

If listening has so many benefits, why aren't more people doing it well?

Most people believe listening is *hearing* and do not listen on a deep level, because they have never been taught how to really listen. Therefore, the focus of their listening is superficial and mostly centred on themselves.

Instead of listening closely to what someone is saying, they often get distracted after a sentence or two and instead start to think about what they are going to say in reply. They are either too busy searching for a comparable experience from their own perspective to really understand the message. Or, they just drift off thinking about unrelated things.

We receive information in what we hear through our ears, but we also listen with our senses and with our intuition. We hear, see and experience sounds, words, images, feelings and energy. Active listening means being fully involved: paying attention not only to the story, but how it is told, the use of language and voice, the pace of the words, the pressure behind the words and how the person uses their body.

Active listening means you are *listening to understand*, it is not a passive process.

"IN THE LAST ANALYSIS, WHAT WE ARE COMMUNICATES FAR MORE ELOQUENTLY THAN ANYTHING WE EVER SAY OR DO."

STEPHEN COVEY

Practical exercise

CORE INSIGHT ACTION

PRACTICE ACTIVE LISTENING

Be purposeful in your interactions, use the following tips to practice active listening. Start with one-to-one conversations.

- Pay attention to what is being said and *how* it is being said
- Notice non-verbal messages (i.e tone and pace of the voice, body language etc)
- Listen to understand
- Suspend judgement of your own ideas
- Ask probing open-ended questions to encourage the person to go deeper and share more
- Seek clarification that you have understood correctly the meaning of what was said
- Be aware of your own inner filters, don't think about what the information means to you and your experiences
- Ask for feedback on how the person felt and experienced the communication.

Review

For each interaction ask yourself:

- What did I notice and understand from the whole interaction?
- What did I experience?
- What have I learned as a result?

"WISDOM IS THE REWARD YOU GET FOR A LIFETIME OF LISTENING WHEN YOU'D HAVE PREFERRED TO TALK."

DOUG LARSON

Chapter 13

FORGIVENESS PART 1: THE VEIL OF DISTORTION

"FORGIVENESS IS ONE OF THE MOST BEAUTIFUL GIFTS THAT GOD OFFERS US, AND WHEN WE ARE WILLING TO GIVE IT TO OTHERS, IT ADDS BEAUTY, PEACE, JOY AND POWER TO OUR OWN LIVES."

JOYCE MEYER

WHY IS FORGIVENESS A DIRTY WORD?

Human interactions across the world are littered with offenses ranging from minor faux pas to major life-changing incidents. Who hasn't been hurt by the actions or words of another, whether deliberate or not? Perhaps a parent constantly criticised you growing up, a colleague sabotaged a project or your partner had an affair. Or maybe you've had a traumatic experience, such as being physically or emotionally abused by someone close to you. These wounds can leave you with lasting feelings of anger and bitterness, even vengeance. So, when somebody says: "I'll never forgive [a person] for what they have done to me", you're likely to see heads nodding in agreement.

Alas, forgiveness is widely viewed as a dirty word. The majority of people still accept that a person is entirely justified to hold on to unforgiveness, because they are viewed as the victim or the aggrieved. And by choosing not to forgive they are somehow empowering themselves.

Through personal experience and in my work as a coach, I have found this to be one of the most fundamental issues that rob my clients of their peace, power and prosperity and the ability to live their best life.

I believe this enduring negative association is because the *action* of forgiving someone is misunderstood and the *impact* of not forgiving someone is widely underestimated. It is not routinely connected to the personal cost the aggrieved person pays when they *choose* to hold onto unforgiveness.

So, what are the most common misunderstandings that people have about forgiveness?

MYTHS

1 Forgive and forget: I cannot forget what this person has done to me, so how can I ever forgive them?

2 This person has not apologised for what they have done to me, this must happen before I can forgive them.

3 If I forgive this person, I will have to reconcile with them, but I do not want to return to this toxic relationship/environment.

4 This person is not sorry for what they have done to me and has shown no remorse.

5 This person is no longer alive, so I don't have to forgive them. I'm stuck with this forever.

6 This person does not deserve my forgiveness.

7 What does it even mean to forgive myself?

8 The offense and hurt is so deep I'll never recover, therefore I will never forgive.
9 Forgiving this person means I am weak because I am letting them off the hook (forgiveness is not the same as justice).

Can you see what's wrong with all of these scenarios?

They all give your power away and put it in the hands of the person who has hurt or offended you. That is the power to heal and move past the offense.

To be able to forgive it's important to understand that only you have the responsibility for your own happiness and peace. This may be a hard concept to grasp for those who believe other people are responsible for their happiness. But the moment you put that responsibility in someone else's hands you have *given away your power* and any hope of living your best life, free from the effects of unforgiveness which is holding you captive to the hurt and pain of the original offense or traumatic experience.

Have you ever met anyone who is truly happy, that is living with unforgiveness? I certainly haven't. But I have met a lot of unhappy, angry, bitter people who view themselves as "hard done by" that refuse to forgive.

THE TRUE IMPACT OF UNFORGIVENESS

"WHEN WE HATE OUR ENEMIES, WE ARE GIVING THEM POWER OVER US: POWER OVER OUR SLEEP, OUR APPETITES, OUR BLOOD PRESSURE, OUR HEALTH AND OUR HAPPINESS."

DALE CARNEGIE

UNFORGIVENESS SIGNIFICANTLY IMPACTS YOUR IDENTITY

To understand the true benefits of forgiveness, it's important to shed light on the wide-ranging personal costs associated with what happens when you *choose* not to forgive. This will help to provide you with the impetus needed to take the action to free yourself from unforgiveness and its effects, one step at a time.

You are connected – mind, body and soul – and it is naïve to think you can work in isolation to yourself. What affects your mind often impacts your emotions and physical health.

If you consider that simply to move your arm, a number of actions must occur that involve the bones, muscles (shoulder, elbow, biceps, triceps) and motor neurons sending signals from the brain through the spine telling your arm to move.

The arm cannot operate in isolation to the rest of you. And in the same way, you are a whole person and you cannot compartmentalise unforgiveness and believe that the residue will not seep out into other areas of yourself. Similarly, when you count the cost of holding onto unforgiveness, there are many ways that it will impact you; from an unproductive and negative mindset distorting your personality and damaging relationships to poor physical and mental health.

THE VEIL OF DISTORTION

Unforgiveness is like a veil that falls over the eyes and blocks out the light. A person is unable to see things as they really are, and lives their life as though a dark cloud is hovering over them all of the time.

While some may be deceived into thinking they can compartmentalise the negativity, this simply isn't possible. Unforgiveness seeps into to your very core and infects your personality, character, decision making and perspective on life. Even if you cannot see it, people around you will. Remember the blinds have come down for you, but not for those around you.

Consider this: a group of cousins see their aunt sleeping and decide to play a prank on her. They put some strong-smelling cheese under her nose. When their aunt wakes up, she complains that the room stinks! She goes from room to room trying to get away from the stench, complaining about the smell. But the stench follows her everywhere. No one in the house can smell what she does and after hours of complaining, she realises the smell is coming from her.

As plausible or implausible as this story may seem to you, this is a similar scenario for people living with unforgiveness. The whole world can seem like it stinks to you. But this sentiment isn't shared or even seen from the perspectives of those around you. More seriously however, living with unforgiveness causes deep inner wounds in the soul; and the longer you hold on to it, the greater chance it has to pervade every part of you. Unforgiveness and misery – its faithful companion – are able to completely fill the human soul and conscious mind.

YOUR TRUE PERSONALITY CAN BE DISTORTED BY UNFORGIVENESS

The following definitions of *unforgiving* below are insightful:

- Not disposed to forgive or show mercy; not allowing for mistakes, carelessness, or weakness.
- Unrelenting, ruthless, cruel, heartless, harsh, demanding, grim, pitiless, remorseless, revengeful, unkind, unsympathetic, vindictive, unappeasable.

Notice that the definitions for unforgiving are "adjectives" which are describing words. Thus, it becomes part of a person's character and identity.

Think about those definitions. Would you be happy to be described in this way?

While you may be still navigating one or more of the myths discussed earlier in the chapter to justify unforgiveness in your life, the chances are you will be exhibiting at least a handful of these behaviours and it's also likely that some of these adjectives may have already morphed into your personality and are being projected outwardly – albeit often unsuspectingly – towards others.

What is in the heart does come out of the mouth; and we can learn a lot about ourselves by listening to ourselves.

UNFORGIVENESS PERMEATES YOUR MINDSET

According to Mindset.com: "Mindsets are those collection of beliefs and thoughts that make up the mental attitude, inclination, habit or disposition that *predetermines* a person's interpretations and responses to events, circumstances and situations."

Psychologist Bryn Collins states that a person's mindset is part of their identity: one facet of what makes up their personality. It is the perspective from which a person generally views the world, the filter through which they process new and old information.[19] Your mindset impacts how *you* make sense of *you*.

Unresolved issues that have taken root become a mindset forming habitual way of thinking, impacting your decision making and distorting your interactions and overall view of the world. It can keep you trapped in self-defeating cycles, fed by your attitude, behaviour, emotions, beliefs and values.

For example, if you have been hurt by someone, a partner cheated or betrayed you, and you do not resolve those issues; forgive, heal and move past the offence (forgiveness being paramount), holding the wound can result in developing a mindset that all men are cheaters. Regardless of who you meet, you treat them with the same distain and expectation. Your behaviour models your expectation. Your new partner may find themselves being judged unfairly and paying for a previous partner's offenses. You may also relate to other people and their partners with the same expectation, regardless of any evidence contrary to this belief.

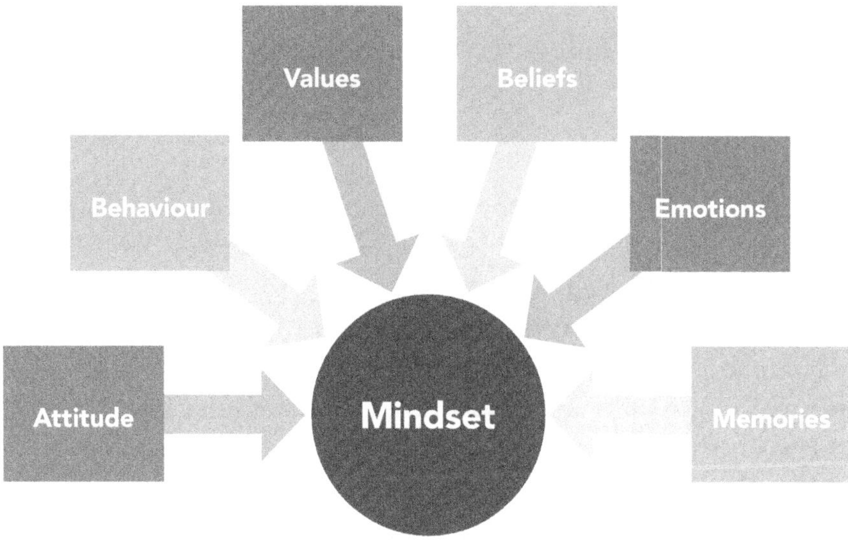

Your mindset shapes your *attitude* and *behaviour* and your attitude and behaviour reinforce your mindset.

Your mindset shapes your *values* and *beliefs* and your values and beliefs reinforce your mindset.

Your mindset shapes your *emotions* and *memories*, and your emotions and memories reinforce your mindset.

And so, the cycle continues.

ANGER

The emotion anger, also known as wrath or rage, is an intense emotional state. It involves a strong uncomfortable and hostile response to a perceived provocation, hurt or threat. It is normal to feel anger; for example, when you perceive that you have been treated unfairly or you feel threatened, attacked, powerless or frustrated. But if the issue or situation is not resolved and anger becomes deep rooted in your soul, it can wreak untold havoc in your life and skew your core identity.

It doesn't matter as much if the offense or issue was small or great, it's the fact that it is *unresolved* that fuels the problem. Unresolved issues become internalised and our subconscious mind develops ways to compensate for this. In the process of burying the issue, your mind, will and emotions work overtime to restore equilibrium. But this really is a smokescreen. The evidence will turn up everywhere.

A quote from Christian author Joyce Meyer, who was abused in her childhood, illustrates this point, as she describes the personal cost of her unresolved anger.

"My relationships were suffering due to my anger and resentment, but I didn't know it. My anger was deeply rooted in my soul. It was in my thinking, in my emotions, my words, and all of my actions because it was part of me. Anger was with me for so long that I didn't recognise it for what it was."[20] Unforgiveness is like drinking poison and expecting someone else to die.

IMPACT TO YOUR PHYSICAL AND MENTAL HEALTH

There is a growing body of research that demonstrates the link between your state of mind and emotions having a significant impact on your health and well-being. Holding onto unforgiveness can affect your metabolism, immune response or organ function and lead to physical disease.[21]

Risks to physical and mental health are palpable; chronic anger puts you into a fight-or-flight mode, which results in changes to your heart rate, blood pressure and immune response. Those changes then increase the risk of depression, heart disease and diabetes, among other conditions.

Chronic stress leads to exhaustion, weakens the immune system and is linked to numerous conditions such as anxiety, depression, headaches, back pain, abdominal pain, skin rashes, shingles and insomnia. Forgiveness, however, calms stress levels, leading to improved health.

An interesting article by Lorie Johnson for CBN news highlighted that some medical books now classify unforgiveness as a disease.

According to Dr. Steven Standiford, chief of surgery at the Cancer Treatment Centers of America, refusal to forgive makes people sick and keeps them that way.

Forgiveness therapy is now being used to help treat diseases, such as cancer. Dr Sandiford says: "It's important to treat emotional wounds or disorders because they really can hinder someone's reactions to the treatments, even someone's willingness to pursue treatment."

Dr Michael Barry, Director of Pastoral Care at the Cancer Treatment Centers of America specialises in the connection between spirituality and health and is author of the book, *The Forgiveness Project*. According to his research, 61% of all cancer patients have forgiveness issues, and of those, more than half are severe.

"Harbouring these negative emotions, such as anger and hatred, creates a state of chronic anxiety," he says. "Chronic anxiety very predictably produces excess adrenaline and cortisol, which deplete the production of natural killer cells, which is your body's foot soldier in the fight against cancer."

SPIRITUALITY

There is also a spiritual side to unforgiveness. There may be many points of divergence, but all of the world's major religions (Christianity, Judaism, Islam, Buddism, Hinduism) teach forgiveness. As a Christian, I have learned it's the biggest obstacle to having a healthy relationship with God.

With all this evidence pointing to the negative cost of unforgiveness, aside from the myths associated with it, why else do so many people hold on to it so keenly and easily find themselves in situations that can cause offense? I believe this is because we live in an imperfect world where people still struggle to have authentic communication with each other. Try as you might, it's almost impossible at some point to escape being offended or hurt by others.

The fear of rejection, betrayal, exposure and insecurity are just some of what fuels these misunderstandings and offenses. Many people believe keeping up a façade is safer than showing their true feelings and emotions. They'd rather hide than be transparent and face an issue head-on. So, as a result they hold on to the hurt and offense, and nurse unforgiveness in their hearts, which goes on to take root in their soul.

But unresolved issues give rise to anger, jealousy, violence and even hatred (in addition to all of the other problems mentioned earlier). And even though, for a short while, it can feel like a comfort blanket of protection, you are really just shutting people out and forgoing healing and restoration. According to Meyer, you can be pitiful or powerful, but you can't be both at the same time.

We were created for human relationships and meaningful authentic connections with others. Humans do amazing things when there is unity, peace and understanding among them.

Adam Hornyak

There is a mesmerising sculpture called *Love* by Alexander Milov, commissioned for the Burning Man Festival in 2015. I have a picture of this on my wall. It depicts two people sitting with their backs touching each other bent over, head down. Inside each person is a child. Both children are standing facing each other, arms outstretched, looking for connection.

The caption under the picture says: "A sculpture of two adults after a disagreement, sitting with their backs to each other. Yet the inner child in both of them wants to connect. Age has many beautiful gifts, but one we could afford to live without is the pride and resentment we hold onto when we have conflicts with others. The forgiving free spirit of children is our true nature. Remember this when you feel stubborn."

REFLECTION

Practical exercise

- Who (or what) are you angry with?
- Is your anger helping you or anyone else?
- Is it solving the problem?
- Is it changing the person you are angry at?
- Is your anger increasing your happiness and peace?

Definition of forgiveness

To understand what it really means to forgive, lets first see what the dictionary definition says. It is important to note that "forgive" is a verb, an active doing word, something that requires action.

- To stop feeling angry or resentful towards [someone] for an offence, flaw or mistake.
- To give up the desire to punish [extract] revenge; to pardon [an offense]; to cancel a debt.

Psychologists generally define forgiveness as a conscious, deliberate decision to release feelings of resentment or vengeance toward a person or group who has harmed you, regardless of whether they actually deserve your forgiveness. Forgiveness does not mean forgetting, nor does it mean condoning or excusing offenses, nor does it mean you think that person had the right to hurt you.

You don't need to make up with the person who caused you harm either, for instance, victims of abuse should not have to reconcile with their abuser. When you forgive someone, you make the *choice* to give up your negative feelings of hostility, resentment and revenge and replace them with positive ones such as compassion, understanding and empathy. Despite your forgiveness there are still consequences your offender must face but forgiving them releases YOU from the pain. You have the power to forgive.

THE BENEFITS OF FORGIVENESS

Letting go of grudges and bitterness can make way for improved health and peace of mind. Forgiveness can lead to:

- Healthier relationships
- Improved mental health
- Less anxiety, stress and hostility
- Lower blood pressure
- Fewer symptoms of depression
- A stronger immune system
- Improved heart health
- Improved self-esteem
- Improved sleep.

CARYS' STORY

While at university studying for my Master's Degree in Journalism, I got talking to a fellow student. Carys was bright, friendly and very sophisticated: she was around a decade older than me and in her thirties when we met and became friends. She was studying as a mature student and was extremely focused and ambitious about her future career in journalism. Having worked as a secretary for many years, she had taken the plunge to venture into unchartered waters to jump-start the underutilised potential within her. Gaining a post-graduate qualification and pursuing a new career path was paramount.

Carys was very amiable and made friends easily. She was always enthusiastic and energetic and took every opportunity to live life to the fullest. She would relay stories of her adventures, like a special person she met while spending a week skiing in the alps. She was full of life and wanted to experience every moment of it.

Then Carys disappeared. A few months later she appeared again but looked very different. She had a baseball cap on and very casual clothes (I'd always seen her in suits or smart dresses). Her skin looked burnt in places. She explained to me that she had been diagnosed with an aggressive form of breast cancer. She'd had a significant lumpectomy and was undergoing chemotherapy. Mentally, she was still very positive, but I could see it had knocked some of the wind out of her.

The cancer went into remission and things were looking up for her. Carys continued with her studies, but after a while the cancer returned more aggressively than before. At that moment I made a decision to pray for Carys and be open to opportunities to support her. Over that time our friendship grew and she began to share parts of her past with me.

Although Carys was a practising Buddhist, she allowed me to pray with her and I started to feel strongly, that the root to the cancer and its return lay elsewhere. She shared that she'd grown up in a volatile home with domestic violence between her parents. At a very early age she moved out of the family home to live with her boyfriend. At just 17, they had a child and she experienced excruciating mental and physical abuse. She shared how her boyfriend would dangle their baby, then just months old, over the banister of the stairs in their home, and threaten to drop him. He would bring her friends home and sleep with them while she was in another room.

While Carys got out of that relationship early on, she never fully recovered from its impact.

Between her upbringing and abusive relationship Carys had deep wounds in her soul. She was hurting inside from the brokenness, shame, dysfunction, rejection and trauma she'd experienced, having buried it deep down. But this turned into bitterness and unforgiveness. Carys did not speak to her child's father and she never forgave him or truly dealt with those issues.

Carys reasoned that she could make a go of her life and tried in practical ways to forget the past. But she was just seeking a new way – having built up a shiny, new façade – and as she rebuilt her life, Carys used the tools she knew; intellect, energy, skill and talent, to mask her past. But as you can guess from Eva's example mentioned earlier in this book, this simply eats away at you.

Although more evasive, Carys beat cancer a second time. But unbeknown to her, the clock was ticking.

As she shared more about her life, we got to the root of her issue. In many cases, wounds of the soul lead to physical illness and this was no exception. Carys hadn't forgiven the father of her child for the abuse and trauma she and her son had suffered at his hands. It had merely grown calloused and was the root to her health issues.

Within months the cancer returned for a third time and spread throughout her body.

She fought valiantly and then she experienced a breakthrough. A big shift in her world occurred when she truly understood that unforgiveness and holding on to the trauma and the old calloused wounds was at the root of her illness. She resolved to forgive. Firstly, the father of her child and then anyone she had issues with. She even became friends with the father of her child, who would shave her hair through the chemotherapy treatment.

Carys experienced a dramatic change. For the first time she said she felt "free, lighter, joyful, amazing and peaceful". Despite the cancer now ravaging her whole body, she spoke to everyone she knew about the power of forgiveness and used her own example to warn people to not hold onto this poison.

She became almost evangelical in sharing her experience and new freedom, saying although her body was ravaged with cancer, she'd never felt so free mentally and emotionally or joyful deep within her.

Sadly, shortly after, Carys lost her battle.

My friend touched many lives with her message and changed the course for many of her friends and family who took heed and acted on her advice. There were many testimonials at her funeral about how her message of forgiveness had changed their attitude and the decisions they'd made to let go of resentment and unforgiveness in their lives.

I didn't know then all that I know now, but Carys' experience was a vivid message to me about the toxic nature of unforgiveness that can steal your best life and the power of forgiveness to free you to live your best life.

Time ran out for Carys, but her message lives on.

Chapter 14

FORGIVENESS PART 2: YOU HAVE A CHOICE!

"Forgiveness does not change the past, but it does enlarge the future."

PAUL BOESE

So far, you have learned about misconceptions that shroud forgiveness. I've shone a light on the negative impact to aspects of your identity [personality, mindset], physical and mental health when you hold onto unforgiveness.

It's easy, but tiring to be led around by your emotions or be unintentionally controlled by other people's negative actions and behaviour. But if you believe your feelings control your actions you have given away your responsibility and empowered them to do so.

You *do* have a choice. And by taking back your power and controlling your own path forward you can heal and gain true freedom and inner peace. The answer lies in your attitude.

In his book, *Man's Search for Meaning*, Nazi concentration camp survivor and psychiatrist Viktor Frankl detailed the horrors and human indignities of being imprisoned. Enduring extreme hunger, cold and brutality, first in Auschwitz and then in Dachau,

Frankl was under constant threat of going to the gas ovens. He lost every physical belonging on his first day in the camps, and was forced to surrender a scientific manuscript he considered his life's work. Frankl's wife, father, mother and brother all died in the concentration camps.

Despite these grave injustices, Frankl was able to survive mentally intact by learning and understanding that he had the power to determine his *attitude* and *internal response* to his circumstances, even if everything else was out of his control. Though he couldn't save the lives of his closest family, he was able to persevere through unimaginable physical and psychological horrors.

He said: "Everything can be taken from a man but one thing: the last of human freedoms – to choose one's attitude in any given set of circumstances, to choose one's own way".

Frankl could have given up, he could have died, or he could have lived the rest of his life bitter from what he had gone through. But instead, he went on to use his suffering and experiences to help others find meaning in their lives.

His model for personal freedom in difficult circumstances has helped millions of people around the world (including me) and his works have impacted generations of new psychotherapists who will spend their lives helping people.

Inspired? Fortunately, your attitude is something you can control. Just like Frankl, you don't have to let someone else's behaviour or actions determine your mood or level of peace and happiness. It was very enlightening for me when I discovered Stephen Covey's Circle of Influence and Concern, a blueprint that enables anyone to learn how to be proactive in taking control of their life and increasing their influence on varied issues that impact them.

In his book the *7 Habits of Highly Effective People*, Covey distinguishes between proactive people – who focus on what they can do and what they influence – and reactive people, who focus their energy on things beyond their control. Reactive people maintain an attitude of victimisation and blame.

When you focus your energy on the issues that are within your control, things change around you and you gain more influence over the wider issues that concern you, piece-by-piece. Your circle of influence starts to increase and you become more empowered. Conversely, if all your energy goes into those things you cannot change your circle of influence shrinks and you feel less effective and more out of control.

"If you're proactive, you focus on preparing. If you're reactive, you end up focusing on repairing."

JOHN C MAXWELL

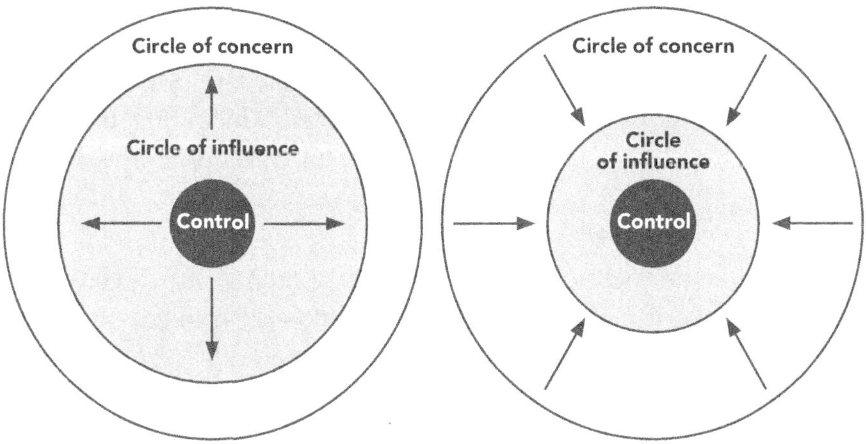

PROACTIVE FOCUS

REACTIVE FOCUS

1 What you can directly control
2 Concerns you can influence
3 Wide range of concerns

MARSHA'S STORY

Marsha has long-term health issues significantly impacting her quality of life. Her mother died just over a year ago and her elderly father, who now lives alone, has a serious health condition. Marsha has siblings and adult nieces and nephews.

A lot of her time had been taken up worrying about her father because he had various needs she felt were not being met adequately. Because her life revolved around hospital visits and treatment, she hadn't been able to do the things she hoped she'd be able to do for her father. Marsha resolved that when her health improved, she would be able to spend more time with him. She was also disappointed and frustrated that, from her perspective, other family members were not providing more assistance to her father.

Then Marsha got the devastating news that her father's cancer may have returned, having been in remission for a year. All of the sudden, the time she hoped that she would have to improve her own health and be able to help her father was put into doubt. She could see clearly that tomorrow was not promised and began to look at the things she could realistically do for him, even with her own health being seriously compromised at the time.

Marsha began spending time with her father during the day in between some of her own hospital treatments. Cooking with him and sharing meals together. Taking care of some of his needs and generally showing him love in practical ways.

This action has transformed both of their lives. Marsha is energised with a new sense of purpose. Doing something, however little, is better than doing nothing and fretting about what other family members were not doing. Her father's mood has significantly improved, his appetite has returned and he is eating better. The bond in their relationship is growing and they are creating precious memories that Marsha will be able to reflect on, whether her father lives for many more years or not.

Marsha made the decision to work on the things she could control and influence. She could not control whether the cancer would return, whether her father would recover or die, or whether her family would do more to help. But she could control her reaction. Instead of being bitter and remaining frustrated, or viewing herself as limited through her own health issues, she took one step at a time focusing on what she could do.

"IT WILL NEVER RAIN ROSES: WHEN WE WANT TO HAVE MORE ROSES, WE MUST PLANT MORE ROSES."

GEORGE ELIOT

JOANNE'S STORY

Joanne is one of eight siblings. The family home in Leicester was always the focal point that gelled the family together. As adults most siblings had moved away from the city to pursue their careers; the family home was where all the memories were made and where all the reunions took place.

Joanne's mother had been seriously ill with multiple sclerosis for many years and had recently passed away. One sister who had remained at home to care for their mother, had not been able to progress her career or life in the same way as her siblings. And since her mother's passing, she had revealed that the family home would have to be sold, as it had been re-mortgaged twice to cover the costs of caring for their mother.

Joanne and the other siblings were stunned. They had no idea this had happened.

So now Joanne was faced with the loss of her mother and the loss of the family home; and having no focal point for their memories or place to anchor, the family dispersed and the sibling feuding began.

When I met Joanne, sometime after the death of her mother, she was bitter, angry and depressed. She told me that she felt she had lost the potential for any future memories of the family environment that she'd always experienced when she returned to the family home from her house in London.

I encouraged Joanne to focus on her *circle of influence*; what was within her power to change. To do this required understanding what was at the heart of the issue, and so, instead of blaming her sister for the loss of their childhood home, Joanne took a look at things from her sister's perspective. Her sister had given up a lot to look after their mother, while the other siblings were all forging their own careers and building their own families without the caring responsibilities that she'd undertaken. None of the siblings had paid attention to the financial situation of their sister or how she was coping throughout their mother's prolonged illness.

Thinking about this enabled Joanne to forgive and release herself from the anger and resentment she'd felt towards her sister. She even gained a new understanding of the difficulties her sibling had faced, which she never fully appreciated before.

The family home had given Joanne a place to *belong*, a place to feel *love* and be *accepted*. It had given her the assurance that – no matter what was going in her life – significant holidays would be spent at that home together with her extended family.

Joanne needed to understand that the elements she felt were lost were not tied up in the family home. When she could highlight the real loss, she could work within her circle of influence to recreate those elements and the feelings associated with it in another way. She set about identifying the people and places in her life where she felt loved and accepted. She also pinpointed close friends in her life that she considered family. She had already shared much more of her life with them than her biological family.

After speaking to these three friends about how she felt, they resolved to create new memories and picked significant dates in the yearly calendar where they would always meet and bond as a "family". At least one time in the year would be a holiday abroad.

Joanne regained her sense of belonging and of feeling loved and accepted by these close friends who had all invested a lot in each other. Over time she became more peaceful and content, because she was no longer feuding with some of her siblings, and so the anger and bitterness had no resting place within her.

Losing the family home was out of Joanne's control. But the thing she craved was not forever connected to the family home. It was within her circle of influence: identifying the issue and taking proactive steps turned the whole situation around for her. Over time it also helped to build bridges with her siblings.

Both Marsha and Joanne were able to get a positive personal result by adopting a proactive approach to the process of forgiveness. A reactive person will wait for circumstances out of their control to change before they enact a change in themselves. They may say something like: "If this happens… then I'll be happy." My partner is responsible for making me happy." Or "I can't move on until I have an explanation or apology from this person". In this place, they remain stagnant or even go backwards.

A proactive person will focus on what they can do to change the situation from what is already within their control, as in the examples of Marsha and Joanne. Both women worked within their circles of influence to make significant positive changes to issues that were negatively impacting them. In the context of forgiveness, both experiences demonstrate how *having the right attitude* and *being proactive* provide the groundwork to forgive. By understanding that only they had the power to change their situation, regardless of the perceived wrong that they experienced, they were able to let go of the resentment and positively move forward with their lives. They learned how forgiving others was a gift to themselves.

REMEMBER THE MYTHS?

1 Forgive and forget: I cannot forget what this person has done to me, so how can I ever forgive them?

2 This person has not apologised for what they have done to me, this must happen before I can forgive them.

3 If I forgive this person, I will have to reconcile with them, but I do not want to return to this toxic relationship/environment.
4 This person is not sorry for what they have done to me and has shown no remorse.
5 This person is no longer alive so I don't have to forgive them. I'm stuck with this forever.
6 This person does not deserve my forgiveness.
7 What does it even mean to forgive myself?
8 The offense and hurt is so deep I'll never recover, therefore I will never forgive
9 Forgiving this person means I am weak because I am letting them off the hook (forgiveness is not the same as justice).

"THE WEAK CAN NEVER FORGIVE. FORGIVENESS IS THE ATTRIBUTE OF THE STRONG."

GANDHI

REFRAMING MYTHS

Practical exercise

If you believe that someone or something else is the cause of your problems, challenges or misfortune, you will be completely disempowered to change anything about your situation. So, with what you have learned so far, let's revisit these myths from a new empowered perspective.

Reframe each myth from a position of personal responsibility (your circle of influence).

I've done the first two for you:

1 Forgive and forget: I cannot forget what this person has done to me, so how can I ever forgive them?

Forgiveness is a gift to me. It is not actually about the other person. It will give me peace and closure so I can be free to live a happier, healthier and more productive life.
2 This person has not apologised for what they have done to me, this must happen before I can forgive them.
I do not have to wait for an apology to forgive. If I wait for what may never happen, they are still holding me captive, and I have given away my power to heal and move on. Letting go of resentment sets me free.

HOW DO YOU RECOGNISE WHEN YOU NEED TO FORGIVE YOURSELF?

It can be difficult to identify and accept that you need to forgive yourself as the necessity is often masked by negative feelings such as guilt, shame and self-loathing. Individuals often blame themselves for bad things that happen in their lives, whether the fault was theirs on not.

For example, children blaming themselves for their parents' divorce, a partner blaming themself for the breakdown of a relationship, or even a crash survivor experiencing guilt and confusion because they survived the accident, but were not able to help others.

Self-forgiveness enables you to *separate who you are from the mistakes you've made*, otherwise you will reject yourself. From this standpoint you can begin to learn from the choices you have made and find ways to make amends where possible; and it will be considerably easier to wholeheartedly forgive others when you start by forgiving yourself.

During the process of self-forgiveness, it's important to understand your emotions; accept responsibility, treat yourself with kindness and compassion, apologise to yourself and find ways to learn from the experience.

"FORGIVENESS IS NOT AN OCCASIONAL ACT; IT IS A CONSTANT ATTITUDE."

DR MARTIN LUTHER KING

Practical exercise

CORE INSIGHT ACTION

REVIEW

How would you describe forgiveness in what you have learned so far? Write it down.

Compare it to the description below:

Forgiveness is the mental, emotional, and spiritual process of letting go of resentment, indignation, or anger against another person for a perceived offense, difference, or mistake.[22]

It is a conscious deliberate decision to overcome the pain that was inflicted by another person.

Forgiveness is a process which takes time to embed, set your intention to forgive and your feelings will catch up. Remember, forgiveness does not mean forgetting or condoning the wrongdoing, reconciling a relationship or legal leniency. You can forgive a person while in no way believing that their actions were acceptable or justified. In addition, forgiveness does not mean letting go, but hoping for revenge.

STEPS TO FORGIVENESS

It's helpful to view forgiveness as a gift to you, not a gift to someone else so that YOU are free to live a happier life. The following exercise will guide you through the process of forgiveness. Think about the areas where you are holding unforgiveness and apply the steps in this exercise for each situation.

Practical exercise

1 Call it out

To improve your understanding of the injustice, and how it has impacted your life, answer the following questions and write your answers down.

- Describe the injustices you have endured. What happened? Why was this treatment unfair?
- What are your actual thoughts, feelings and sensations around the situations?

2 Count the cost

What areas of your life have been affected? Has it stopped you from living the life you once had? Remember that what happened was in the past and the very fact you are continuing to hold on to it will only keep it in the future for as long as you let it.

How have the injustices affected you? Pick any of the examples below that apply and describe them. Add whatever isn't listed:

- Painful emotions (such as anger or shame)
- Changed worldview (such as "all people are scammers")
- Changed behaviour (for example, avoiding new relationships)
- Cognitive rehearsal (recurring thoughts about injustice)
- Practical costs (time, money)
- Physical harm (such as injuries from abuse).

3. Let it go

With your new understanding of forgiveness, spend some time reflecting on what you would gain.

- Thinking about the cost; describe how things might be different if you forgive. Be as specific as possible for each situation you have listed previously.
- Now think about what you stand to lose in the future if you do not forgive and things remain the same.

or

- What are the pros and cons of practicing forgiveness in each situation you have listed?

4. Review and reflection

Practical exercise

The reflection phase of forgiveness enables you to further decrease the negative emotions associated with the injustices (leave some time for reflection before you complete this segment). You may find meaning in the experiences and recognise personal growth.

HOW HAVE YOU BENEFITTED BY FORGIVING OTHERS?

Consider how forgiveness has benefited your mindset, emotional health, behaviour and the time and energy spent thinking about the offence.

Describe how you have grown because of the injustices you endured and your efforts to forgive. How has your world view changed? Are you stronger than you were before deciding to forgive?

Remember, *journaling* is a great way to reflect and process your honest feelings; to see and acknowledge your growth over a period of time. It will also highlight areas that need further work or attention.

Practising forgiveness frees you to attract more positivity into your life. From personal experience I've learned to be quick to forgive so as to not enable the negative effects of unforgiveness to become embedded in my soul. The more I value and understand myself, the easier it has become. In the same instance, I have learned to create healthy boundaries for myself to not engage with toxic behaviours and unhealthy situations.

The **checklist** below will help you to assess your progress.

How you will know:

- You do not constantly repeat talking about the offense and speak about the offender in a negative way
- You are able to see your growth and learning that has come out of the adversity

- You have more peace, less anxiety and anger; there are fewer negative emotions
- You are able to see a way forward where you are in control of your wellbeing and happiness
- You can exercise choice: you're no longer a "pending item" in your own in-tray
- You've given up expecting things from your life from people that they do not give you
- Your energy is directed towards ways to get your positive goals met, instead of focusing on the experience that has hurt you (circle of influence)

Remember that a well-lived life is an ultimate revenge: look for love, beauty, and kindness. Put your energy into appreciating what you have instead of what you don't have.

"TO FORGIVE IS TO SET A PRISONER FREE AND DISCOVER THAT THE PRISONER WAS YOU."

LEWIS B SMEDES

Chapter 15

RELATIONSHIPS: WE'RE ALL PLAYING ROLES

"SOMEONE TO TELL IT TO IS ONE OF THE FUNDAMENTAL NEEDS OF HUMAN BEINGS."

MILES FRANKLIN

Humans are social beings; we are wired for connection and the quality of our relationships affect our mental, emotional and physical health.

According to professor and author Brené Brown: "A deep sense of love and belonging is an irreducible need of all men, women and children. We are biologically, cognitively, physically, and spiritually wired to love, to be loved and to belong."

No one can exist alone for very long. We are all inter-dependent. If I were the only person left on the planet, what would I do? There would be no doctor to fix my ailments, no one to talk to or to socialise with. How would I repair my car and how would I get electricity? The list goes on. I wouldn't even have the means to leave the island of England to venture to another continent. Would I even want to be here if I were all alone?

As an individual person you have a number of significant relationships and play a particular role in each of them. For example, you may be a daughter, mother, sister, wife and best friend. All these relationships run concurrently and may add varying levels of richness to your own life. They could provide a sense of love, connection, responsibility, happiness, challenge, belonging, acceptance, companionship and safety (to name but a few). These are just some of the benefits we idealise and strive for in relationships.

Relationships are good for your health and wellbeing. Numerous studies have shown the benefits to include longer life, a stronger immune system, lower blood pressure, better recovery from illness, reduced stress and a stronger heart.

Social contact helps us cope with stress and major life changes like a divorce, redundancy, bereavement and moving house. And knowing that we are valued by others is an important psychological factor in helping us to forget the negative aspects of our lives and think more positively about our environment.

A 2010 study in the Journal of Health and Social Behaviour by sociology researchers Debra Umberson and Jennifer Karas Montez, found evidence linking a low quantity or quality of social ties with a host of conditions, including the development and worsening of cardiovascular disease, repeat heart attacks, autoimmune disorders, high blood pressure, cancer and slowed wound healing.

HEALTHY RELATIONSHIPS ARE THE NECTAR FOR LIFE

Teddy Pendergrass, a hugely successful American soul singer's life took a dramatic turn in 1982. Aged just 31 and at the height of his fame, he was involved in a car crash where he suffered a spinal cord injury, leaving him paralysed from the chest down. The disability not only impacted his lifestyle, but also his career, as he lost the ability to sing and entertain as he had before. Pendergrass described how he contemplated suicide and could not see a reason to go on. Then, an ingenious idea by his friend and therapist to stage his own funeral while he was still alive came about.

Pendergrass, attended his own funeral and heard from people that he loved and cared about, on how their world would change if he wasn't in it. He was so moved by what he heard, and that was the turning point for him to realise his intrinsic value to so many people, which gave him a reason to push through. From that day forward, he abandoned all notions of suicide and went on to live a productive and fulfilling life. Pendergrass was a son, husband, father, cousin and friend and many other roles besides. These relationships provided a mutual richness to his existence.

Professor Brown says: "When these needs [for social interaction] are not met, we don't function as we were meant to. We break. We fall apart. We grow numb. We ache. We hurt others. We get sick. There are certainly other causes of illness, numbness, and hurt, but the absence of love and belonging will always lead to suffering."

If relationships have so many benefits, why do we find them so difficult to maintain and nurture? Relationships can become fractured, strained, distorted or even toxic. Few find true "nirvana"' in their relationships. Why do we feel compromised, misunderstood, suffocated, side-lined, unappreciated and even abused?

At the heart are issues with your core identity. When you don't know who you really are, you experience relationships from a foundation that isn't authentic or stable. You are open to all kinds of compromise, falsehood, resentment, disillusionment, confusion and insecurity that can build up and choke a potentially good relationship from developing. It is often the issue at the heart of relationships breaking down. This is because you do not take your *true self* into these relationships and before long, the cracks will emerge.

When you are unsure of your core identity, you are unsure of your boundaries. When you operate from an often unintentionally inauthentic place, it's easier to compromise and fulfil the needs of others without truly understanding your own needs. When you don't know who you are, others will tell you directly or indirectly who they think you should be. And that premise will form the basis of your interactions.

Each relationship provides an opportunity to look in the mirror and see what is reflecting back.

JANE FONDA

Activist and Oscar winning actress Jane Fonda, now in her eighties, has lived a very colourful life. Fonda has spent the majority of her life trying to find meaning and more specifically, connect with her core identity and live out the truest expression of herself. In her early sixties, she took the plunge and divorced billionaire Ted Turner after a decade-long marriage. This was her third marriage.

In her bio-documentary *Jane Fonda in Five Acts* she says the recurring theme in all three marriages, was her tendency to fade into a passive role and mould herself according to what her then-husband wanted her to be, but there was always a centre to herself that they never touched.

In her own words:

Ted feels like he is getting small when he is alone. Ted can't be alone and so my whole life had to be about him. It was rare that I could go to a conference. The women's conference in Beijing I really had to negotiate. I began an organisation called the Georgia Campaign for Adolescent Pregnancy Prevention. There was a lot that I wanted to do that I couldn't do. It was very important to me.

As we moved through the decade that we spent together I became more of a feminist so my focus was more on women's empowerment. But it's hard to be a complete feminist if you are in a marriage that doesn't quite work. None of my marriages were democratic because I was too worried about pleasing. I had to be a certain way for them to love me. I had to look a certain way and I looked different for all of them. I wanted to be living as a whole Jane, a fully realised Jane. I hoped that Ted would be okay about it because I really loved him and I was hoping it would be forever but that's not the way it turned out.

When you reside within your own skin you can feel it. You are holding all of you, your anger, your kindness, your judgmental-ness.

Everything that makes you what you are including that you may be braver and stronger than the man you are married to. I remember when I said to him, 'Ted this isn't going to work unless there are changes.' We were in a car and all the oxygen left the car and I knew it was not going to happen. It was awful. I could hear a voice saying 'God, Fonda come on, he is handsome he is sexy you'll never have to work again, lighten up come on.' Over here there was a softer voice 'saying if you stay you will never be authentic you will never be able to be whole.'

It wasn't until I was finally single at 62 that I began to feel whole, feel that I was where I was supposed to be.

It took real courage for Fonda to fight to honour her true self. The trappings of wealth, security and genuine love were not enough to quiet the inner stirrings of a soul that was striving to discover and express its true identity. Fonda's example shows that the years do not diminish the inner conflict that occurs when we do not live out the truest expression of ourselves. To discover and then honour her true self was the route to achieve real freedom.

"ALL DISCOMFORT COMES FROM SUPPRESSING YOUR TRUE IDENTITY."

BRYANT H. MCGILL

AZURA'S STORY

Azura, a pastor's wife, was lost. A highly intelligent and capable woman was buried in a sea of depression and inner emptiness. She had placed the values of her husband, family and the church members above her own needs and desires.

It came at a cost; by bowing to perceived cultural and church members' expectations of being dutiful and always helping others to a sacrificial level, Azura had had lost all sense of her identity. She could not enjoy her children or husband fully. She felt put upon and not comfortable in what seemed like a pre-defined role of what a pastor's wife should be. Azura was unable to say "no", or even identify how to fix the void or the unease and dissatisfaction growing within her.

But before Azura was a wife, she was a complete and whole person within herself. The fact that she was not fully in touch with that person meant it was easy to morph into what she believed was expected of her when she married. Azura didn't consider that exploring, owning and expressing the strengths and natural talents within her *would not* put her into conflict with her roles as a wife, mother, church leader or even a friend.

In fact, it would make her more effective in those roles; honouring her unique self, unsuppressed and free would bring her personal happiness and fulfilment that would also radiate outward. It would enable Azura to make better decisions for herself and the future roles and responsibilities she *chose* to take on, and even re-evaluate her behaviour in her existing roles and the responsibilities she would choose to retain.

The turning point came when Azura's youngest child was about to start school. With more time on her hands, she could no longer hide behind the outer façade of busyness. She felt an increasing since of dissatisfaction and she needed to find a way out.

Coaching was the path to self-awareness and enlightenment for Azura where she was given the space to transform into *who she really was*. Azura went from not even knowing what music she liked to giving herself permission to own her vast array of talents and explore the latent desires and passions that she previously believed did not fit into the role she had taken on as the wife of a pastor.

Through coaching, Azura explored her interests, passions, talents, values and personality. She discovered that she had a passion for adventure and spontaneity and she had a flair for sports;

Azura was already an accomplished swimmer. She was also gifted at researching, editing and teaching, which she enjoyed. She understood more about her personality. She no longer viewed her introversion as a deficit and learned how to work to the strengths of her personality traits, rather than work in opposition to them, which is what had led to the previous inner conflict.

Azura learned that she could be authentic and be an even greater asset to her husband, family and church members. Just in a different way; a way that also honoured who she truly was.

This meant, no more childminding as a day job and stepping in to look after church members' children a short notice. It meant saying no more often when it didn't fit with her own agenda and goals. This meant discovering and honouring her own values first, rather than conceding to the values and expectations of others.

Azura went from depression to enlightenment and expression. Azura transformed.

She moved from childminding to a ministry of researching and teaching God 's word to others, which led to a number of speaking engagements. The solitude she craved was utilised in researching and preparing teaching materials which fuelled her own personal growth as well as fulfilling her desire to impact others and enable them to grow as Christians. She harnessed her sporting ability to train and take part in triathlons; and new-found "me time" was spent training which provided numerous benefits for her mental health.

Azura's sense of adventure and spontaneity was fulfilled with trips that often involved the whole family. For example, a trip to Disney World.

She also dealt with the obstacles in her way. With serious introspection she identified, challenged and reframed the beliefs holding her back and making her miserable. Azura was able to view herself through a new untainted lens and the new possibilities became endless. She understood more about the importance of identifying and honouring her core values and aligning her decision making with those values in mind.

No longer lost, Azura found herself on the path of operating in her authentic purpose, happy and fulfilled. She was a more contented wife, mother, leader and friend. All of her significant relationships benefited from the transformed Azura, who was operating out of her unique self, fulfilled, with a new inner freedom that radiated around her.

There were no more false compromises.

We are all unique and have something great to offer to society when we turn up authentically.

When Azura identified and honoured her personal values and the beliefs that were limiting her potential, she was able to get in touch with her core identity to gain congruence and carve out a purposeful and fulfilling life.

"DON'T LET THE NOISE OF OTHERS' OPINIONS DROWN OUT YOUR OWN INNER VOICE."

STEVE JOBS

JENNICA'S STORY

Jennica has a complex relationship with her mother. Although she is an independent adult in her forties with a successful career of her own, she has held tightly to the apron strings of her mother.

Jennica's parents split up when she was young, and she remained at home with her mother. After the separation, her father became an irregular presence in her life thereafter and she felt the loss profoundly. A strong sense of rejection and unworthiness had stemmed from this perceived abandonment. Her mother was a stern no-nonsense personality that had remained bitter and angry at the break up of her own marriage and could be very negative about relationship issues. Her mother had not let go of the past and was somewhat controlling over her children's lives.

The trauma Jennica had experienced in early life had distorted the dynamics of the relationship with her mother. She was trapped in a childlike cycle of need and acceptance, without the courage to form or explore an independent identity separate from her mother. Instead, she had taken on the values and beliefs of her mother without questioning them and it was clearly impacting her own ability to parent her children effectively.

While there was a strong need to remain close to her mother, the relationship was not bringing out the best in her. She felt out of her depth and unworthy as a mother and a spouse. Jennica said: "I don't know who I am without my mother". She lived in a constant fear that she would not be able to cope or even lose herself if something were to happen to her own mother.

But Jennica could not uncover her core identity while she was trapped in this cycle; and because she was not charting her own course she felt out of control. Her loyalty to her mother was unwavering, so any question of going against her advice was unthinkable. However, there was a cost.

At the time of coaching Jennica was struggling with anxiety, stress, stagnation, mild depression and excessive alcohol consumption. In addition, the relationship with her teenage children was suffering and causing Jennica great distress. Jennica was stagnant in her ambitions and goals and confused about her abilities. She was afraid of stepping out further to new opportunities that went against the values and beliefs of her mother.

She lacked confidence in her abilities as a parent and felt like she was "play acting" as a mother and out of her depth. She could not trust her own basic mothering skills and her intrinsic value because she didn't understand where this began and her own mother's ended.

THE PAIN OF CHANGE VERSUS THE PAIN OF STAYING THE SAME

Jennica was in deep conflict, she knew that she didn't feel right, but realigning relationship boundaries with her mother would feel like cutting off her right and left arm and venturing into an abyss of the unknown where she would have to take full responsibility for herself and grow up emotionally. She would have to relinquish the need to be parented and feel secure as a child, as she was now the adult. She would have to refrain from "rescuing" her children and allow them to learn from their errors. She would have to develop her own parenting skills, less rigid, controlling and critical. She would have to take off the mask and discover who she really was to uncover the authentic base where she could anchor and then grow.

Although the process of transformation seemed insurmountable to Jennica, she would not be able to evolve and discover who she really was and what she really wanted while she remained being a pseudo extension of her mother. In this role she would not be her whole self and settle the inner conflict that was willing her on to take the plunge and cut the apron strings.

The perceived comfort zone of a Peter Pan-esque existence was robbing Jennica of true happiness, contentment, peace and confidence. It was impacting many of her most important relationships negatively and distracting her from fulfilling her true potential. Ultimately it was blocking Jennica from discovering and accepting who she really was as an adult.

"ONE OF THE GREATEST REGRETS IN LIFE IS BEING WHAT OTHERS WOULD WANT YOU TO BE, RATHER THAN BEING YOURSELF."

SHANNON L ALDER

KELLY'S STORY

Kelly had successfully left a 10-year abusive relationship where she had almost lost her life two years prior. Although she had physically removed herself and her two daughters from this volatile environment, she had not made the same shift in her head. Mentally and emotionally, she felt trapped in negative cycles of thinking and behaviour and had great difficulty interacting with the father of her children while trying to co-parent.

To meet Kelly, an outwardly confident, outgoing person with a sunny disposition, you would have no idea the ordeal her life had been through from the years of domestic abuse and even through childhood. Through coaching, Kelly discovered that the sexual abuse she'd experienced as a young child at the hands of an older sibling and her mother's subsequent ineffective handling of the matter had shaped her outlook and behaviour in successive relationships. Her mother failed to protect or support her when the abuse was discovered and instead behaved as though nothing had happened. No help was given to Kelly or her sibling. They were just left to get on with things without support or intervention. Her mother was visibly emotionally distant towards her from that point onwards.

By the time Kelly met her partner, an older man, she was happy to escape the family and start a new life with him. Things turned sour quickly but instead of seeking help, Kelly learned how to subconsciously pretend everything was okay, as deep inside she didn't believe it would get any better or anyone would rescue her. After all, isn't that what happened when she was a child; pretend everything is alright and get on with things? She had learned a level of normalisation to the abuse because of the way the early trauma had shaped her thinking and beliefs about relationships.

Through coaching Kelly understood on a conscious level how this childhood trauma had impacted her identity, choice of partner and subsequent decision making. By facing the real cost to her life and the lives of her children, she was able to take steps to healing and discover who she really was, free from the baggage of abuse and trauma that was weighing her down mentally and emotionally, long after she had physically removed herself from that environment.

Without the inner work, Kelly would have found herself moving from one toxic situation to another, despite the obvious signs of danger. The inner blindfolds needed to be removed for Kelly to see clearly and operate differently in future relationships. This can only happen when you have a true grasp of your core identity, unencumbered by the obstacles that seek to obscure the view of your true landscape.

As a result, Kelly has been better able to advocate for herself within her extended family, in her work and her friendships. There is a new inner love that comes with the revelation and acceptance of her unique self.

Each relationship nurtures a strength or weakness within you; relationships can be vibrant and life giving or stagnant and even draining. But what matters most is how you as an individual turn up in that relationship, which will play a large part in directing how the relationship will go. When you are unsure of who you really are, it is almost inevitable that you will compromise and lose yourself to the expectations and desires of others. But it really isn't their fault. They don't know who you really are!

"THE BEGINNING OF LOVE IS TO LET THOSE WE LOVE BE PERFECTLY THEMSELVES, AND NOT TO TWIST THEM TO FIT OUR OWN IMAGE. OTHERWISE, WE LOVE ONLY THE REFLECTION OF OURSELVES WE FIND IN THEM."

THOMAS MERTON

CORE INSIGHT ACTION

Practical exercise

MY ROLES IN RELATIONSHIPS AUDIT

Pick **five** important relationships in your life. Ask yourself the following questions for each relationship:

- What role am I playing?
- Can I freely express myself?
- What are the restrictions?
- What am I compromising in myself to experience any of the following: love, connection, happiness, challenge, acceptance, companionship safety, security etc?
- If there were no restrictions, how would I express myself?
- What needs to change?

Chapter 16

THE LONG SHADOW OF SELF-REJECTION

"BECAUSE TRUE BELONGING ONLY HAPPENS WHEN WE PRESENT OUR AUTHENTIC, IMPERFECT SELVES TO THE WORLD, OUR SENSE OF BELONGING CAN NEVER BE GREATER THAN OUR LEVEL OF SELF-ACCEPTANCE."

BRENÉ BROWN

At the time of writing this, a new series of *I'm a Celebrity Get Me Out of Here*! has begun. The game show puts individuals together in the Australian jungle – most having never met each other before – and they must live together and work as a team to survive. Mostly horrendous individual and group challenges must be undertaken to provide food for their camp mates.

There is no question the show is very entertaining. The challenges are daring and funny and can have you at the edge of your seat. There are multi-layers of interest for viewers. This year I have been paying attention to the group dynamics, how contestants/teammates interact with each other, and how bonds are formed. The psychological pressure of being in an environment where social rejection can break you down and the lengths contestants will go to, to be accepted in the group are evident. Also, the trauma of being away from partners, family and friends where they experience acceptance and real connection coupled with an added layer of wanting the approval of the viewers is huge.

The behaviour of an individual impacts the whole group. Anyone rejected in the group would not be able to survive for long. In instances where rejection has taken place, viewers witness a rapid discombobulation of the ostracised contestant. All their personal game strategies are thrown out of the window and their vulnerabilities, warts-and-all, are laid bare.

One might say these are celebrities used to living life in the public eye, but ego will only carry them so far. If they stay in the jungle long enough, the real person emerges; and careers have either soared or crashed and burned as a result of the show.

We are wired to belong. Just as we have needs for food and water, we also have needs for positive and lasting relationships. This need is deeply rooted in our ability to survive in social groups. When this doesn't happen and we feel rejected, there are all sorts of mental, emotional and physical consequences to our wellbeing.

WHAT IS REJECTION?

The Latin noun rēicere, which means "to throw back'" is the ancestor of the word rejection.

According to the Cambridge English Dictionary, rejection is defined as the act of refusing to accept, use or believe someone or something.

Common synonyms of rejection are spurning, dismissal, elimination, abandonment, expulsion, disowning and denial. In the field of mental health care, rejection most frequently refers to the feelings of shame, sadness or grief people feel when they are not accepted by others. It is no wonder then, that humans hate rejection and go to great lengths to avoid it.

The fear of being rejected is so powerful, the majority of humans are happy to live behind a mask of inauthenticity as they perceive this as the only way to be accepted in social groups and even in more intimate relationships. According to author Miguel Ruiz: "Just being ourselves is the biggest fear of humans. We have learned to live our life trying to satisfy other people's demands. We have learned to live by other people's points of view because of the fear of not being accepted and of not being good enough for someone else."

REJECTION CAUSES PHYSICAL PAIN

Research has shown a relationship between hurt caused by rejection and body pain. Kip Williams and colleagues at the University of Toledo conducted an experiment which indicated that rejection triggers the same area of the brain that is active when we feel physical pain. DeWall, Eisenberger and colleagues, conducted research to find out if pain due to rejection could be treated in the same way as physical pain. They found that people who took Tylenol [Paracetamol] in the experiment as opposed to people who took placebo pills had less activity in the pain related areas of the brain when subjected to rejection.[23]

THE EFFECTS OF SOCIAL REJECTION

Rejection also has serious implications for an individual's psychological state and for society in general. Social rejection can influence emotion, cognition and even physical health.

According to DeWall, social rejection increases anger, anxiety, depression, jealousy and sadness. It reduces performance on difficult intellectual tasks, and can also contribute to aggression and poor impulse control. Physically, too, rejection takes a toll. People who routinely feel excluded have poorer sleep quality, and their immune systems don't function as well as those of people with strong social connections.

Research has linked social isolation and loneliness to higher risks for a variety of physical and mental conditions: high blood pressure, heart disease, stroke, obesity, a weakened immune system, anxiety, increased stress, depression, drug addiction, alcoholism, anti-social behaviour, cognitive decline, Alzheimer's Disease and even death.

It causes a discomfort in our body which tells us that we are not wanted, that we don't belong. Rejection usually hurts more than we expect it to. And even if a wounded soul seeks isolation to protect themselves, it does not bring happiness.

But, despite the hurt of rejection people still crave connection. There is neural evidence that shows positive social interactions release opioids for a natural mood boost, according to Eisenberger.

EXTERNAL REJECTION LEADS TO INTERNAL REJECTION AND THE DISTORTION OF YOUR TRUE SELF

Psychologist and author, Sidney Jourard said: "We camouflage our true being before others to protect ourselves against criticism or rejection. This protection comes at a steep price… we are misunderstood. When we are misunderstood, especially by family and friends, we join the 'lonely crowd.' Worse… we tend to lose touch with our real selves."

While the impact of social rejection can have a range of negative repercussions to an individual, far worse is the *self-rejection* that emerges from this, which has a direct impact on your core identity. *The greatest damage from rejection is mostly self-inflicted.*

According to psychologist Guy Winch, the common response to being excluded or side-lined is not just to nurse your wounds but to become intensely self-critical. You may convince yourself that you're not "good enough" and become preoccupied dwelling on your failures or flaws, whether they're big or small. You may call yourselves names, lament your shortcomings, and feel disgusted with yourself. Just when your self-esteem is hurting most, you go and damage it even further. Doing so is emotionally unhealthy and psychologically self-destructive, yet Winch believes every single person has done it at one time or another.

Self-rejection magnifies and prolongs feelings of low self-esteem. It distorts your true personality and can lead to behaviours that seek to overcompensate or withdraw. In either case, these behaviours are inauthentic and do not honour who you really are. When you reject yourself, you are open to all forms of self-compromise associated with people pleasing, and your mask just becomes more elaborate. The more you reject yourself with negative self-talk and feelings of unworthiness, the more people will be able to take advantage of you and the more you will lose touch and become disconnected from your core identity.

It's one thing to hear someone else reject you, but it's a completely different thing to hear those words come from your own mouth, or to feel those thoughts run through your own inner consciousness. Think about it. You can't get away from yourself, or ignore your inner self-talk. You are with you all of the time, the most persistent and constant voice you hear is your own.

Worse still, whenever you reject yourself, you paralyse yourself before you've even tried. You isolate yourself from people and opportunities, which means that you stay stagnant and leave yourself with no chance of getting the result you actually want. But this only happens because you've blocked your own path.

Self-rejection is a form of self-sabotage.

"We have the need to be accepted and to be loved by others, but we cannot accept and love ourselves. The more self-love we have, the less we will experience self-abuse. Self-abuse comes from self-rejection, and self-rejection comes from having an image of what it means to be perfect and never measuring up to that ideal. Our image of perfection is the reason we reject ourselves the way we are, and why we don't accept others the way they are."

The quote above by author Miguel Ruiz powerfully encapsulates Isobel's experience of self-rejection which distorts the core identity and leads to self-sabotage.

ISOBEL'S STORY

Isobel now in her fifties has struggled throughout her adult life with self-acceptance. Despite many years of outward success with her business venture which led to multiple international awards, Isobel was unable to be at peace with herself.

The mask

Isobel was attractive, outgoing, funny, creative and innovative. Wherever she went she found favour with people and had many opportunities throughout her professional life that others could only dream about. She was fun to be around on a surface level and could hold good conversations on a range of topics. She was stylish and well-travelled. The mask she constructed was thick and elaborate, but unsustainable. Destructive patterns of behaviour gave her away.

Behind the mask

Isobel had struggled with a difficult and abusive childhood; rejection from her mother and physical and mental abuse from her father. In addition, she was sexually abused as a minor, something she refused to deal with or receive the subsequent healing that would come from confronting the trauma. Instead, Isobel internalised these traumas and used them to reject herself.

She created an elaborate façade for her mask. There was a huge void between the public face she presented and the inner person that had no self-love and critically low self-esteem. Isobel was insecure; she constantly compared herself to others and because of the self-rejection she held so tightly to, naturally she always came up short. This led to consistent feelings of insecurity and the need to *compete* with others she deemed were *better than her.* As a consequence, she was unable to sustain lasting authentic friendships or healthy business connections for any length of time. Her sense of worth was negotiated by a "trading mentality", that she was accepted by what she could do for others and vice versa. *Her ONLY value was in what she could do* and not in who she was.

In reality Isobel's self-rejection and denial led to a distortion in her personality. She was emotionally unavailable, unable or unwilling to empathise with others or feel the human emotion of others. However, she expected empathy from others. Her behaviour was often narcissistic, selfish, self-serving and stubborn; unwilling to accept the wisdom or genuine assistance from others. Everything had to be on her terms, but unfortunately her terms were misshapen.

Self-rejection had distorted Isobel's core identity and her ability to find true peace and fulfilment in her life. Her attempts to behave as though she was sorted was exhausting and eventually left her in freefall, disconnected from her true self and buried under a veil of deception that altered her reality. The long shadow of self-rejection had led Isobel to disempower herself.

When you deny who you are, you absolve yourself from taking any responsibility. It's easy to see yourself as the victim and those around you as your oppressors. That's where the stagnation takes root.

In Isobel's case, over a period of time – unable to keep up with the demands of her façade – coping mechanisms such as drinking alcohol overcame her. Her mental and physical health suffered along with her ability to take an honest look at what the impact of her divergent and dual lives (inner and outer) had taken from her.

The deception was so great, that she was unable to see a way out of her quandary. It was catch-22, a vicious circle. A bright individual full of promise that refused to deal with her inner struggles became a shadow of a person governed by fear and denial.

I have included this story because it is a cautionary tale that could have had a different ending if Isobel had had the courage to honestly tackle the self-rejection that led her down this destructive rabbit hole. Reading and consuming information on self-help and transformation is not enough, it needs to be diligently put into practice. Only then will the personal benefits become evident.

Remember, you can't get away from yourself. When you reject key parts of who you are, what you say you believe and what you act out may be in direct conflict to who you really are.

> "THE GREATEST TRAP IN OUR LIFE IS NOT SUCCESS, POPULARITY OR POWER, BUT SELF-REJECTION."
>
> **HENRI NOUWEN**

THE ANTIDOTE TO SELF-REJECTION IS SELF-ACCEPTANCE

It is true, throughout life it is impossible to avoid rejection of various sorts, but you can control your response to it, most importantly how you manage and respond to what goes on inside your own head. Self-acceptance is key.

Ruiz explains: "Once you forgive yourself, the self-rejection in your mind is over. Self-acceptance begins, and the self-love will grow so strong that you will finally accept yourself just the way you are. That's the beginning of the free human. Forgiveness is the key."

Clinical Psychologist Maury Joseph PsyD says: "Self-acceptance does not promise us the sense of purification, perfection, and control that self-rejection tempts us with. And in that sense, it may be less attractive in moments when the need for change feels dire. However, if we've tried self-rejection, seen its results, and understand why we thought it was a good idea at the time, perhaps we can begin to accept ourselves and see what happens then.

"Self-acceptance is not guaranteed to cure anything or to even feel good. All self-acceptance guarantees us is that we will be in touch with the clearest and most realistic picture of ourselves in this moment, beyond our fantasies of how we should be."[24]

This leads back to the importance of discovering who you really are, free from the obstacles that seek to obstruct and distort that discovery. It's the obstacles of limiting beliefs, skewed values, unforgiveness, people pleasing and so on, that distort your core identity. Often what you are rejecting is the person you think you *should be* that you are not living up to [the mask you have carefully tried to construct over time] rather than who you really are. When you discover this and live out of its truth; you exhale and become comfortable living in your own skin. Remember, your sense of belonging can never be greater than your level of self-acceptance.

> "WHEN YOU KNOW YOURSELF, YOU ARE EMPOWERED. WHEN YOU ACCEPT YOURSELF, YOU ARE INVINCIBLE."
>
> **TINA LIFFORD**

CORE INSIGHT ACTION

Practical exercise

REFLECTION

- Think of a time you were rejected.
- How did you feel?
- How did you respond outwardly?
- How did you respond inwardly?
- What was your inner self-talk?
- What were your outer actions?
- How far was the gap in between?
- How will you apply what you have learned so far about your core identity and operating within your circle of influence to help you navigate future inevitable rejections?
- Record your learning in your journal.

Chapter 17

CHANGE PART 1: THERE IS NOTHING PERMANENT EXCEPT CHANGE

"Change is inevitable. Growth is optional."

JOHN MAXWELL

When you think back to a significant period of change in your life, how do you feel? What emotions rise up in you?

Change is commonly linked to big emotions like excitement, fear or even panic. Big changes like moving house or even country, a new job, marriage, divorce or redundancy come with a trailer load of the unknown. There will be many issues to navigate, to learn and respond to. You may feel ill-equipped for many of these challenges, simply because they are unfamiliar and you are going into new territory.

But change is where progress happens and where growth occurs. On my website and in my business material I use this quote: "In unchartered waters there are endless possibilities, venture in..." Stepping forward and charting an unknown course is often necessary to fulfil your potential and achieve your purpose.

Whether we like it or not, things are constantly changing. To grow and develop we must go through transition. Even a baby must physically grow, develop and learn the skills that will enable them to become a fully functioning independent adult. There will be physical, mental and emotional changes to navigate. We humans have a vast capacity for growth and achievement; while the popular principle that we only use 10% of our brains is unfounded; there *is* a great depth of untapped capacity in us that lies dormant unless triggered by a new situation, issue or challenge.

When you put your mind to something, you can learn new things and there is increasing evidence in the area of neuroplasticity showing that this changes the brain by creating new connections between nerve cells. But to do this you have to step out of your comfort zone and the familiar to embrace change.

> "I HAVE ACCEPTED FEAR AS PART OF LIFE, SPECIFICALLY THE FEAR OF CHANGE. I HAVE GONE AHEAD DESPITE THE POUNDING IN THE HEART THAT SAYS: TURN BACK."
>
> **ERICA JONG**

So, if change leads to positive results, why does it make us so uncomfortable?

Change is linked to *uncertainty and fuels fear.* We get comfortable with what we know, with what is familiar whether it is actually helping us or not. But change doesn't happen in the comfort zone. FEAR is "*False Evidence Appearing Real*". We fear the unknown, simply because it is unknown and we perceive in our minds various scenarios fuelled by the things we seek to avoid that cause us discomfort. Ever heard that saying: "better the devil you know"? Well, what makes a familiar devil better than one that may not even exist on the other side of fear?

The human brain values certainty and predictability. The brain can overvalue the present and undervalue the future. You can feel out of control if you are unsure about what a future change will mean for you or what will happen next. Given the choice between a payoff today and in one week's time, humans seek safety; taking the easier option. For example, you may stay on the sofa instead of going to the gym; the reward of being warm and cosy in the present trumps the future reward of feeling healthy.

Change is associated with *loss and grief.* It can mean letting go of something we treasure for something different or, something familiar for something better. For example, you are offered your dream job, but it means relocating to another country leaving friends, family and your home comforts behind to start afresh in the unknown.

The popular TV franchise *90 Day Fiancé* focuses on individuals who relocate to other countries to be with their future spouses. It involves leaving behind family, jobs, friends and a whole lifestyle, sometimes even their native language to take a shot at love and the future life they hope for with their new partner. The couples often have to overcome huge cultural barriers among other things to progress the relationship. One of the hardest things the person who has relocated talks about is what they have left behind, what was comfortable, familiar and predictable. A period of feeling out of their depth occurs before the transition is complete. But the couples who make it and weather the storms of transition are blessed with a whole new life and go on to make new discoveries, creating new memories together.

It's emotional. Big emotional reactions are linked to change which can lead to extreme behaviour and poor decision making. Solely using emotions to guide your response to change is often unhelpful because feelings are ever changing and often linked to fear which can pop up at any time without warning.

THE CYCLE OF CHANGE

The *change curve* derived from the work of Elisabeth Kubler-Ross, describes the internal emotional journey that individuals typically experience when dealing with change and transition. This journey consists of a number of stages that people go through: *shock and denial, anger, blame, bargaining, depression, acceptance and meaning*. There are many bumps through the transition to acceptance.

Kubler-Ross change curve

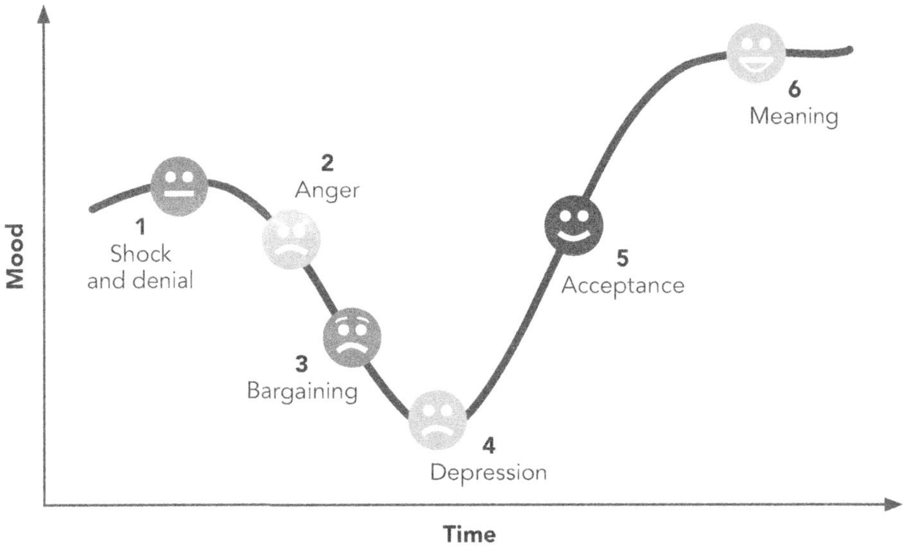

Let's look at these elements in relation to the 2020 Coronavirus Pandemic.

People reacted to this unprecedented global pandemic in a variety of ways, depending on their internal response to change and facing the unknown.

Initially some people believed it wasn't real and refused to prepare for lockdown or even comply with its restrictions. Others were terrified, began stockpiling, disinfecting and sanitising everything and anything in their sight, while consuming numerous conspiracy theories on social media about an impending Armageddon.

Some people focused their attentions on looking for a scapegoat, someone to blame. In the early stages of the pandemic the Chinese community, their culture and lifestyle, were vilified by some politicians, the press, social media, and – in turn – by some people, for "creating and spreading" the virus.

Some people, however – when the initial shock subsided – got creative and embraced the change that lockdowns provided. Those people became innovative and developed businesses and initiatives to help others. Whole communities galvanised and joined in efforts to support the most vulnerable; volunteering in foodbanks, making deliveries and sewing scrubs for medics, among others things.

As the reality of the "new normal" of lockdown-life set in, some people suffered with mental health problems and struggled to come to terms with the many issues impacting their way of life that was out of their control.

Many people experienced great personal loss; the loss of income, career, lifestyle, loved ones and even hope for the future. Self-doubt, anxiety and depression rose significantly. There were unimaginable restrictions to personal liberties that were inconceivable just a short year before, yet everyone had to weather these changes.

Change happened regardless. There have been positive and negative outcomes from it, depending on an individual's perspective and approach to the change itself. This determined their ability to navigate the many circumstances that were outside their control.

"If you don't like something, change it. If you can't change it, change your attitude."

MAYA ANGELOU

YOU ARE ALREADY EQUIPPED – HARNESS YOUR RESOURCES!

The example of the pandemic illustrates that major change can often be imposed on you as a result of issues beyond your immediate control. How can you embrace change and make it work for you, even in the worst situations? The answer lies in your perspective and utilising the stability of your core identity. While everything around you may be changing, or you may have to deal with a significant issue of transition in your life, there is one thing that remains stable which can help you to positively navigate transition. Your core identity.

Understanding *who you really* are and operating out of it is the passport to navigating change successfully.

When you harness the many resources that are found at your core, you can be in control of your personal process of change and gain stability, rather than only reacting to events or firefighting to maintain a status-quo that no longer exists.

These resources include understanding your *strengths and natural talents*, aspects of your *personality*, your *passions and interests* and the compass of your *core values and guiding beliefs* to understand what *motivates* you to achieve.

Your circumstances may change and provide new challenges: you may change your perspective or direction of travel, but your core identity doesn't change, it only evolves. You can apply the constant things in your core identity to enable you to navigate change without feeling like a deer in the headlights, or by burying your head in the sand when change is happening all around you *(See career change case study in Chapter 18)*.

When you are unable to positively embrace change with a clear understanding of who you are, you lose out on opportunities to grow and evolve, and are unable to utilise new opportunities and adapt. For example, changes in innovation and technology could enable you to exploit opportunities that would have an authentic benefit when approached from a positive perspective.

It is never the change itself, but your attitude towards it.

The term "Luddite" is used to describe a person opposed to new technology or ways of working. Sarah refuses to use Facebook, Linkedin or any other form of social media, she views this new technology as sinister and believes it will have a negative impact on her wellbeing and her privacy if she participates in it. While it is true, social media can have a negative impact on an individual's mental health and privacy; social media itself is not a negative invention. Many people have positively benefited from engaging with it for professional or personal reasons.

Sarah has approached her decision as though she has no control or say over how she will engage with and use these platforms. As a result, she is being left behind. Her aversion to social media means that her newly launched business is struggling, because it is invisible online. Her reluctance to create a professional profile on Linkedin means potential clients or partners are unable to connect, find out what she does, or utilise her business's services.

If Sarah were clear about who she is and what she stands for, she could engage in social media on her own terms and not believe she would get carried away with the tide. She could set her own parameters and stick to them. Her mindset and perspective have held her back and stalled progress in her business venture.

LEAH'S STORY

Dealing with change without a good awareness of who you really are at your core can be confusing, frightening and unproductive. Leah's identity crisis came about through a period of major transition. She had no authentic foundation and struggled through a significant life change.

When Leah, a career woman in her early thirties, became a new mother, she was like "a fish out of water", completely shell shocked about the changes in her circumstances, emotions and choices. Instead of feeling joyous, she was confused and needed meaning and stability. She was fearful about this unknown new life and grieving the old life she knew and understood.

Her identity was previously tied up in her career as a broadcaster and the outward trappings of success. Although she'd physically prepared and read many baby magazines and books, this did not deal with the inner tsunami rising up inside her. Everything had changed, she was at home with a crying baby and she didn't have the option to just get up and go out without thinking of anyone else. The usual activities and distractions were no longer an option.

The transition between being a career woman and a full-time stay-at-home mother was overwhelming and Leah felt lost and alone. None of her friends or colleagues had babies, so even her friendship groups were compromised, leading to a period of soul searching, transition and, inevitably, a crisis in identity.

Being away from work and something she was good at which defined her, to being a complete novice at being a mother freaked her out. She didn't know how to exist in this new identity or how to think of herself. As a result, she couldn't make any plans as before (an unpredictable baby was involved now) and things felt like they were out of control, and every day was a journey into the unknown. She felt conflicted and dissatisfied.

Leah had a tough time making the transition to being a mother because she didn't know who she really was. Her core identity was something to still be discovered and understood, so she was unable to access this to give her any stability through the major change that was happening in her life.

The first year of being a parent (navigating internal and external firefighting) was not as enjoyable as she'd envisioned. Leah gave a lot of mental space to striving to find a foundation that made sense, on which she could build. Her old (unstable) foundation for her identity was obliterated when she left work and became a mother.

When you build your identity *on what you do* rather than *who you truly are*, navigating change can be an uphill struggle and many people give up along the way, as the constant changes mean there is no place to anchor for any prolonged period of time.

The reality is that what you do and your circumstances are always prone to change. You cannot guarantee you will have the same career your whole life, or work for the same company. You cannot guarantee you will always live in the same location or be someone's wife (if that is how your identity is defined).

Life is full of unexpected twists and turns. Understanding your core identity and your subsequent perspective will determine how successfully you navigate change.

THE PAIN OF CHANGE VERSUS THE PAIN OF STAYING THE SAME

The story of Moses and the Israelites

The Israelites had been enslaved by the Egyptians for 400 years and Moses was leading them out of captivity. They got to the Red Sea and were hemmed in as the Egyptians were chasing them. At this point, faced with a dilemma that they were unsure how to navigate; they had two choices, to figure out how to overcome the obstacle of crossing the Red Sea, or to give up. The Israelites lost their resolve and starting complaining to Moses that he should have left them in captivity because they were better off there. It was something they knew and were familiar with. Even though it was oppressive, the fear of the unknown meant in their panic, they were willing to surrender their opportunity for freedom and return to a life more familiar, even though it was oppressive and soul destroying. (Exodus 14)

Can you relate to this?

> "Growth is painful. Change is painful. But nothing is as painful as staying stuck somewhere you don't belong."
>
> N.R. NARAYANA MURTHY

CORE INSIGHT ACTION

Expand your circle of influence

The circle of influence and concern (below) can be used to help you become more flexible and proactive when dealing with change.

It will enable you to focus on what is already within your control and the things you can influence. You will no longer waste time and energy on the myriad of concerns that you can do nothing about.

Remember, reactive people focus on their circle of concern. Proactive people focus on expanding their circle of influence.

When you focus your energy in the realm of what you can influence, it will expand. By default, your circle of concern will decrease, extending the control and influence you have over your own life.

Practical exercise

1 Take a sheet of paper and draw three concentric circles like the illustration to the right
2 In the centre ring list those things **you have** control over right now
3 In the middle ring list those things you are concerned about that you can influence
4 In the outer ring list those the concerns that you can't control or influence.

Review

- Where will you now focus your time and energy?
- What specific actions in those areas will you take to expand your circle of influence?

Circle of Influence Example

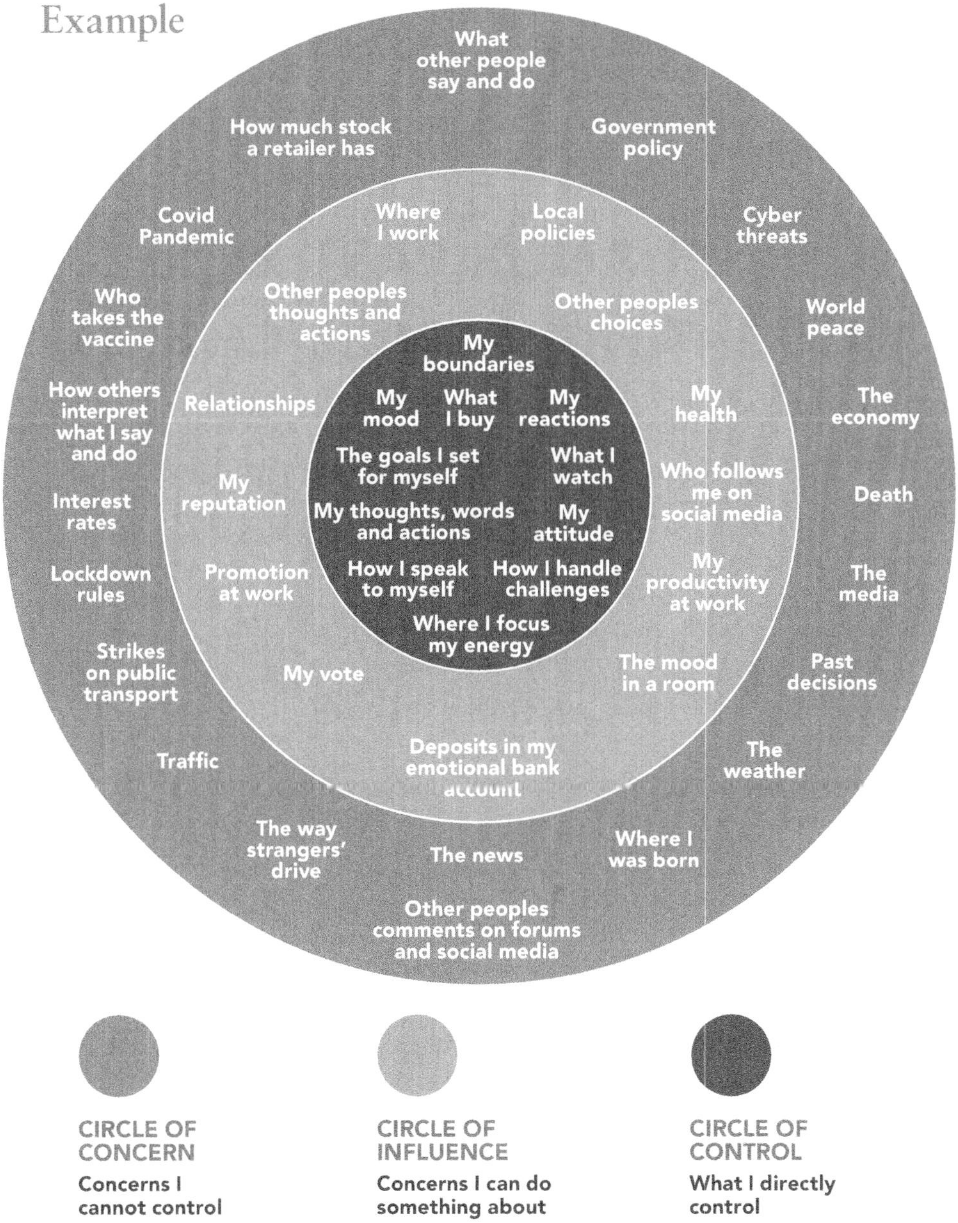

Chapter 18

CHANGE PART 2: NAVIGATING CAREER CHANGE

"IN ANY GIVEN MOMENT WE HAVE TWO OPTIONS: TO STEP FORWARD INTO GROWTH OR STEP BACK INTO SAFETY."

ABRAHAM MASLOW

CASE STUDY
TONI

Toni came for coaching two years after graduating from university with a Business degree. She was working as a trainee accountant with a media firm. Toni considered herself fortunate to land such a good opportunity relatively quickly after graduating, as many of her peers had not been so lucky.

On the surface, Toni was a young, intelligent professional on her way to a lucrative career in finance. The company was paying for all of her training and there were even free overseas trips thrown in. Friends and family – her father in particular – were extremely proud of her career choice. For the first year, Toni almost enjoyed her role, but then things started to change.

Every day began to feel like Groundhog Day, Toni was no longer thriving. She found the repetitive tasks and even the environment of her workplace suffocating and soul destroying. She began failing a particular accountancy exam over and over again. Slowly, the lights were going out and depression was setting in. Toni felt trapped and unable to see a way out, and so she plodded on with the job that was slowly sucking the life and vibrancy out of her.

What was the problem, I hear you say? Surely Toni could just take her qualifications and experience and pursue another career path. If only it were that simple.

As the previous chapter has highlighted, change at the best of times can be difficult. Deeply held beliefs and values, often on a subconscious level, as outlined previously in this book, can play a major role in our ability to act and embrace positive change. Toni was no exception.

Toni was experiencing an *identity crisis*. There was incongruency between who she thought she SHOULD be and who really was. The problem was that Toni didn't know who she really was: she only knew something wasn't right about the career path she was on, and it was impacting all areas of her life. This was a void that could not be filled with other activities and diversions.

Beneath the surface there were many subconscious limiting beliefs that were directing Toni's choices. Before she could tackle what seemed like the daunting and frightening task of changing her career path, she had to discover *who she was* and face head on the limiting beliefs she was held hostage by.

DIGGING DEEPER

Through coaching Toni was able to uncover the most damaging limiting beliefs that were holding her back. She had spent so much of her childhood, teenage and young adult years fulfilling other people's expectations of herself, that she hadn't stopped long enough to discover if their expectations and values were also her own. She was keen to please the adults she respected so that she could feel accepted by them. In particular, the acceptance of her father, who had been an intermittent presence in her life throughout her childhood.

NOT CONNECTING WITH HER REAL SELF

From a young age Toni had been given a lot of responsibility for her younger siblings and she hadn't had freedom to develop her own interests and cultivate hobbies. Even as an adult she became the person the extended family would call on and expect to help out, particularly with their children. She found it hard to pinpoint what her passions and interests were, as she had not given herself the room to explore them, and her needs had always taken a back seat to others.

FULFILLING OTHER PEOPLE'S EXPECTATIONS

The influence of her father was one of the biggest stumbling blocks. Her father was someone she respected, but he was also materialistic with a value system focused on money bringing happiness and fulfilment, rather than valuing job satisfaction and genuine self-expression. His ethos of "do what you need to do to earn money and buy expensive things that will fulfil you" was a mantra he lived by, and to which she had been exposed to from a young age. Because of the respect she had for her father, she didn't dare inwardly challenge these values and even accepted his suggestions for career choices to achieve the same end-goal.

But were these really Toni's values? In the absence of knowing her core identity, it was very easy and almost inevitable that she would accept and not question the values and influence of such a significant person in her life.

Part of the reason Toni spent longer than she needed to unhappy and languishing in her job was the fear of telling her father her career path was not working for her and that she wanted out. She feared his rejection and disappointment above everything else which seemed even more unbearable than her current unhappiness.

The cost of limiting beliefs

- I cannot live the life I want without a high paying job caused Toni to focus on material things above happiness and fulfilment.
- I cannot start a new career or go back to university caused Toni to be sad, angry and demotivated at work.
- I cannot apply for a job I don't have experience in caused Toni to miss out on opportunities that were possible through transferable skills.
- I cannot disappoint my father, he may reject me caused Toni to deny her own needs and not pursue her interests, becoming increasingly lost.

When Toni uncovered the beliefs holding her back – exposing what they were costing her on a daily basis – she was motivated to embark on the process of career change, understanding that those beliefs could be challenged and replaced with more authentic and accurate ones. Challenging those long-held beliefs and values would also contribute to knowing herself.

WHAT DID TONI LEARN?

- Her talents would be wasted and she wouldn't be utilising her strengths.
- Without challenging herself, she'd be stuck in her comfort zone.
- She might miss out on what matters most if she was constantly chasing money.
- Opportunities would pass her by.
- The fear of rejection and need for approval was NOT worth more than her own happiness and fulfilment.

What should she choose, the pain of change or the pain of staying the same?

Given the journey above it would seem obvious which way Toni would go, but change can be scary and even more so when you don't know what you are trading it for. If you don't know your true purpose, you don't know where to direct that change and can easily waste more time and effort journeying in another different, but wrong, direction.

For Toni and many others embarking on a career change, or any other type of major change, understanding your core identity is the impetus you need to find your authentic purpose. Your core values, guiding beliefs, personality, strengths and natural talents, and your passion and motivation is the guide to connect with your true self and fill in the missing pieces of your own puzzle.

DISCOVERY – CONNECTING THE PIECES OF TONI'S PUZZLE

The discovery process enabled Toni to harness parts of her core identity to provide an insightful and stable basis for transition, and connect with her own beliefs and values, not just the inherited or dysfunctional ones.

Toni gave herself permission to let go and dream, without limitations. She started with creating a vision board[26] that represented her ideas, interests and inspirations. This provided a visual picture to begin to see patterns linked to her identity and what was most important to her in life. Toni's vision board gave her the freedom to explore her interests in a relaxed way and pinpoint what areas ignited the passion and motivation within her.

PERSONALITY

Toni completed a variety of personality tests to enable her to understand her motivation and behaviour and the optimum environments and situations where she would thrive. Being aware of her specific personality traits and preferences enabled her to understand how she communicates and perceives the world, in addition to how she understands and connects with others. A clearer understanding of what made her "tick" enabled Toni to make better decisions and build more meaningful relationships as she also understood how she was perceived by others.

This is an important building block along the road to discovery. No two people are exactly the same. Understanding your specific traits and preferences brings validation that being different to those around you is not being "wrong". Each personality has something great to offer, especially when working to their strengths. *(More about personality in chapter 21)*

STRENGTHS AND NATURAL TALENTS

Toni took a deeper look into her strengths and natural talents. She looked beyond what she had done in her career to *who* she had been in what she had done. Uncovering what was natural and inbuilt in within her was a powerful way of guiding her towards a true sense of her unique purpose. Through this detailed introspection a pattern emerged that gave Toni an understanding of her natural abilities, the things she did without effort that she enjoyed and executed with an ease as leisurely as breathing. These were innate skills connected with her core identity and when utilised instinctively, they gave her a sense of contentment.

Shifting your identity from *what you do,* to who you are is key. You will get a sense of your natural abilities in terms of *who you are* and feel more of a sense of purpose that can propel you to turn your work into something you love, step by step.

PASSIONS AND INTERESTS

Analysing the messages and patterns from her vision board enabled Toni to actively pursue interests and activities that aligned with her values and personality. She set challenges and stepped out of her comfort zone to experience new things including competing in an all-terrain obstacle course, presenting in a company meeting, leading an exercise class and being more assertive.

Toni paid attention to what ignited a passion and energy within her and used the learning from these activities to fine tune her chosen areas of focus and then set meaningful goals. This new awareness also enabled her to discount and say "no" to what did not align with her authentic interests and direction. She was understanding her WHY.

VALUES

When Toni was living out other people's values and not consciously connecting with her own, she experienced incongruence and was deeply unhappy and dissatisfied. But when she connected with her core values and understood what they gave her on a daily basis when utilised; she was *motivated* to make the required changes to honour them in her future choices and endeavours.

Toni's understanding of her core values enabled her to connect with her true self and gave her permission to display authentic behaviours and attitudes she would have previously subdued in order to please or align with other people's expectations and priorities. Toni could exhale!

Through this process Toni was able to define her mission and used this as a guide to direct her authentic career change.

MISSION

"My mission in life is to help people lead an active and healthy life, so they are able to live longer, delay any health issues and in the process become body confident. I'd like to focus on 12-18 years olds as they'll already be taking part in some kind of physical activity at school. The earlier we start building these habits, the more likely these kids will remain active throughout their adulthood. Leading an active and healthy lifestyle is all about an individual's mentality, perspective and consistency."

VOILA! FROM FINANCE TO PE TEACHER

Toni was able to make the transition from a career in finance to teaching PE and finding true purpose in her career by going through the discovery process. At the heart of this was uncovering her core identity and building a new foundation from this authentic place. The process was not overnight, but gained through a detailed introspection, full of new learning and revelation. The result was a young woman who was more comfortable in her own skin with genuine confidence and excitement about the future. A woman who was clear about her purpose and excited about the journey to fulfil it.

In her own words:

My mentality now is 'do it if you thoroughly enjoy it, do it if it means a lot to you and do it unapologetically'. Whereas, before coaching I had a level of self-doubt and allowed external voices to have undue influence, so I didn't have enough motivation and drive to follow through. I intend to strive for happiness in everything I do from now on especially when it comes to work. If it doesn't bring me any kind of joy then I don't want to know. My last job taught me this and I realise there's no point in going through all of that for a desired salary, it's not worth it! My overall mood has changed, a weight has been taken off my shoulders and I'm genuinely happy nowadays.

CHANGE IN ACTION

Toni discounted the belief that she could not start again and learned the value and impact of her strengths and natural talents and how they could be harnessed effortlessly, in fact, tailor-made for her chosen career.

Being aware of who she really is and all the valuable assets and resources that were contained within her core identity provided a compass to follow that would lead her to her authentic destination.

The task was no longer daunting, but a fun exercise of discovery that provided inner freedom and a genuine excitement for the future.

This was not an overnight exercise. It took months of introspection and practically trying out new things. For example, once the passion for sport and fitness was discovered, along with understanding her natural talent for teaching, instructing and nurturing young people, Toni became a fitness instructor. She spent time working a leisure centre and embarked on shadowing opportunities with physiotherapists in different sectors and with PE teachers in secondary schools among other things, before she was sure which path to take. The decision to become a PE teacher aligned with all aspects of her core identity. When Toni was moving in her authentic purpose, all the stars aligned. The opportunities came thick and fast and a tailor-made trainee teacher role was created for her to learn on the job, which didn't require her to go back to university and "start all over again".

Toni was being fitted for her bespoke suit!

Chapter 19

PURPOSE: FILL YOUR JAR WITH THE MARBLES YOU HAVE LEFT

"THE SOUL WHICH HAS NO FIXED PURPOSE IN LIFE IS LOST; TO BE EVERYWHERE, IS TO BE NOWHERE."

MICHEL DE MONTAIGNE

"There are four things we can never recover in life; a stone after it has been thrown into the valley, words once they have been spoken, an opportunity once it has been missed and time once it has gone."

Those words are from Gaur Gopal Das in a powerful message of living a purposeful life with the time you have left. The video shows a jar with 840 marbles, representing the number of months an average person has to live on this earth (if they are fortunate enough to reach 70). Each month the jar is emptied of one marble, until there are none left.

The image was stark. If you were 40 years old, there would only be 360 marbles left in that jar. That's 360 months. When you have a visual reminder of the amount of time you have, that time is finite, how would you rearrange your priorities, what would you focus on?

WHAT IS PURPOSE?

To have a purpose means to have a sense of drive that helps you accomplish your goals in life. Having purpose means knowing yourself, knowing your priorities, and aligning your behaviour with your desired outcome. It provides the motivation to keep going. Purpose creates meaning that can guide the direction of your life.

The late Dr Myles Munroe cautioned: "The greatest tragedy in life is not death, it is life without purpose." Without a clear understanding of your purpose, life becomes an experiment, activity has no meaning and time and energy are most definitely misused. Knowing your purpose protects you from doing something good at the expense of doing what is right.[26]

I believe we all have a unique purpose inside of us, waiting to be realised, something that will make a difference to our own life and the lives of others.

According to Jeffery A Williams, author of *Knowing Your Why*: "Right outside your door awaits problems for which your gifts, talents and experience are perfectly situated to solve. Everything and everyone are created to solve a problem."

But most people are not consciously aware of their purpose. They try doing different things that they like or avoiding things they don't like and believe that being busy is accomplishing their purpose. One of the main reasons people struggle to know their purpose is that they are programmed to "just do" without consciously knowing why they are doing it in the first place.

Being good at lots of things doesn't make it your purpose. Your authentic purpose encapsulates and expresses aspects of your core identity. We are all designed to express the strengths and talents we have, aligning them with our values, beliefs, personality and passion. But if what you do causes you to supress key parts of your core identity, you will be unable to achieve your authentic purpose.

Discovering your purpose is critical to living a fulfilled life. It is the link to joy, satisfaction and success. When you discover your purpose, it drives you and causes you to stay focused on the things that are important. You will not be wasting the remaining marbles in your jar.

> "YOU MUST FIRST BE WHO YOU REALLY ARE, THEN DO WHAT YOU NEED TO DO, IN ORDER TO HAVE WHAT YOU WANT."
>
> **MARGARET YOUNG**

YOUR PURPOSE IS INEXTRICABLY LINKED TO YOUR CORE IDENTITY

When I was a newly qualified coach, the emphasis from my training was to assist clients to set and achieve their goals, and navigate the obstacles that were in the way. This meant looking at a client's environment, behaviour, capabilities, beliefs, values and so on.

A useful model was Robert Dilts' neurological levels of change, which illustrates the different levels that an individual experiences the world (see diagram on page 220).

The pyramid's six levels are organised in a hierarchy, the function of each level being to combine, organise and *direct the interactions on the levels below it*. Whatever is on top, runs through everything underneath. Changing something on a higher level means lower levels *must* also change to support it. However, change at a lower level does not necessarily affect an upper level.

For instance, making changes to your environment [level 1], where you work for example, does not guarantee a positive change in your behaviour [level 2] at work. However, improving your knowledge and skills [level 3] to achieve a promotion at work would have a distinct impact on your behaviour and your environment.

Neurological logical levels of change overview

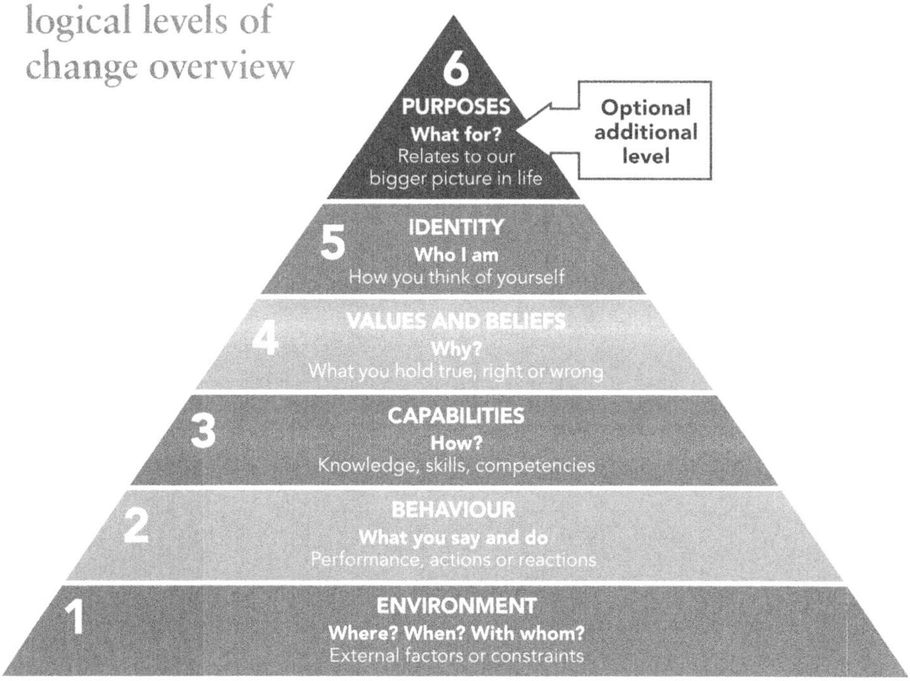

I quickly realised that coaching clients to achieve their goals by working on the lower rungs of the pyramid first was not the most dynamic approach. Goals could be achieved, but change was not embedded or sustainable in the long term, because my clients needed a deeper introspection. I didn't want them to come back to me like a boomerang when a new issue emerged. I wanted them to develop their own skills to tackle life challenges and continue to achieve their goals long after the coaching was over, and to positively impact other people in their lives (principally through their visible success and how they shared what they had learned).

Then I noticed a pattern with my clients, regardless of the issues, fears or goals that they came to coaching for, they didn't know who they were. And as a result, they were living out a pseudo version of who they thought they should be, therefore making inauthentic life and career choices. Those choices were causing misery, confusion and dissatisfaction; the result being a feeling of disconnection that would not go away.

Without an understanding of your core identity and honouring it in your life, you will not achieve your true purpose. Instead, you are going to waste time climbing a ladder that is "leaning against the wrong wall" or helping other people achieve their purpose at your own expense. According to Dr Miles Munroe, abuse misuse and neglect await those who do not know their purpose.

"THE PERSON WITHOUT A PURPOSE IS LIKE A SHIP WITHOUT A RUDDER."

THOMAS CARLYLE

In reference to Dilt's model, the primary aim of coaching for all of my clients is to work on unlocking and revealing level five on the pyramid: *identity*. Once achieved, I noticed the lower levels of the pyramid were also unlocked and this made achieving goals relating to environment, behaviour and capabilities very easy. More importantly their goals became authentic.

And once the clients' core identity was revealed, their authentic purpose emerged. However, without this excavation, nothing authentic and truly meaningful could be released from that roadblock on level five: identity.

MOTIVATION

Living in your authentic purpose provides the motivation to achieve your goals. There is an energy that flows and captivates you. When you are living out your true purpose, life has *real* meaning. You are at one with yourself, you are "on flow".[27] You have zeal, focus and reason. You are able to positively navigate the obstacles that will inevitably come your way. The life of a person living in their authentic purpose is almost unrecognisable as their life was beforehand.

German philosopher Friedrich Nietzsche said: "He who has a why can bear almost any how."

If you know why your life is important and your goal is a positive one, you can suffer through almost any defeat without giving up or quitting.

This was literally the experience of Frankl who used Nietzsche's theory as the blueprint for his survival while imprisoned, when so many thousands around him in the same circumstances had perished. He held onto thinking about his purpose and directed all of his mental energy towards his reason for living.

Frankl believed humans to be motivated by the desire to find meaning in life. He argued that life can have meaning even in the most miserable of circumstances and the motivation for living comes from finding that meaning. This was certainly played out in his own life experience.

Think of the difference between someone who loves their work and doesn't consider it work, even though they are working hard, they are energetic and optimistic about it. They are the *round peg in the round hole*. It doesn't matter so much about the status or financial rewards of the work, it's really whether that work is right for them. For example, aid workers who give up their home comforts to live in difficult, often war-torn countries and places of conflict, but are completely content and even willing to risk their own lives.

Then consider how it would be if this satisfaction and meaning could be applied to all areas of a person's life? That's what authentic purpose can give you, the ability to exhale, be at one with yourself and enjoy the journey and reward of a truly intentional life.

KNOWING YOUR "WHY" IS POWERFUL

Living your life with a unique purpose; breathes new life into you. It effectively gives you an eternal, perpetual, unending "second wind" to push through and not give up. Consider that idiom for a moment; a second wind means a "renewed state of vigour". In distance running such as marathons, an athlete – out of breath and too tired to continue – suddenly finds the strength to press on at top performance with less exertion. Some scientists believe the "second wind" to be a result of the body finding the proper balance of oxygen to counteract the build-up of lactic acid in the muscles.[28]

Similarly, when you live your life in your *authentic purpose* everything becomes easier, you are moving with the current of the wind rather than against it, propelling you forward. You are not fighting against yourself.

THE EMPTINESS OF INAUTHENTIC GOALS

Successfully achieved goals always have a purpose and motivation behind them. It's very difficult to achieve any meaningful goal without motivation, and if your goal doesn't chime with your values and beliefs, motivation will struggle to make an appearance.

A word of caution, that doesn't mean to say that motivation is always positive. It must be linked to a clear understanding of your core identity. Your purpose and goals must be connected to the right motivation that flows from an unencumbered understanding of your core identity.

When we see the success of others from the outside looking in, the picture can be very deceptive. I have coached many clients who portray a very attractive veneer of having it all together because of outward material success. But those goals were inauthentic, not feeding the true purpose of their soul, so the inner emptiness and conflict persisted.

TAYLOR SWIFT

In the documentary, *Miss Americana*, Grammy award-winning singer-songwriter Taylor Swift talks about the inner emptiness, conflict and then realisation that her goals, motivation and purpose were set from a place of inauthenticity. She had strived for success to "prove a point", only to realise when she had achieved it, it was in fact an empty victory.

Her perceived humiliation by controversial rapper Kanye West at the 2009 Video Music Awards, when collecting her Best Female Video Award, was well documented. West gate-crashed her moment on stage to claim that someone else, Beyonce was more deserving of that particular award, to which the crowd erupted in a sea of "boos". The 17-year-old Swift thought those boos were directed at her.

In the documentary she says: "For someone who's built her whole belief system on getting people to clap for you, the crowd booing was a pretty formative experience. This was a catalyst for a lot of psychological paths I went down and not all of them were beneficial. It was fuelled by not feeling like I belonged there. I am only here because I work hard and I am nice to people. So, I thought I'm going to prove myself and show that I deserve to be here. When you are living for the approval of strangers and that is where you derive all of your joy and fulfilment, one bad thing can cause everything to crumble."

This motivation fuelled Swift's relentless quest to prove herself. Her single focus was to achieve a Grammy award for her album. The following year she was awarded the *Album of the Year* Grammy for the second time.

She recalls: "I remember thinking, oh my God, that was all you wanted and that was all you focused on. You get to the mountain top and you look around and you are like 'oh God what now?' I don't have a partner that I climbed it with, there was no one I could talk to that could relate. I had my mum but I thought shouldn't I have someone that I can call right now? I had to deconstruct an entire belief system for my own personal sanity."

Can you see the missing link here? Talent ✓ Passion ✓ Motivation ✓ but the ladder was facing the wrong wall. The love of what she was born to do and had clear ability to do, was obscured and muddied by the wrong motivation that was able to grow from the lack of clarity over her core identity and the beliefs and values attached to this distorted picture.

> "EVERYONE HAS BEEN MADE FOR SOME PARTICULAR WORK AND THE DESIRE FOR THAT WORK HAS BEEN PUT IN EVERY HEART."
>
> **JALALUDDIN RUMI**

DISCOVERING YOUR "WHY?"

We are all here to solve a problem, our job is to discover what that is. We all have some talents, skills and abilities that come naturally to us and when we use them, we feel good, free, it flows from us with ease and there is a great inner satisfaction.

But even when you are on the right track, your purpose doesn't just hit you in the face, like going from zero to 100: it's an incremental exercise, a journey. As you discover the elements of your core identity your purpose will flow out of that. You will have the awareness and skills to act on the messages and opportunities that come your way with a clear understanding of how they honour who you are.

In the days before GPS maps, have you ever been lost while driving your car? You stop a passer-by to ask for directions and fortunately they can direct you. They tell you about 10 manoeuvres you need to take, straight down, left at the second exit, right at the roundabout, straight for two miles... You set off again, happy to be on the right track, but then after the third or fourth manoeuvre you've forgotten the rest of the verbal directions you were given and get lost again. Likewise, it's through a step-by-step journey of discovery that your authentic purpose is revealed.

Think about driving and seeing that there is a right turn ahead. You cannot see what is on that road until you make the right-turn and actually manoeuvre onto the road. Similarly, as you take positive steps in the right direction, your next move will be in your vision. When you know who you are, you will know where you are heading. You already have the road map and will see the destination ahead of you, one manoeuvre at a time.

I love the word discovery, life itself is a series of discoveries, "there is nothing new under the sun" from the conception of the world; everything that is here now, was there in the beginning and there to be discovered. One discovery has led to another, one invention has built on the discovery and/or invention of another. For example, the concept of telecommunications went from homing pigeons and telegraphs to mobile phones and the internet.

I describe the journey of me uncovering my purpose as a series of discoveries, where one authentic action led to another. The key phrase here is *authentic action*. Some of those actions took place simply because I was following my interests and what felt good to me and gave me meaning. This inner feeling trumped fulfilling other people's expectations of me, and even though my level of self-awareness wasn't so developed in the earlier years, in a subconscious way, looking back, I was still working towards my purpose because I was *honouring my core identity, even though I didn't know it.*

My strengths, natural talents, interests, capabilities, beliefs, values and personality were all leading me towards my purpose. For example, from a very young age I was a deep thinker, I was always interested in how the world worked, why it was the way it was and why people were the way they were. I also felt emotion very deeply and was very intuitive.

Today I would describe myself as a modern philosopher, or lover of wisdom. In a broad sense, philosophy is an activity people undertake when they seek to understand fundamental truths about themselves, the world in which they live and their relationships to the world and to each other.

As a child, I had demonstrated gifts for poetry, reading, writing and music. I won competitions for poetry and reading. But because I hadn't recognised the value of these gifts by the time I got to secondary school, these talents became stunted. When I attended sixth form college and was able to choose my topics, I chose subjects that interested me (Politics, Economics, Sociology, English Literature). I did remain an avid writer of poetry, but because writing came so easily to me, I didn't recognise its value. As mentioned previously, a limiting belief I had at that time was that if I didn't work hard for it, it wasn't valuable.

Moving through to university I abandoned a Law degree after the first year because the human, inquisitive and creative part of me refused to be moulded in that way. Instead, I completed a Politics degree, which I thoroughly enjoyed because I was following my interest. From there I studied journalism and worked as a journalist for many years. During that time my colleagues would comment that I added an additional "human" aspect to my news and feature articles that they did not, even if the topic was on a government white paper or a management initiative.

At the time I didn't fully comprehend what my colleagues meant. But I noticed people in the office and my social circles would share very personal issues with me that they wouldn't speak to anyone else about. When I interviewed people, they would open up to me more than they had intended to. I found people really interesting and enjoyed in-depth conversations and interviews as well as learning something new all the time.

When I discovered coaching, I realised that I had been a coach for most of my life without realising it and the qualification just added a name and validation to it. Growing awareness of my personality, strengths, dealing with limiting beliefs and being clear about my core values was pushing me in the right direction. I was taking *conscious* steps to embed positive change and live authentically. Then through coaching, I discovered the niche of identity coaching.

Writing this book is in my purpose, combining my skills of writing, research and people development with my passion to take women on a journey of transformation to get to the core of who they really are to live a genuine life with passion, clarity and purpose.

I love coaching clients; it is challenging but it energises me. I am on flow when I'm doing this.

It expresses my values of freedom, personal growth, honesty and creativity. I have great satisfaction in seeing lives transform for the better. I love words and writing as a vehicle for self-expression and transformation.

Because I paid attention to how I felt about things and had the courage to pursue my genuine interests even when I wasn't that self-aware, I was moving towards discovering my purpose bit by bit. I couldn't see the whole picture but I was on the right track.

As I honoured key aspects of my core identity, my authentic purpose emerged. But if someone told me at college or at university, I would be a transformational coach, I wouldn't have had a clue what they were talking about. But as I continued through my own personal journey of developing my talents, working to the strengths of my personality, honouring my values hierarchy, freeing myself from limiting beliefs, my purpose emerged. Each part was a jigsaw piece needing to find its place to create the full picture.

CONSOLIDATE YOUR LEARNING

The preceding chapters have raised your awareness of what the core identity is. You have gone on a journey to remove the obstacles that have impacted you discovering and honouring your core identity. You will be clear about your most important values, you will have reframed many of your limiting beliefs, your heart will be lighter and health significantly improved as you have unburdened yourself from unforgiveness and people pleasing. You will be aware of the positive and negative influences in your life and taken steps to remove the negative ones. You will be more equipped to deal with change and not shrink back from the fear that can seek to paralyse you from moving out of your comfort zone. You will be inspired by the stories of real people in these chapters that have overcome many life challenges, some of which you can directly relate to. Your communication skills will have improved along with your ability to deal with conflict. You've gained the awareness and confidence to empower yourself in relationships.

It is essential you complete those exercises to be ready for the process of discovery that will lead to your purpose. Hopefully as you've had a recap of the benefits, you will be motivated to go back and complete any exercises, reflection and the subsequent actions required.

The remaining chapters this book will take you on a journey of discovery to fit the pieces of your jigsaw together. Now you have removed the obstacles that were holding you back and skewing or blocking your core identity.

Fill your jar today with the number of marbles you have left and use your time wisely.

"MUSICIANS MUST MAKE MUSIC, ARTISTS MUST PAINT, POETS MUST WRITE IF THEY ARE ULTIMATELY TO BE AT PEACE with themselves. What humans can be, they must be."

ABRAHAM MASLOW

Chapter 20

THE UNMASKING: BRIDGING THE GAP FROM OBSTACLES TO DISCOVERY

"I WASN'T SEARCHING FOR SOMETHING OR SOMEONE... I WAS SEARCHING FOR ME."

CARRIE BRADSHAW

The *persona* (or mask) is the public face or role a person presents to the world. It conceals your real self like an actor. In psychology, persona is defined as the personality that an individual projects to others, as differentiated from the authentic self.

At this point, if you've been diligently doing the exercises to remove the obstacles that have masked your core identity, you'll be ready for the next stage. It's time to take off your mask and shed the remnants of your fake persona.

The unmasking is the bridge to enable you to discover the remaining elements of your core identity and create a road map that will lead you towards your authentic purpose.

Each step of the way is beautiful: the liberation from the straight jacket you've been trapped in. There are wonderful insights and discoveries along the way.

Before you get started, I've included Jane's journey from living in a fake *pretty girl* persona to transforming into her authentic self and harnessing the power of her core identity. Despite numerous challenges, Jane's story shows that no obstacle is too great to overcome in the journey to self-discovery and being who you really are. By operating within her circle of influence with challenge and honest introspection, Jane got fitted with her bespoke suit.

"IT TAKES COURAGE... TO ENDURE THE SHARP PAINS OF SELF-DISCOVERY RATHER THAN CHOOSE TO TAKE THE DULL PAIN OF UNCONSCIOUSNESS THAT WOULD LAST THE REST OF OUR LIVES."

MARIANNE WILLIAMSON

Before transformation Jane's core identity was defined by the limitations of her illness. From a young age she was diagnosed with sickle cell anaemia disease and suffered from frequent bouts of severe sickness which caused major and unwanted disruptions to her life.

As a young child Jane's illness meant she was the centre of attention within her family and received special treatment to compensate for the challenges of her condition. At home, her mother in particular sought to provide validation for Jane, reminding her that she was "pretty" and that her looks would "carry her". She held tightly to Jane and placed a protective ring around her, vetting potential friends and acquaintances. Her life was sheltered.

But as she grew older, the psychological and physical challenges increased. By the time Jane went through school, she was impacted by the realisation that she was *different*. She'd missed significant portions of schooling due to illness and struggled to form lasting friendship bonds. Jane became a loner and there was a growing emptiness inside. She longed for connection and to belong.

As a teenager and young adult, Jane experienced rejection from boys, who – initially attracted to her looks – were put off by the challenges of her health condition. She would constantly be told "You're pretty BUT you're sick". Even her mother would caution that her health would impact any future hopes of marriage and was suspicious of the motives of potential boyfriends.

Jane's teachers advised her to abandon any hopes of a career or meaningful work and medics predicted her life expectancy would not move beyond 30 years old. All these factors impacted Jane's belief system, her values, personality, self-esteem and self-worth and formed the basis for an elaborate mask.

Jane's persona was fuelled by the need to belong and to fill the emptiness of what was missing in her life. Away from college and people who knew about her health condition she hung out with friends from a local housing estate. With them she could be who she wanted to be without the "label and limitations of sickle-cell". She felt accepted and learned to do superficial relationships well. To protect herself, Jane became whoever she needed to be to mask her vulnerabilities and avoid being rejected.

But there was a price to pay for this acceptance. Jane supressed key parts of her identity to gain the perceived acceptance of these friends. This behaviour led to a steady chipping away of Jane's soul, and a denial of her true self. In seeking acceptance and validation she would be around people and go to certain places even if she didn't want to be there. She encouraged attention from men which fuelled her ego and gave her a false sense of validation. She consistently manipulated men to her perceived advantage. Jane would hide behind wearing the latest fashions and she became more materialistic and egocentric (self-absorbed). Being "cool" bought acceptance. On a subconscious level, Jane did what she needed to do to *fit in*.

However, there is a big difference between fitting in and belonging that comes from real acceptance, firstly of yourself and then from others. A quote from Brené Brown sums this up beautifully: "Fitting in is about assessing a situation and becoming who you need to be to be accepted. Belonging, on the other hand, doesn't require us to change who we are; it requires us to BE who we are."

Jane found a semblance of stability by creating a world where everything revolved around her and what situations and people she could manipulate and control. And control was a big element of Jane's thinking and behaviour. By controlling how her home was organised and nurturing relationships and friendships only on her own terms gave her a sense of reassurance and comfort. For example, Jane made a big deal over the tidiness and cleanliness of her home. If a visitor used the kitchen sink and didn't leave it bone dry, there was a problem.

But believing these lies led to self-destructive behaviour. For instance, when experiencing symptoms that needed medical attention, she would prolong seeking help, ignoring the situation until it reached crisis point when an ambulance would be needed, followed by a hospital admission. If she had sought help in a timely way, she wouldn't have delayed the required treatment and avoided the situation deteriorating.

In reality, Jane wasn't really in control of her health or anything else. Living with sickle cell was very challenging and, in her experience, many people didn't understand or didn't want to understand it.

"IT TAKES COURAGE TO GROW UP AND BECOME WHO YOU REALLY ARE."

E.E CUMMINGS

TRANSFORMATION

Living behind a mask did not provide the belonging, fulfilment or peace Jane was searching for. Inside, she always knew she needed change, but didn't know how it would happen. Everyone around her was sinking too. She was never challenged and only had friends that agreed with her regardless, rather than being honest with her. But honesty is what Jane needed; to take a sober and honest look at her situation in order to make the changes that were needed.

The turning point for Jane came when she found faith, became a Christian and developed a relationship with God. At last, she could be honest and vulnerable, and could trust and feel safe in her vulnerability. Her beliefs and values were challenged.

As Jane gained self-awareness, she began to process and identify her limiting beliefs and unhelpful behaviours and their negative impact on her. She was no longer governed by the mental boundaries and limits of her views about her health that had imprisoned her.

Jane gained the tools to discover who she really was and the courage to remove the obstacles that had obscured that discovery previously. Principally, Jane's mindset changed. She confronted and reframed limiting beliefs, she uncovered her true values, she learned to live within her circle of influence and abandoned the need to control and manipulate people and situations.

LETTING GO

Jane was no longer afraid to be alone and got rid of the "hangers on" that were negative influences in her life. She cut the apron strings with her mother. Although Jane had left home a few years prior, she was not in control of various elements of life, such as her finances (which were still managed by her mother). She explains: "It was a physical thing, but also a spiritual severing needed to take place. I gained emancipation. I was stepping into being my own woman, who God created me to be."

Through spiritual growth, coaching and positive genuine challenge, Jane dealt with one issue at a time. This included the courage to take leaps of faith into new territory and learn news ways of doing things which was "liberating". She no longer filled the need to be seen and validated by manipulating men for attention. As she discovered her core identity, she began to genuinely love and appreciate herself. It was no longer all about her, the egocentric behaviour was gone.

A key period of reckoning came when Jane was diagnosed with vitiligo[29] and in just over a year of dealing with the resulting patchy discoloured skin, all of the pigmentation in her skin was lost. This was initially another blow to her beauty, which was a big part of her perceived identity and brought another vulnerability. She explains: "That stripped me. I had to get to know myself again without having a mask to hide behind. Although vitiligo had its own challenges, I saw my own personal growth. I learned to love me and no longer needed acceptance from anyone anymore."

REWARDS OF TRANSFORMATION

Jane no longer defines herself through the limitations of her health. Her mindset has totally changed now the obstacles that were obscuring her vision have been removed.

In her own words:

The song, "I found love in a hopeless place" encapsulates my experience of finding myself and having God in my life. I have hope. Without this I'd probably be dead. I am now aware of who I really am and my role in society. I do not have to devalue myself in anyway, which is what I'd done previously. I have more inner confidence, its real. There is no longer a mask to hide behind with a façade of confidence.

I'm aware of my gifts and talents. I place more value on them and explore and nurture them. I can speak freely, boldly and confidently. Before I would tiptoe around, I didn't confront things to avoid rejection. I'm able to see myself more truthfully, the person beneath the layers. I'm able to stand up for myself and eliminate people pleasing behaviour. I'm more willing to have authentic conversations and not use manipulation. I realise that I'm not dependent on other people's responses for my wellbeing; I have a new inner strength that is real. My values have changed, I view vulnerability as a strength, BUT I use it wisely.

I have learned that I am unique. I can see the benefit of both inner and outer beauty. Not just focusing on superficial outward appearance to seek validation. I am free to be who I was created to be and I understand how God sees me and how I am loved.

I have shed a lot of my former persona. Today I can describe myself as caring, kind, confident, funny, creative, nurturing, self-aware, reflective, and soft. I'm not afraid to show vulnerability but am wiser about who sees it. I'm better at seeing things from different points of view; it's no longer all about me, me, me.

The advice I would give my 16-year-old self would be, love yourself. Don't let anyone tell you that you cannot. Live your best life within the boundaries and perimeters that you have (circle of influence). Don't believe the lies of society about women's sexuality. You are unique and multi-dimensional.

"THE GREATEST DISCOVERY IN LIFE IS SELF-DISCOVERY. UNTIL YOU FIND YOURSELF YOU WILL ALWAYS BE SOMEONE ELSE. BECOME YOURSELF."

DR MYLES MUNROE

Jane's Before Mask

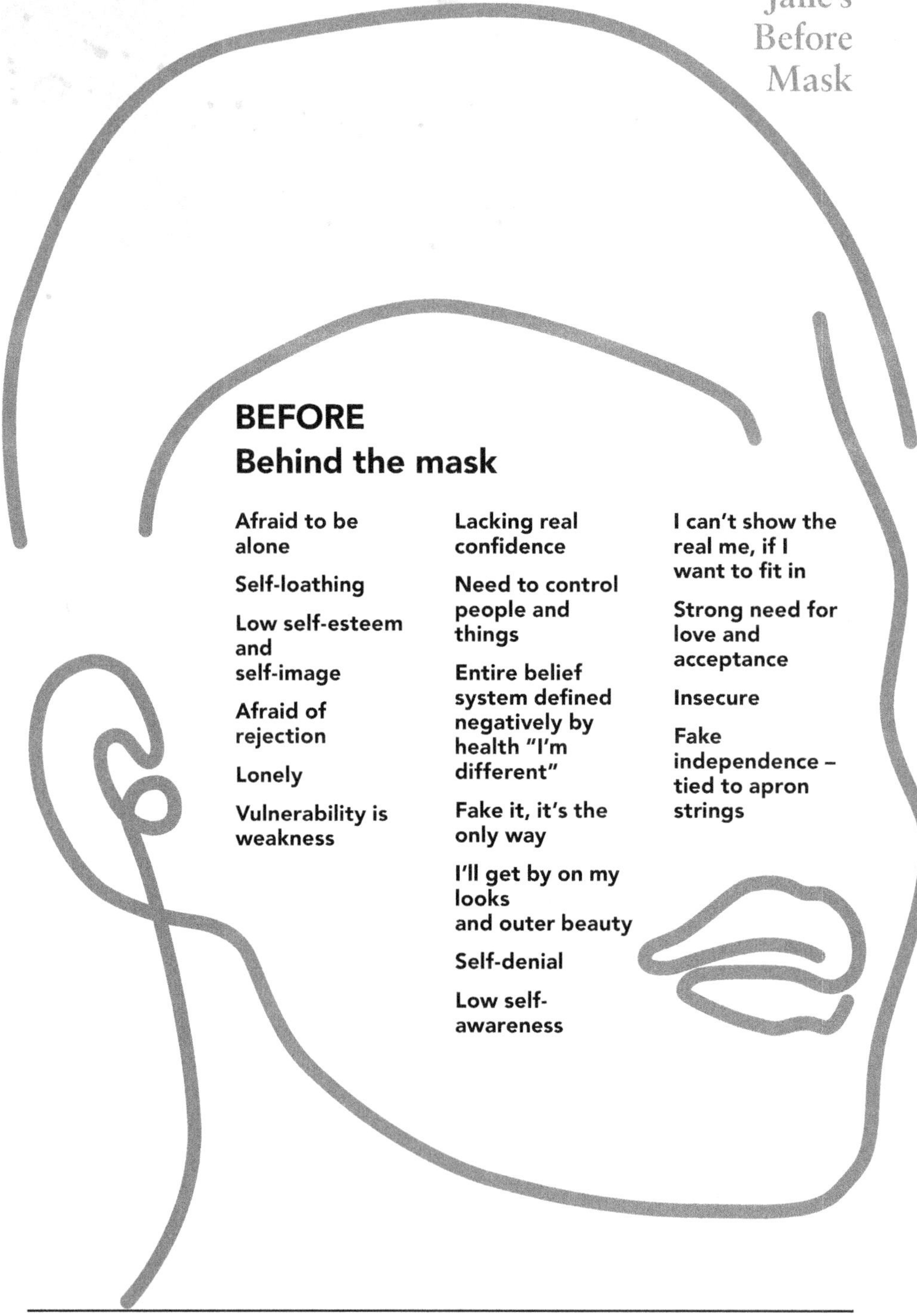

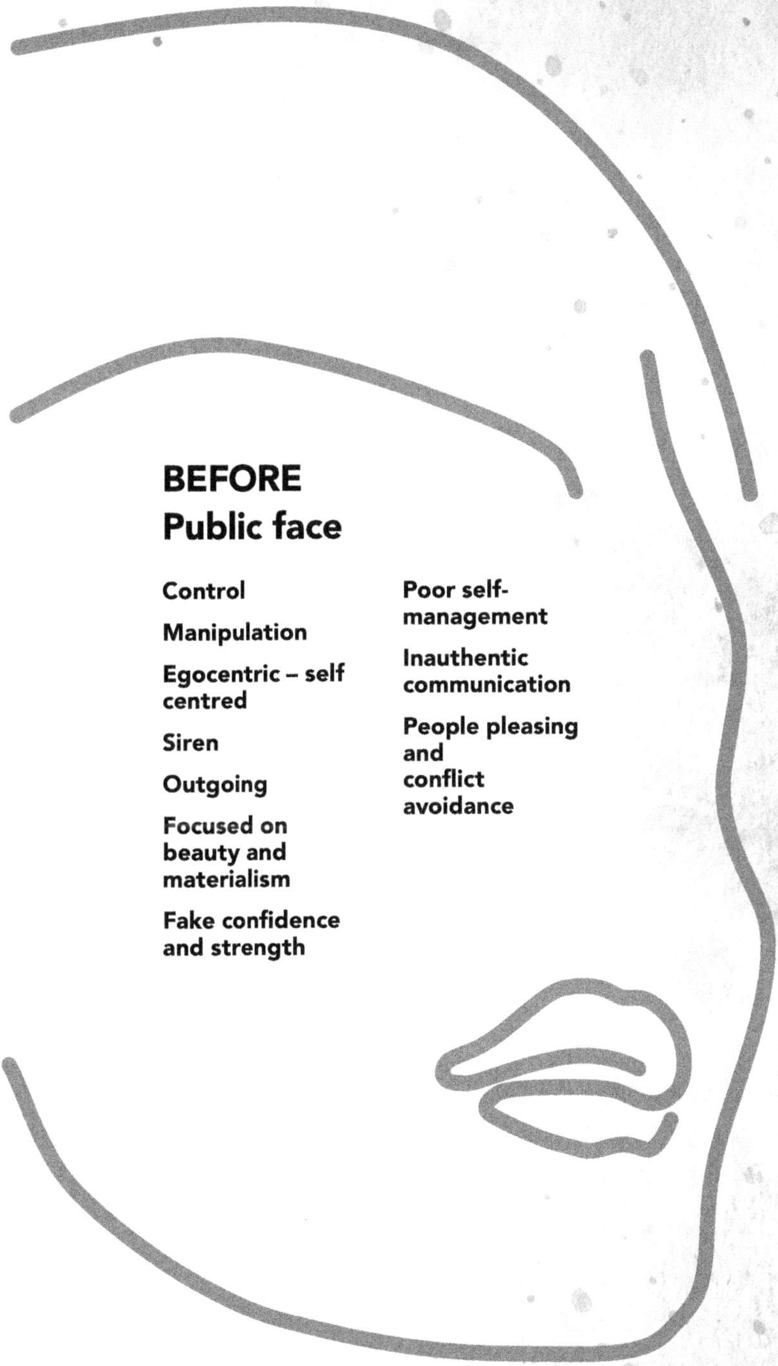
BEFORE
Public face
Control
Manipulation
Egocentric – self centred
Siren
Outgoing
Focused on beauty and materialism
Fake confidence and strength
Poor self-management
Inauthentic communication
People pleasing and conflict avoidance

Jane's After Mask

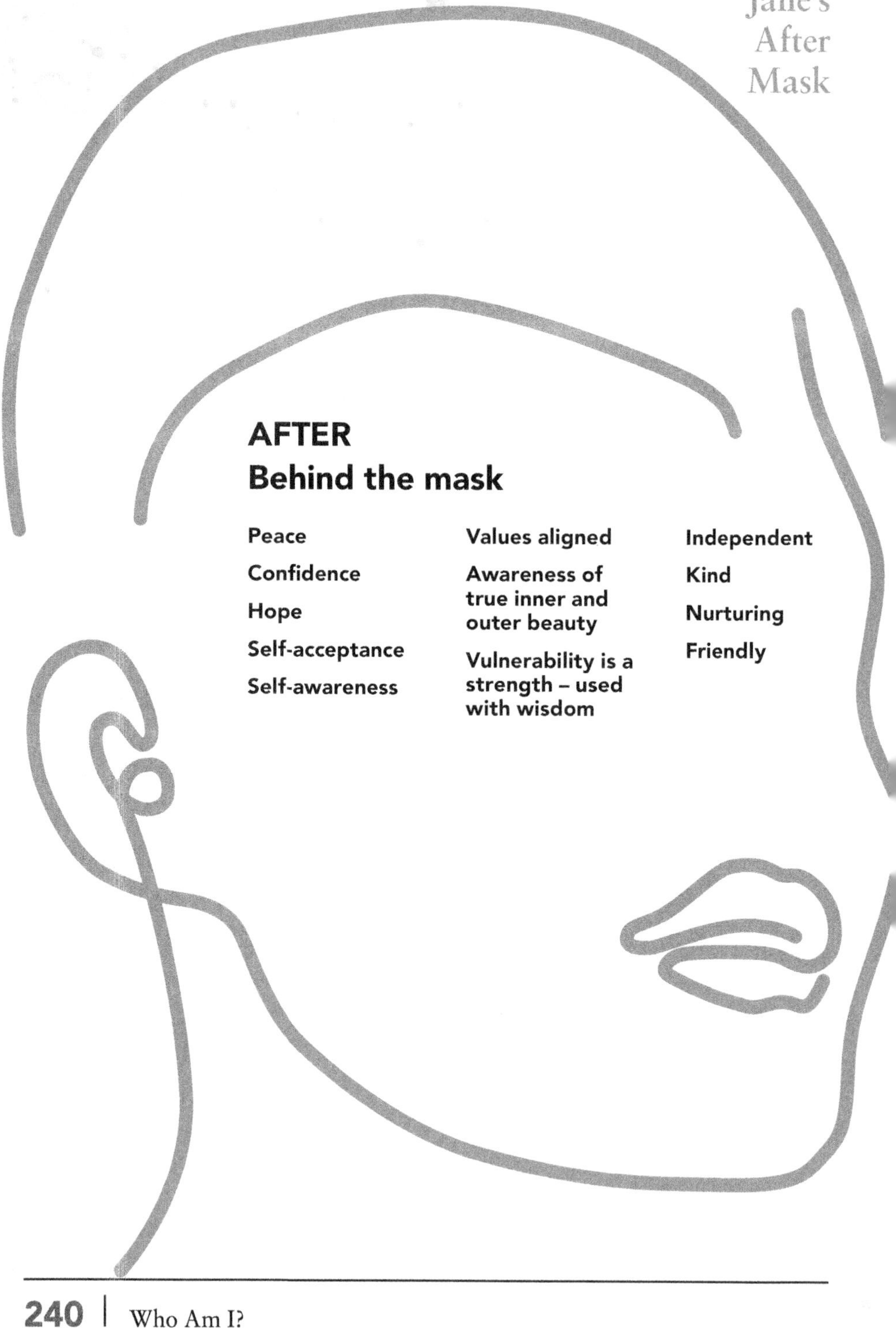

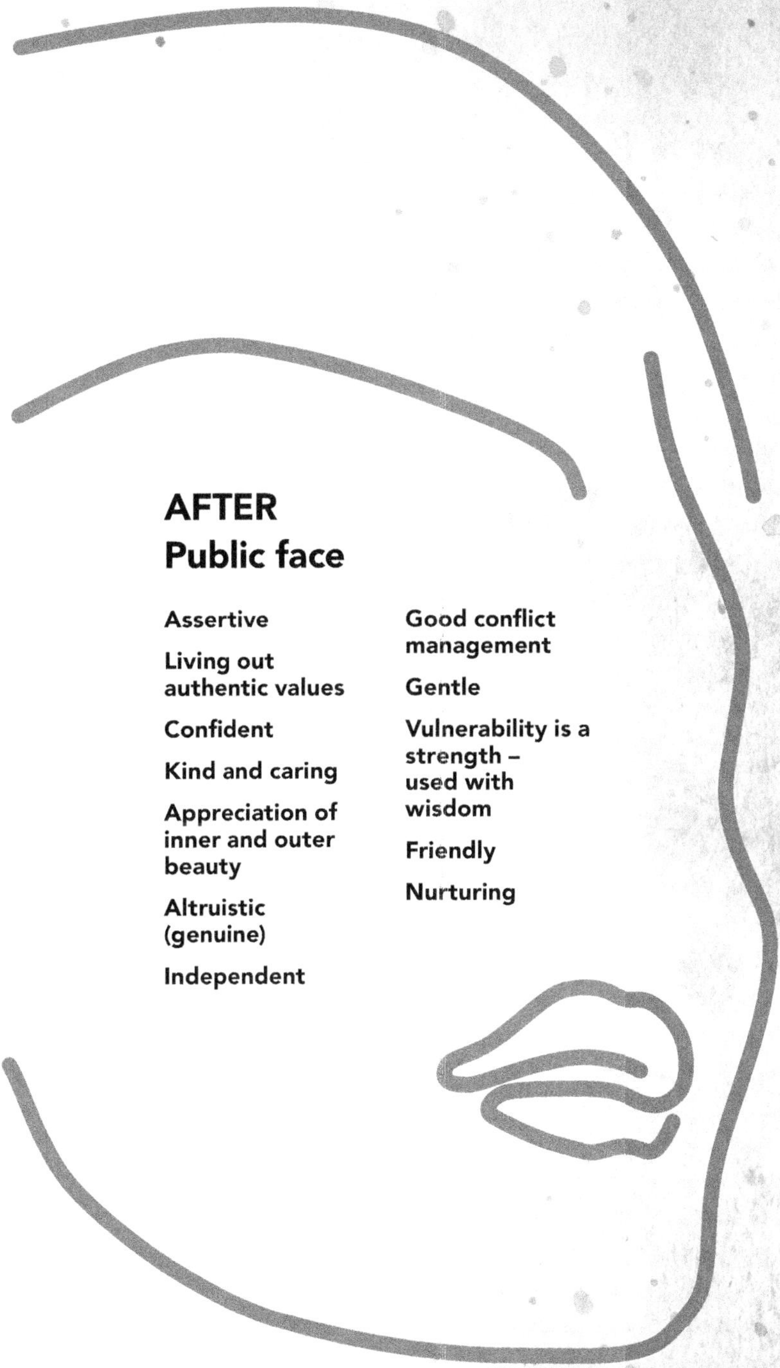

AFTER
Public face

Assertive

Living out authentic values

Confident

Kind and caring

Appreciation of inner and outer beauty

Altruistic (genuine)

Independent

Good conflict management

Gentle

Vulnerability is a strength – used with wisdom

Friendly

Nurturing

"WHENEVER TWO PEOPLE MEET, THERE ARE REALLY SIX PEOPLE PRESENT. THERE IS EACH MAN AS HE SEES HIMSELF, EACH MAN AS THE OTHER PERSON SEES HIM, AND EACH MAN AS HE REALLY IS."

WILLIAM JAMES

Jane's story highlights the difference between how we see ourselves, how other people perceive us, and who we REALLY are. When we live inauthentically a growing inner conflict gains traction. The wider the gap between the inner and outer person (mask) the more disconnected you are with your true self.

For Jane, her whole belief system was interpreted through the lens of *you're different*, which distorted her own self-perception and provided currency for the fake *pretty girl* persona. Jane was in conflict with herself until she gained the tools to take off her mask and free herself.

It's time to take off your mask… and step over the bridge towards your own journey of discovery.

Practical exercise

CORE INSIGHT ACTION

THE MASK: Where am I now?

Think of this exercise as a review or spring clean to make room for more of the true person (your core identity) to emerge through the *discovery phase*.

- Illustrate your **public face** with what you think you project publicly in general (true or false)
- Illustrate **behind the mask** with what you keep hidden (what you really think and feel)
- Use whatever words, images and colours you like to illustrate both aspects of your mask.

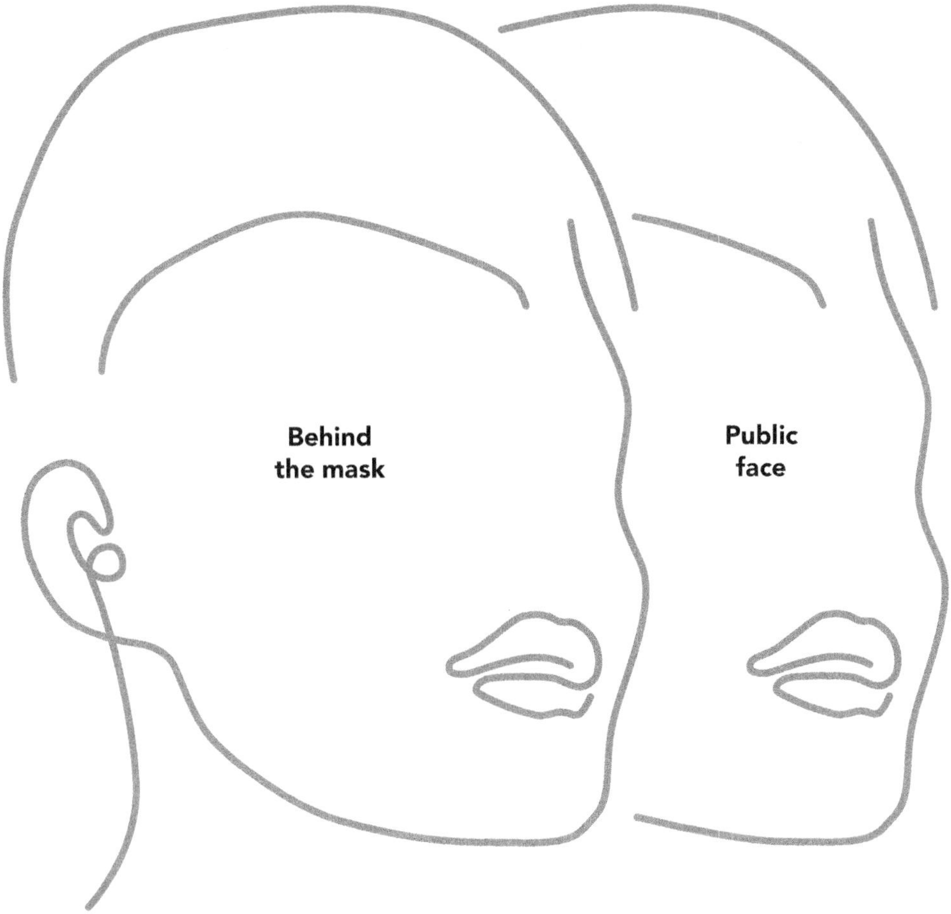

Review

Compare both masks and answer the following questions:

- What have I shed?
- Where is the synergy?
- How have I benefited?
- Where are there significant incongruencies?
- What areas need more work?
- What is missing?
- What have I learned?

Practical exercise

What you are presented with is a reformed version of what is behind the mask. Hopefully by this stage there is more synergy between your public face and what is behind the mask. This will encourage you to complete the final stages to uncovering your core identity.

> "THE JOURNEY TOWARD SELF-DISCOVERY IS LIFE'S GREATEST ADVENTURE."
>
> **ARIANNA HUFFINGTON**

Part Three

DISCOVERY

"When I discover who I am, I'll be free."

RALPH ELLISON

"Our insights transform us in several ways. They change how we understand, act, see, feel, and desire. They transform our thinking; our new story gives us a different viewpoint. In some cases, insights transform our abilities as well as our understanding."

GARY KLEIN

THE CORE IDENTITY MODEL: DISCOVERY

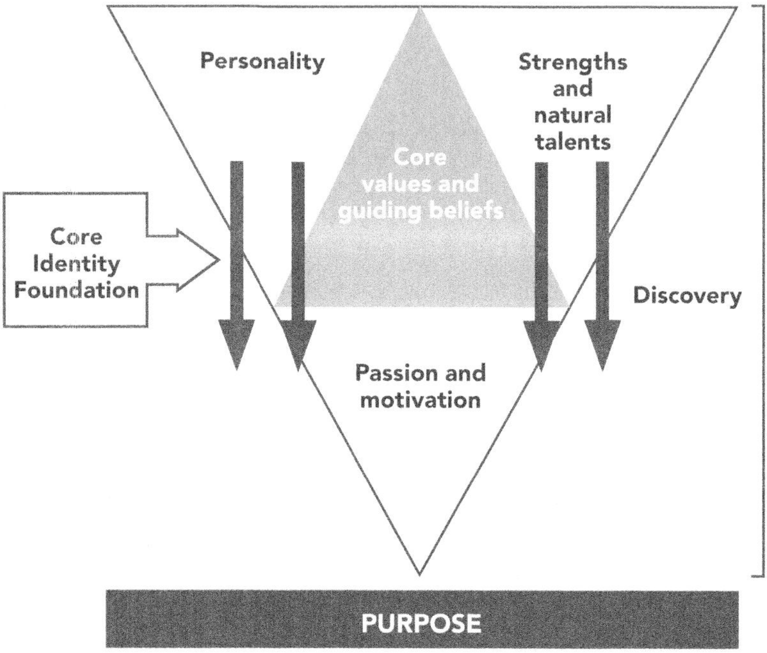

Chapter 21

PERSONALITY: YOU ARE UNIQUE, HOW DO YOU ENGAGE WITH THE WORLD?

"IF YOU HAVE ANYTHING REALLY VALUABLE TO CONTRIBUTE TO THE WORLD IT WILL COME THROUGH THE EXPRESSION OF YOUR OWN PERSONALITY, THAT SINGLE SPARK OF DIVINITY THAT SETS YOU OFF AND MAKES YOU DIFFERENT FROM EVERY OTHER LIVING CREATURE."

BRUCE BARTON

The word personality also stems from the Latin word "persona", which refers to a theatrical mask worn by performers in order to either project different roles or disguise their identities. At its most basic, personality is the characteristic patterns of thoughts, feelings, and behaviours that make a person unique. It is believed that personality arises from within the individual and remains fairly consistent throughout life.[30]

Most definitions of personality focus on the patterns of a person's behaviour and characteristics. Personality embraces the traits and preferences that direct your thoughts, feelings and behaviours. For example, do you get energy from being around lots of people, or does too much interaction drain you? Do you make decisions based on the big picture and how things feel, or do you prefer solid facts and figures? Do you find it easy to empathise and understand people's emotions or does it feel like you are walking across a minefield? Do you like to keep your options open and look for possibilities or do you prefer things clear cut?

There are no right or wrong personality traits or preferences. The key is in understanding what your authentic ones are and how you can utilise them to be most effective and to gain a better understanding of yourself.

Explanations for personality can focus on a variety of influences, ranging from genetics to the role of the environment and lived experiences.

For the purposes of this book, I am focusing on the most important aspect of your personality *found in your core that is genetic in its nature*. The traits and preferences you were born with that have developed (unencumbered if you are lucky) as you have grown up, or have been misshapen through the unhelpful influences of nurture and environmental factors that have led to a distortion or confusion of your true personality.

I view much of these environmental aspects as not part of the core personality but developed as an add-on, usually linked to obstacles such as limiting beliefs that alter behaviours. For example, major trauma at any stage of life can significantly impact a person's personality. But this impact does not have to be permanent. When work is done to deal with the root cause of the trauma and heal, it allows the core personality to come up for air and breathe unencumbered.

PERSONALITY VERSUS CHARACTER

Although character and personality are both used to describe a person's behaviours, the two examine different aspects of an individual. Personality is generally defined as illustrating a set of distinctive inborn traits and personal qualities. The word character is usually used to describe a person's level of integrity; a set of morals and beliefs that defines how we treat or behave with others and ourselves. *Your personality is more visible, while your character is revealed over time*, through varying situations, but both are directly related to your attitude and behaviour.

YOUR AUTHENTIC PERSONALITY IS A KEY PART OF YOUR CORE IDENTITY

Why you prefer certain ways of doing things over others, why you are drawn to certain people, what energises you and drains you, what gives you joy, are all linked to your personality and *the level of freedom you have to express it.* This is part of your core identity and one of the key linchpins that holds your identity together.

It is important to understand your true personality traits and preferences to be able to express yourself authentically and enhance the quality of your life. This leads to more satisfaction, better life choices and overall success in both personal and professional spheres.

This knowledge and self-awareness are part of the compass of life that guides you. Everyone's personality is unique and without a clear understanding and acceptance of your own preferences, going through life can be extremely difficult and confusing.

"PERSONALITY BEGINS WHERE COMPARISON ENDS."

KARL LAGERFELD

WHY KEY ASPECTS OF YOUR PERSONALITY CAN GO UNNOTICED AND UNDERVALUED

When you do not know and understand your true personality (what makes you tick) and connect with the strengths in your traits, from early on you are likely to be set adrift, influenced by the personalities around you that are deemed to be more favourable by the significant people in your life. You see evidence of this when parents condition or force certain behaviours on their children, or when adults inhibit their own feelings and deny themselves the sensation of reality – *their true feelings.*

If those favoured personality traits do not align with the traits you are exhibiting, this can set the catalyst in motion for a lifetime of inner self-talk that as you are; you are not good enough. This may subdue the real you, for a caricature version that seeks to mould into something outside of yourself that you are not, and dumbing down the value in your own unique personality which you have not been able to see. The cycle continues through the messages of society that promotes the narrative of a one-size-fits-all approach to acceptability and value.

However, your core personality is still there. It has merely been supressed through learned behaviour and the pressure to conform to imposed standards that are outside of yourself. This creates the inner conflict which you may or may not be aware of. It could be just a nagging feeling that something is off, not feeling comfortable in your own skin, feeling like you have to work too hard to be something that you are not to be acceptable to others and to fit in. All this takes you further away from your true personality and only by expressing the real you will you feel that sense of wholeness. But for many, it is a journey to get there.

People have different strengths and needs and so do you. The more you understand your personality, the more you connect with your personality, the more able you are to judge what motivates yourself and others. You will have more awareness of how others perceive you and how they react to your own personality style. There will be more quality and depth to communication. Understanding you own unique way enables you to accept yourself and work to your strengths. Making sense of your personality helps to point you in the direction of your true purpose.

PAY ATTENTION TO INNER FEEDBACK

Paying attention to your inner feedback gives you important messages to guide your discovery.

When I applied to study an undergraduate degree, I didn't have that much conscious awareness of my personality strengths or preferences. I decided to study Law on the basis that it was a career that would pay well and give me a good lifestyle. I had studied Law at GCSE level, but had not selected it for my A-Level (I chose Sociology and Politics). But law seemed like a reasonable career choice based on the financial reward and the fact that I would be able to get the required grades, so I went ahead.

I remember sitting in a contract law lecture and listening to the ruling of a particular case and becoming frustrated that the verdict of the case was the end of the story. I was more interested in how those people's lives changed as a result of winning or losing the case, I had so many questions and no answers.

I recall being in a property law seminar and being told to write in a specific formulaic dry way. No emotion, no creativity, just the facts and arguments for and against. Well, it felt like I was being asked to cut off my hand.

Something was wrong, I didn't understand what. But I knew it wasn't right for me. I wanted to express myself in the work I produced. I was interested in people's lives and how various events impacted them and how they overcame things. I wasn't big on just dry facts; I liked subjective and creative ideas. Law was not stimulating me. I couldn't think of anything worse than spending three years studying a topic that didn't inspire or motivate me and then going on to have a career that would do the same. On the premise of, well it pays well.

Even though I didn't have the knowledge and understanding I have now about who I was and what would suit my personality and skills, I knew enough through the *internal feedback* of my mind, emotions and behaviour that something was off and that the path I had chosen would not work for me.

With that realisation, I decided that I was going to switch degrees. I didn't know what career path to take, but I opted for a topic that I would at least enjoy spending three years out of my life studying. Even though it had no clear career path as law had done. I chose a Politics degree.

I had no idea at the time what I would do as a career at the end of it. But I was revitalised. All the negative internal feedback subsided. It felt right. It was many years later when I had developed better self-awareness that I understood why that choice was so important and relevant to my personality and strengths.

Now, a few of my fellow students were also unhappy and dissatisfied with the degree. It didn't suit them either. But they ploughed on, reasoning that they just had to get through it. A few years later I bumped into one of them who was then working as a solicitor. They had invested time, money and energy to qualify in a profession, and guess what? They hated it just as much as they did at university, it just wasn't right for them either and those feelings of dissatisfaction and unfulfillment had not gone away.

When we go against those internal messages that our true personality is sending to us, we are going against ourselves. For example, if you work in a busy office with lots of activity and noise and everyday feels overwhelming, pay attention, your personality may prefer a quiet, calm environment to bring out your best. Do you allow yourself to pursue hobbies and interests that fascinate you, or do you go along with the pack and engage in what is on trend, whether you like it or not?

Adele was getting over a difficult break up. She decided to travel on her own to Dubai for a short holiday. This was the first time she was entirely on her own on holiday and could choose to do whatever she wanted. Adele spent time just being still watching the sunset. She found great satisfaction from this. However, she was torn; feeling duty bound to do the kinds of things her friends and family would expect her to do on holiday. So, she forced herself to visit a few tourist attractions, but this didn't really give her any satisfaction. When I questioned her motivation, she replied that she didn't want to appear boring and people wouldn't understand if she explained how much she enjoyed the sunsets; she would have nothing to say that was interesting to others about the trip.

But it could have been a true moment of discovery and freedom for Adele, to find out more about why she enjoyed that experience, what it gave to her and how it contributed to helping her to understand more about her personality, likes and dislikes.

Can you relate to this? Adele felt she had to do what she enjoyed in secret. She was satisfied when she allowed herself to engage in something that appealed to her true self. However, she did not have the confidence or acceptance of that part of her personality to openly express her genuine interest.

How many holidays have you been on that do not fit, or a festival or activity you go along with to meet the wants of others without truly exploring if it is right for you? As mentioned before, it is easy to get swept away with current trends or the preferences of others when you do not understand the preferences, likes and dislikes of your own authentic personality.

When you are able to express the truest form of your personality, the inner conflict diminishes and you can better understand your place in the world. You are more at peace. In turn you'll understand better how to relate to others and express yourself more effectively.

> "THE SHOE THAT FITS ONE PERSON PINCHES ANOTHER; THERE IS NO UNIVERSAL RECIPE FOR LIVING."
>
> **CARL JUNG**

YOU ARE UNIQUE, HOW DO YOU ENGAGE WITH THE WORLD?

You can't be good at everything and be all things to all people. Have you ever heard the saying "Jack of all trades, master of none"? You are unique and the key is to connect with your true personality and harness those strengths to improve the quality of your day-to-day life. Be less concerned with what you think you should be and give your real personality room to come out and breathe.

There are no good or bad personalities. Some traits and preferences are just suited to individual forms of expressing and relating. It's generally the character of a person and their level of integrity that determines whether they are perceived to be good or bad.

There is value in difference, different personalities complement each other. For example, how many couples do you know that have similar personality traits and preferences? I usually find they are more likely to be opposites that complement each other in different ways. Such as, an introverted husband with an extroverted wife. Personalities that have similar traits often butt heads; I find that parents tend to get along least with the child that is the most like them in personality.

> "YOUR REAL PERSONALITY IDENTITY IS NOT AN OPTION; IT IS THE FOUNDATION FOR YOUR HAPPINESS AND HEALTH."
>
> **DIANA DENTINGER**

Personality tests are a useful broad guide to help you understand more about who you are, why you do many of the things that you do and how to harness your strengths. I'd heard of personality assessments and psychometric testing and I was sceptical and avoided them. But when I started training as a coach and I came across it again and completed some trait-based personality tests, I was fascinated at the insight that it gave me about my own behaviour. In what seemed like an instant it enabled me to dispel many of the limiting beliefs I subconsciously held about my personality and it gave me validation.

For example, growing up I was constantly told I was different as though it was a negative thing. I was also told that I was shy and didn't like people, and an introvert. I didn't question this, even though as a teenager and adult working as a journalist and in my social life I displayed the complete opposite behaviours. The older I got, the more these messages were in conflict with what I was experiencing. It was that *off feeling*, but I didn't get the full realisation until those assessments. Then the light bulb came on at 100 watts!

My personality profile helped to fill parts of the jigsaw puzzle of my core identity; I understood why I did things the way I did, why I was different and how these behaviours could be perceived by others. It led to a clearer understanding of my identity and a confidence to capitalise on directing my preferences and strengths to maximum benefit in my personal and professional life. It also helped me to understand what to avoid and minimise in my life. I gained even more clarity around decision making, communication and what motivated me.

Even little things made more sense. I used to wonder why I had such difficulty preparing an outfit the night before to wear to work the following day. Many of my friends were able to do this and I could see how this could potentially save me time in the morning, but I had an aversion to this. It wasn't that I was indecisive, as this is a strength of mine. The strong "feeling/perceiving" part of my personality meant I like to leave things open ended and would choose things based on how I felt on the day. When I made the connection, I no longer viewed that behaviour as negative and enjoyed the element of the unknown in deciding on the day how I would express myself through my choice of clothes.

Yes, I was different but well suited to my purpose. I became more at peace with myself.

DISCOVER YOUR PERSONALITY TRAITS

There is a vast array of personality tests available of varying quality and accuracy. Used appropriately these tests can be hugely beneficial in improving knowledge of yourself (and others); your motivations, strengths, weaknesses, preferred thinking and working styles and also preferred styles for communication, learning, management, being managed and team-working. They are a great tool for personal development.

I have found the most useful types personality profiles are based on the theory of Carl Jung and Myers Briggs® (MBTI® model). This is a (trait-based) method for understanding personality and preferred ways of behaving. It is *not* a measurement of intelligence or competence, emotional state, mental stability or maturity.

A trait-based model studies the degree to which people exhibit certain preferences. It is *not* a type-based model that that creates a number of subjective and indiscriminate categories and attempts to fit people within them. People who fall within the 16 categories of MBTI will display varying degrees of a particular trait. For example, a person could be mildly extrovert or very extrovert.

The MBTI system describes a person's personality through four opposing personality functions commonly known as preferences or dichotomies. The following summary from Truity.com describes these functions:

Extraversion vs Introversion: How do you gain energy? *Extraverts* like to be with others and gain energy from people and the environment. *Introverts* gain energy from alone-time and need periods of quiet reflection throughout the day.

Sensing vs Intuition: How do you collect information? *Sensors* gather facts from their immediate environment and rely on the things they can see, feel and hear. *Intuitives* look more at the overall context and think about patterns, meaning, and connections.

Thinking vs Feeling: How do you make decisions? *Thinkers* look for the logically correct solution, whereas *Feelers* make decisions based on their emotions, values, and the needs of others.

Judging vs Perceiving: How do you organise your environment? *Judgers* prefer structure and like things to be clearly regulated, whereas *Perceivers* like things to be open and flexible and are reluctant to commit themselves.

One selection from each of the four preferences creates a four-letter code which sums up your personality style. For example, someone with a preference for Introversion, Sensing, Feeling and Judging would have the code 'ISFJ'. There are 16 possible combinations or personality types.[31]

It is helpful to think of preferences as *your preferred way of thinking* and doing things. It happens subconsciously and with ease. It like a default or reflex action.

To test this, take a pen and paper and write your signature. Now use your other hand and write your signature. Can you see the difference in the difficulty of doing the same task? Your dominant *preferred* hand could do the task without much thought. But your other hand struggled, you had to focus and take your time, it probably looked very different to the first signature. The second time you were not using your preference.

Remember, personality tests are not the *only* predictor of behaviour in personality. True personality emerges when limiting beliefs, unforgiveness and other obstacles described in this book that distort your real personality are dealt with. However, the tests are a broad guide that I found useful to help you understand yourself better.

Time to find out how you engage with the world. Have some fun and gain some new discoveries by completing a few personality tests. Remember there are no right or wrong answers, the more honest you are with your responses, the more accurate your results will be. And the more knowledge and awareness you'll have to enable you to get closer to understanding your true self.

A list of recommended tests is included on my website and in the resources section of the book.

"ALWAYS BE YOURSELF, EXPRESS YOURSELF, HAVE FAITH IN YOURSELF, DO NOT GO OUT AND LOOK FOR A SUCCESSFUL PERSONALITY AND DUPLICATE IT."

BRUCE LEE

Practical exercise

CORE INSIGHT ACTION

REVIEW YOUR RESULTS

When you have done one or more of the recommended tests. Complete the following reflective exercise.

- What surprised me the most?
- What have I learned about my personality?
- What makes me tick?
- What validation have I gained?
- What do I agree with strongly?
- What do I disagree with strongly? Why?
- What learning will I utilise? How?
- Write down your most important discoveries in your journal, *you'll need them later on in the book.*

Chapter 22

WHAT FASCINATES AND ENERGISES YOU?

"YOUR VISION WILL BECOME CLEAR ONLY WHEN YOU CAN LOOK INTO YOUR OWN HEART. WHO LOOKS OUTSIDE, DREAMS; WHO LOOKS INSIDE, AWAKES."

CARL JUNG

PART 1
CONNECT WITH YOUR VISION

At the time of writing this chapter, the painfully sad news of the sudden death of Jamal Edwards MBE, at just 31 was announced. Edwards was the founder of SBTV, an online urban music platform which helped launch the careers of artists like Dave, Ed Sheeran and Jessie J.

His story is an inspiration to young and old. When he received a much-wanted video camera from his mother for Christmas at the age of 15, he began filming his friends performing grime music and uploading the clips to YouTube. His vision was to showcase the music of his generation that wasn't being represented in mainstream media.

By following his passion of music and media with a singular focus he was able to achieve a phenomenal amount in his short life. Although young, Edwards had the belief, confidence and drive to pursue his passion. Many artists whose careers were launched after exposure on SBTV are now household names. And although there were naysayers and setbacks along the way, these were just obstacles to be overcome.

Edwards once said: "'Be the change you want to see in the world' is one of my favourite quotes and something I'm trying to live by. If we can look at music and culture in the same way, people won't be told 'no you can't do that' they will chase bigger dreams and be free to express themselves how they want."

Edwards' unwavering love for music and passion for showcasing talent was evident in his work with emerging artists. One of his many tributes described his legacy as unparalleled: "He was one of our generation's founding fathers of UK black media. He changed the blueprint for a lot of people and gave creative room for them to thrive in our culture in a way that nobody was really able to crack before."

Thanks to his impressive achievements, Edwards was appointed an MBE for services to music in 2014 and was also an ambassador for the Prince's Trust, a youth charity run by the then Prince of Wales which helps young people set up their own companies. He also reopened four youth centres in his hometown through his charitable endeavours. Edwards was an entrepreneur with limitless creative bravery, and an example of what can happen when vision and belief collide with passion.

Inspired? Edwards' story shows what can be achieved when you fully connect with your passion.

But not everyone is able to know their vision at such a young age or connect with and explore their true passions. These may have been obscured through the various obstacles outlined in part two of this book. But when you allow your true desires to come to the fore, your passion will guide you.

"IF YOU ARE WORKING ON SOMETHING EXCITING THAT YOU REALLY CARE ABOUT, YOU DON'T HAVE TO BE PUSHED. THE VISION PULLS YOU."

STEVE JOBS

In a recent television interview Dwayne Fields, the first black explorer to reach the magnetic north pole was asked if he always loved the outdoors. He explained that as a young boy growing up in Jamaica, he was always out exploring nature and wildlife. But when he became a teenager in inner city London he subdued this passion, because being outdoors and in nature was not "cool" and he wanted to *fit in* with his peers.

Fields reconnected with his passion as a young adult and has achieved success as an adventurer, naturist and TV presenter. Now his personal goal is to engage inner-city youth in particular, with adventure in the UK countryside and the outdoors, while encouraging environmentally friendly behaviours. His work has led to taking on a variety of projects with some household names like actor Will Smith and astronaut Tim Peak.

Fields' passion was subdued in his teenage years through peer pressure (identity negotiation) but not eliminated completely. But when he courageously allowed his authentic interests and passion to come to the fore, overcoming the fear of rejection, he was able to enjoy success in his authentic purpose.

YOUR UNIQUENESS IS *YOUR* SUPERPOWER!

Identifying and fine-tuning your vision starts with your passion and interests; paying attention to what motivates you, what you enjoy and what you feel strongly about. Through this your vision (and purpose) will come into focus.

If you Google the word "vision", a number of definitions appear, from the rudimentary physical ability of sight, to the power of the imagination to conceive things that do not yet exist with the natural eye. Some definitions from the *Merriam-Webster dictionary* include: a thought, concept, or object formed by the imagination; a supernatural appearance that conveys a revelation and a manifestation to the senses of something immaterial.

When you apply your vision to the future it's possible to create a mental picture that can be harnessed to direct your actions. Vision can also be used as a mechanism to gain clarity and connect the dots between what motivates and fulfils you. It can serve as a guide to direct you towards your purpose.

When some of my clients first start coaching, they have become so disconnected from their true selves, losing touch with their likes and dislikes and with no concept of a personal vision or what motivates them. Creating a vision board is a great way to begin to articulate and clarify what motivates and energises you, it helps to clarify part of your core identity and can be the first step in the direction towards setting meaningful goals aligned to your core values.

Images are powerful. The adage "a picture is worth a thousand words" summarises the wonder of how multiple and complex ideas can be conveyed by a single still image. Images have a remarkable ability to convey meaning or essence, making connections in your conscious and subconscious mind. And when images are collected in the form of a vision board, they illustrate pieces of your story to date, helping you to gain a deeper understanding of who you are, where you are and what will help you on your future path.

CORE INSIGHT ACTION

CREATE YOUR VISION BOARD

In this exercise, the vision board will be used to bring together your passion, interests and desires to gain a better understanding of *what* fascinates and motivates you and *why*. Some of you will never have asked yourself these questions before; you may consider some of your interests as frivolous or not important, particularly if they do not fit in with the general consensus of your social circles or family.

However, your genuine and honest discoveries will aid the bigger picture of revealing your true identity which will guide you towards your authentic vision. It's like taking a journey and traveling in the right direction because you have a map, rather than taking off in a car and guessing where you will end up through luck and chance. This exercise will help to position you on the right road with map in hand so you can find the right fit. Your brain will work tirelessly to achieve the messages you give your subconscious mind.

Practical exercise

Get Creative!

1 Find items that represent or symbolise the experiences, feelings and possessions that inspire you and include your hopes and dreams for the future. Place them on your board.

2 There are no rules!

3 Have fun with the process. Use photographs, magazine cut-outs, pictures from the internet, fabrics, objects, colours or whatever inspires you. Be creative. You can include anything that speaks to you, as long as it fits on the board.

4 Consider including a picture of yourself. If you do, choose one that was taken in a happy moment.

5 You may also want to post your affirmations, inspirational words, quotations, and thoughts here. Choose words and images that inspire you and make you feel good.

Review

When complete, place your vision board somewhere you will see it continuously. Spend time reviewing each item on it and asking yourself the following probing questions. You will find connections.

Practical exercise

- How do I feel about...?
- What is important to me about this?
- What was happening to me when...?
- What emotions and thoughts come to mind?
- Why have I picked the particular item?
- What interests me about each item?
- How does this interest or desire connect with my values?
- What does this image tell me about myself?
- On a scale 0-10 what is my emotional response?
- What does that emotion/s give me?
- What connections do I see between these items?
- If some of the images are aspirational, include reflection questions like:
- How will my life change as result of achieving this?
- How will this bring me fulfilment or satisfaction?

Reflection

- What have you learned about your passion and motivation?
- What does this tell you about yourself?
- *Keep a note of your insights, you'll need to refer to them again later in the book.*

PART 2
DISCOVER YOUR STRENGTHS AND NATURAL TALENTS

"IF YOU DO WHAT YOU'VE ALWAYS DONE, YOU'LL GET WHAT YOU'VE ALWAYS GOT."

ANTHONY ROBBINS

Most people believe they have a pretty good idea of their skills and abilities. They usually view these as the aptitudes they have spent many years cultivating that are carefully documented on their CV. But, this only paints part of the picture. It will demonstrate what you've already done, but not necessarily illuminate the wealth of untapped talent bubbling away under the surface that's waiting to be utilised.

I have coached many clients who – when looking for their next career move or career transition – initially believed their only draw was to look at what they'd already done to determine their future choices. But this only works if you are 100% fulfilled in your current line of work and aren't yearning for the elusive "something else".

But what if you want to do something new and desire more fulfilment and purpose? Being aware of your strengths and natural talents which are part of your core identity is key to gaining fulfilment and purpose. It enables you to extract more of your potential in both your personal and professional life. The more authentic you are, the more successful you will be.

Your strengths and natural talents are the things you do with ease; you may not even realise the value or impact they have on others. But you feel good when operating from this sphere.

Your Dictionary defines *strengths* as "tasks or actions you can do well". These include knowledge, proficiencies, skills and talents.

Natural talent is defined as "an innate or inborn gift for a specific activity, either allowing one to demonstrate some immediate skill without practice, or to gain skill rapidly with minimal practice".

The 80-20 rule (Pareto Principle), applied to human potential says most people, operate on just 20% of their potential. So, there's a whole 80% of potential waiting to be untapped that can lead you to greater career fulfilment. So how do you uncover that hidden potential, living under the surface that's invisible to your untrained eye? Don't look at what you have done, but *who you have been in what you have done.*

Honouring what is natural and inbuilt in you is the easiest path to gain a true sense of your unique purpose. *Shifting your identity from what you do, to who you are provides the key.*

Feeling inspired? It's time for a mental workout.

CORE INSIGHT ACTION

Practical exercise

DISCOVER YOUR NATURAL TALENTS

Consider the questions below. Write down your responses and spend some time reflecting on the insights that emerge.

- What have employers and colleagues come to rely on you for?
- What have people in your life naturally come to you for?
- How have people used you? Who have you been for them?
- Have people come to you because they needed a listener or needed to solve a problem?
- Have people come to you to inspire creative ideas or model successful risk taking?
- What have you achieved? What did you enjoy about it? What person were you in this?

Now, armed with these key insights, you are ready to take the next objective step to find out who your colleagues, close friends and family say you've been to them.

DISCOVER YOUR IMPACT

Practical exercise

360° Feedback, is not just for executives. You can use this exercise to uncover your strengths and find your purpose. It's a great way to discover the impact you have on others. Try this exercise on trusted close friends, relatives and colleagues, ask them to respond to the questions below with the first thing that comes to mind.

- What is the first thing you think of when you think of me?
- What do you think is most interesting about me?
- What do you think my greatest accomplishment is?
- What do you value most about me?
- What do you perceive to be my strengths?
- What do you perceive to be my weaknesses?
- If I were to be on the front cover of a magazine, what sort of magazine would it be and what would the article be about? OR If you could imagine me in any career/role, what would it be? And why?

Review

Once you've looked through the feedback, analyse the responses.

- What surprised you most about the answers you received?
- What differences are there between how others see you and how you see yourself?
- What common themes emerged?
- What are the key insights you've learned?
- What will you do with these insights?
- List the strengths and natural abilities that were highlighted.
- What will you do more of?
- What will you do less of?

Be honest and open-minded. When you begin to get a sense of your strengths and natural talents in terms of *who you are,* instead of what you do, you will feel more of a sense of purpose and gain clarity regarding this part of your core identity. All new experiences require new challenges, step out of your comfort zone and move beyond what you already know.

PART 3
LEARN FROM YOUR PEAK EXPERIENCES

"THE WAY TO RECOVER THE MEANING OF LIFE AND THE WORTHWHILENESS OF LIFE IS TO RECOVER THE POWER OF EXPERIENCE, TO HAVE IMPULSE VOICES FROM WITHIN, AND TO BE ABLE TO HEAR THESE IMPULSE VOICES FROM WITHIN — AND MAKE THE POINT: THIS CAN BE DONE."

ABRAHAM MASLOW

Think of a time when you felt energised, indomitable, exceptionally motivated and completely immersed in the task or activity at hand. Was this a peak experience? Peak experiences can be described as powerful meaningful moments when you are the happiest and most fulfilled; when you are at one with yourself and the world.

A peak experience cannot be conjured up, it occurs as a natural consequence of intrinsically doing the right thing, such as doing an activity where many of your talents, skills, abilities and top values are present. For example, a gifted musician could have a peak experience while playing or composing music. A dancer may experience it when choreographing and performing a dance routine. A sailor may encounter it when using their abilities to overcome choppy waters. Learning from peak experiences can aid you in the discovery of your true self.

According to Gayle Privette, all peak experiences have the following three characteristics:

Fulfilment – they generate positive emotions and are intrinsically rewarding.

Significance – they lead to an increase in personal awareness and understanding and can serve as a turning point in a person's life.

Spiritual – during a peak experience, people feel at one with the world and often experience a sense of losing track of time.[32]

So, what exactly does it feel like to have a peak experience? Think of total immersion and then exhaling. In a peak experience you are at the crest of your power, using all your capacities to your best and fullest. You exhibit a higher level of perception; stronger and more intelligent than you normally are in everyday life. There is no inner conflict or restraint; no fear, worry, self-doubt or self-consciousness. You feel completely illuminated as though you could go on forever.

You've heard of the term "being in the zone". This comes from the concept of "flow"– a state of mind when people become so involved in an activity that the world seems to fade away and nothing else seems to matter. In this state, time seems to fly by, the focus becomes sharp and people experience a loss of self-consciousness. Flow is often a component of having a peak experience.

Peak experiences happen subconsciously, you may simply be following an interest and become totally immersed, experiencing the fulfilment, significance and the spiritual flow described by Privette. Even if you are unaware that it was a peak experience; you will not forget the way you felt when your uninhibited passion and motivation connects and fuses with your most valued talents and abilities.

Because your response is subconscious it means that you are operating from your most authentic self. Psychologist Harriet Learner says: "We'll always be disappointed if we believe that we can plan for a peak experience and make it happen. True joy can't be anticipated or planned. It just strikes."

HOW CAN PEAK EXPERIENCES HELP YOU UNDERSTAND MORE ABOUT YOURSELF?

In Abraham Maslow's popular theory of human motivation, individuals are their most true selves when they achieve self-discovery which is the highest level of human need. Learning from peak experiences enables you to put another important piece of the core identity jigsaw puzzle in place.

Peak experiences are closely linked to your values, personality, talents, abilities and interests, whether you are aware of it or not. When you are "in the zone" your emotions and your body speak to you, feeding back key messages and insights from your core that signals to what is most important in your life. When you pay attention, there are valuable lessons and pointers directing you towards your authentic purpose. Subsequently your mind will start making connections when you ask yourself the right questions.

In writing this chapter, I had a little brainstorm of my own. I couldn't immediately pinpoint my own peak experiences and had to ponder on this for a while. The conclusion I arrived at was that peak experiences come in many forms. The two I'll mention here contain the fulfilment, significance and spiritual elements Privette describes.

Fourteen years ago, I'd been searching for a new career path, something more meaningful, I was ready for a change. I attended a weekend introductory course in life coaching, not sure what it was all about. While there, I remember a distinct feeling of exhaling, as though all the stars aligned and thinking: "oh my God, this is me!" I didn't even know there was a name and profession for what I already was. Everything resonated with me there was no hesitation. I just knew it from my core, that this was the path for me to take.

It was as though someone took a pin and popped all the air out of the balloon of conflict that had been steadily growing inside of me.

As mentioned in the previous chapter, I'd been sceptical about personality profiling and previously avoided them. But when I completed my own assessments, I had a distinct awakening. What I learned about myself smashed right through a leading limiting belief I had about myself that had impacted many of my actions over the years.

In my examples, both peak experiences awakened something in me, which enabled me to understand more about my core identity. The lights went on! I experienced connection with what seemed like disparate parts of myself. They were part of a series of realisations that enabled me to understand and accept myself and discover my authentic purpose. That is why I classify them as peak experiences.

CORE INSIGHT ACTION

IDENTIFY YOUR PEAK EXPERIENCES

This exercise has its roots in the teachings of Abraham Maslow, and in the techniques of neuro-linguistic programming (NLP). It aims to identify those moments when you are absolutely at your best, when you are in the zone. It will help to pinpoint what you are most passionate about and your favoured talents and abilities.

Peak experiences are when:

- You are not conscious of time passing because it is going so quickly and you are so absorbed.
- It is easy and effortless.
- There is core enjoyment present and just thinking about it now creates a warm feeling.
- Everything is going well; you know it will be successful.
- There is a kind of joyousness and fun in the activity; it is serious but playful.
- There is no self-doubt present, you are free of inner conflict
- You are using all of your learned and innate talents and abilities.

- There is spontaneity, expressiveness and naturally flowing behaviour not uninhibited by conformity.
- A free mind that is flexible and open to creative thoughts and ideas.
- Complete mindfulness of the present moment without influence of past or expected future experiences.

Practical exercise

Part 1

Get a pen and paper (or your journal) ready to write down your answers.

Think about some times in your life where some of the above conditions were present. Recall experiences that gave you joy, a thrill where you felt you were at your best. It may apply to a particular event or to a whole period or project.

Try to identify **at least four** strong candidates from different aspects of your life both personal and professional (i.e., education, work, relationships, leisure). Describe the experience. **Tell the story.**

1 What feelings did the experience create for you? (i.e., Joy, pride, confidence, excitement, comfort, accomplishment...)

2 Vividly recall the situation; where were you, who were you with what could you see, hear, sense?

3 What did that mean for you?

4 What makes that so important?

5 What was your part in what happened?

6 What was special about that?

7 What actions did you take to create the outcome?

8 What skills did you use that enabled you to take those actions?

9 How did your personality express itself?

10 What was important about how you felt?

11 How can you utilise those skills again? What else can you do with those skills?

12 Look for patterns – similarities in the actions and skills, that help define who you are and your capabilities.

Part 2

Practical exercise

- What have you learned about your skills and abilities; the way they dovetail with your personality and how your values operate?
- What are your top skills and abilities (identify between 6-10)?
- What motivates you?
- What are you passionate about?
- Keep a note of your responses. You'll need them to complete the next chapter of the book.

Be totally honest with your answers. It will be a powerful foundation from which to build the understanding of your core identity. This knowledge can also help you to navigate future challenges and provide motivation for your desired future.

Remember, what fascinates and energises you are a key part of your core identity and you will not feel truly fulfilled unless you are able to express this more fully. Going after your passion is not *just a dream* reserved for someone else. A dream is a goal with a date and a road map of how to get there, step by step.

"DISCOVERING WHO YOU ARE TODAY IS THE FIRST STEP TO BEING WHO YOU WILL BE TOMORROW."

DESTINY'S ODYSSEY

Chapter 23

Practical exercise

INVENTORY: PIECING IT ALL TOGETHER

"THE GREAT SOLUTION TO ALL HUMAN PROBLEMS IS INDIVIDUAL INNER TRANSFORMATION."

VERNON HOWARD

PART 1
REVEAL YOUR CORE IDENTITY

The life cycle of the butterfly symbolises transformation. A caterpillar has limited capabilities. It crawls from plant to plant and is limited by gravity. It is not particularly attractive.

One day, the caterpillar stops eating, hangs upside down from a twig or leaf and spins itself a silky cocoon or moults into a shiny chrysalis. Under the right conditions, hormones are released that trigger a *metamorphosis* (a Greek word meaning transformation or change in shape).

Within its protective casing, the caterpillar radically transforms its body, eventually emerging as a butterfly. The butterfly is beautiful. It has the ability to fly way beyond the heights that its former self could, no longer confined by the grip of gravity.

If we apply this metamorphosis to humans, the caterpillar represents a person before they become aware of their core identity and the obstacles suppressing it. The cocoon stage is the period of self-discovery and awareness, and the subsequent actions taken to free oneself to live authentically from their core identity. The butterfly, in all its glory, is a representation of the inner and outer freedom the person has gained. They are no longer *crawling* but have gained *freedom wings* to soar, discover and fulfil their true potential.

This transformation is a powerful and visual portrayal of what happens to people when they have the courage to do the work that enables them to take off their mask and live authentically. It's beautiful and empowering.

Now you've completed the work in part one and part two of the book, it's almost time for the big reveal; but first you must piece everything together by making an inventory of what you've learned so far. The following summaries will help you.

Guiding beliefs

Beliefs are the stories we tell ourselves about why we can and can't do certain things in life. They are not based on fact, and often remain unchallenged throughout life. In the earlier chapters on beliefs, you uncovered the limiting beliefs that were holding you back and have taken action to challenge and reframe those beliefs. You now have a set of true accurate and honest positive beliefs you hold about yourself, which I hope you are actively implementing.

LIST YOUR TOP 5 POSITIVE GUIDING BELIEFS.

Values

Values shape your character and reside in the core of your identity; they have a primary influence on your behaviour and attitude. Values provide the motivation to change or remain stagnant.

Your **personal values** furnish you with broad guidelines for all aspects of your life. They tell you who you are and what is most important to you in life, reflecting your needs and desires, enabling you to live in alignment with your values.

LIST YOUR TOP 5-10 CORE VALUES.

Personality

Personality expresses a set of distinctive inborn traits and personal qualities. The characteristic patterns of thoughts, feelings, and behaviours that make a person unique. There are no right or wrong personality traits or preferences. The key is in understanding what your authentic ones are, and how you can utilise them to be most effective and to gain a better understanding of yourself.

From the exercises in the personality chapter, you would have gained some important insights about your own personality and have a list of your most important discoveries.

LIST YOUR DOMINANT PERSONALITY TRAITS AND PREFERENCES.

Strengths and natural talents

Your strengths and natural talents are the things you do with ease; you may not even realise the value or impact they have on others. But you feel good when operating from this sphere. This knowledge gives you a better understanding of yourself and how you operate at your best.

To recap, natural talent is an innate or inborn gift for a specific activity, either allowing one to demonstrate some immediate skill without practice, or to gain skill rapidly with minimal practice. Strengths are tasks or actions you can do well.

Through the exercises in the previous chapter, you now have a good understanding of your strengths and natural talents.

LIST YOUR TOP 10 STRENGTHS AND NATURAL TALENTS.

Passion and motivation

You learn a lot about yourself by paying attention to what you are passionate about and how you are motivated. Your authentic passion and motivation can be used to fuel your vision and guide you towards your unique purpose. Vision uses the power of the imagination to conceive things that do not yet exist with the natural eye. Much of realising your true and full potential rests on your ability to harness your understanding of what motivates you, aligning it with your values and beliefs and then capitalising on it to pursue your authentic goals. Use your learning from the exercises in the previous chapter.

LIST WHAT YOU'RE PASSIONATE ABOUT AND WHAT MOTIVATES YOU.

COMPLETE THE WINGS OF THE BUTTERFLY TEMPLATE WITH YOUR LISTS

Congratulations. You now have all the components of your core identity. It's time to illustrate them on your butterfly. Enjoy yourself! You can make it as colourful as you like.

The butterfly template is available from my website: **www.suzannesimmonslewis.com**, or you can get creative and design your own.

When you've completed the wings of your butterfly that illustrates all the important aspects of your core identity, add your name to the body of the butterfly *or* pick one word that symbolises your essence and write it there instead.

CORE IDENTITY DECLARATION
I AM A PERSON THAT...

The beautiful butterfly represents your metamorphosis from the previous cocoon that was suppressing your core identity. Now you have dealt with the obstacles that were in the way and quieted the inner conflict that was in opposition to your true self, the butterfly which captures your core identity can emerge.

Look through your completed butterfly and spend time thinking about how each part represents you. Take a moment to reflect on how you feel about seeing all this information about who you are in one place. It may be the first time you've ever seen it in this visible and profound way.

Here's an illustration of my core identity

VALUES AND GUIDING BELIEFS

Creativity

Freedom

Openness/connection

Humour

Challenge

Growth/knowledge

Stability

Peace

Health

Integrity/loyalty

Focus only on what is within my control

I will be the change I want to see in the world, it starts with me

Seek peace and pursue it

There is a solution to every problem

I am fearfully and wonderfully made

My uniqueness is my superpower

My natural abilities are my most valuable assets

I am loved

PASSION AND MOTIVATION

Explore new ideas and push boundaries

Human behaviour and what makes people tick

Language and words to inspire and transform lives

Meaningful and deep connections

Continuous learning

Seeing clients transform and fulfil their potential

The power of love for self-acceptance and transformation

My son (my mirror)

PERSONALITY

Creative
Open-minded
Funny
Warm
Solution focused
Adaptable
Direct
Determined
Insightful
Challenging
Caring
Loyal
Wise
Intuitive
Compassionate
Imaginative
Empathic
Values driven
Assertive

STRENGTHS AND NATURAL TALENTS

Easily see new perspectives
Transformational leader
Encourager (inspire and motivate)
Coach and teach
Philosopher
Innovative
Storyteller
Humour
Persuasive
Wordsmith
Strategist
Empathy
Curiosity
Interpersonal
Versatile
Networker
Action oriented/ initiative
Perceptive
Communicator
Visionary

Now, write a few paragraphs that sum up who you really are that captures each part of your core identity illustrated on your butterfly's wings. For example, *I am passionate about......... My guiding beliefs are......* and so on.

To give you an idea, I completed my sentences below.

MY CORE IDENTITY DECLARATION

Passion and motivation

I am fascinated by human behaviour and what makes people tick. I thrive on creating opportunities to explore new ideas and push boundaries. I use language and words to inspire and transform lives. I am most happy when I'm able to make meaningful and deep connections. For me, learning never stops and I am greatly motivated by daily opportunities to learn and grow.

I am inspired by the power of love for self-acceptance and transformation. I thrive on enabling women to swap their straight jacket for a bespoke suit and achieve their full potential.

My relationship with God is my greatest inspiration and my beautiful son is the motivation that pushes me to fulfil my purpose. My son is my mirror.

Guiding beliefs

- I will always operate from my circle of influence and focus on changing only what is within my control. I am not responsible for and cannot control other people's responses or actions.
- I will be the change I want to see in the world, it starts with me.
- I will always seek inner peace and pursue it. (Psalms 34:14)
- There is a solution to every problem.
- I am fearfully and wonderfully made, great are your works Lord. (Psalms 139:14)
- My uniqueness is my superpower.
- My natural abilities are my most valuable assets, (not what I had to work hard to achieve). I was born this way!

The *values* I honour most deeply are:

- Creativity
- Freedom
- Openness/connection
- Humour
- Challenge
- Growth/knowledge
- Stability
- Peace
- Health
- Integrity/loyalty.

Personality

I am open and share my authentic self, preferring transparency and real connection. I am receptive to new ideas and information, intellectually curious, creative and imaginative. I easily see new perspectives. I have a strong desire to explore, discover, and grow; always investigating something new and as a result I'm constantly building knowledge.

Humour makes everything better; I can find humour in almost anything and love to make my friends laugh. My warmth puts people at ease; they feel comfortable talking and sharing their secrets with me. I am resourceful, preferring to work on the solution than dwell on the problem. I'm not a quitter and I am single-minded and determined in my ability to get things done and achieve goals.

My friends say I consistently challenge them to be honest with themselves. I like to push myself and others out of their comfort zones to achieve their goals and potential. I'm direct and prefer straight talking, it's easy for me to see through nonsense. I make decisions based on my values and being true to myself and not compromising what is most important to me, even in the face of difficult challenges.

I'm intuitive and easily understand the emotions and needs of others to provide emotional and/or practical support. I'm flexible and adaptable and always open to new possibilities. I easily understand the big picture and how things fit together and make sense of the world by interpreting patterns, possibilities and meaning.

The strengths and natural talents I value most are:
Encouragement – the ability to inspire and motivate others to transform and achieve their goals, with hope, courage and confidence.
Wordsmith and storyteller for self-expression and to inspire self-awareness, personal freedom, transformation and evoke change.
Humour – laughter is a good medicine "A cheerful heart is good medicine, but a crushed spirit dries up the bones". (Proverbs 17:22)
Innovation and creativity – in unchartered waters there are endless possibilities… Just because it hasn't been done before, doesn't mean it can't be done!
Resourcefulness and determination – having the ability to find quick and clever ways to achieve solutions and overcome difficulties. Versatile.
Empathy – the ability to emotionally understand what other people feel and see things from their point of view.
Decision making – the ability to be decisive and make quick decisions connected to values and an instinctive understanding of patterns, possibilities and meaning.
Curiosity – very inquisitive and questioning with a strong desire to explore, discover and grow. A modern philosopher instinctively seeking wisdom and enlightenment.
Coach/teach – the ability to communicate effectively and positively to influence others to unlock their personal potential and achieve their goals.
Network – the ability to make and sustain meaningful connections with people from all walks of life.

PART 2
WHAT'S YOUR STORY?

"ASKING THE PROPER QUESTIONS IS THE CENTRAL ACTION OF TRANSFORMATION. QUESTIONS ARE THE KEY THAT CAUSES THE SECRET DOORS OF THE PSYCHE TO SWING OPEN."

CLARISSA PINKOLA ESTES

Ever wondered why biographies are so popular? We are fascinated with the voyage of people's lives, particularly those who have experienced a diverse journey, filled with twists and turns, with major struggles that were overcome. This combination can be captivating. That person becomes relatable, we gain hope. To understand someone is to know their story.

When I was working for a political magazine as a journalist, I remember attending a business luncheon event for the magazine's contributors. I had the good fortune to be seated next to a columnist that I hadn't met before. An unassuming man, but as we got chatting, I was distinctly enamoured by his story, which I remember all these years later.

From very humble beginnings he succinctly explained his rise to prominence in his chosen field, with the twists and turns that got him there. He went from a modest working-class Yorkshire upbringing to the printing press, then local news reporter to lawyer (mostly self-taught), and then from CEO to knight of the realm. Even though so much in his life had changed, including his now well-honed and crisp upper-class accent, the continuity of his core identity weaved through his whole story, it was the glue that held the divergent pieces together. It was easy to get a sense of his guiding beliefs, values, talents, passion, warmth, good humour and determination among other things. His core identity remained intact through his successful career and personal life over decades that cumulated in him receiving a royal knighthood.

At the time of writing this chapter, I am eagerly anticipating reading and thoroughly enjoying his memoir that will soon be published.

When my clients are going through a career transition, I work with them to craft a credible and compelling story to convince potential employers that while they may be out of their comfort zone, they ARE perfectly suited to the new role. It links their past personal and professional experiences with their chosen career path and provides the gateway to their new endeavour.

Piecing together the disparate threads of your career and experiences into a story that honestly illustrates how you got to be where you are and where you are going, including your key turning points can make listeners believe in your credibility and care about your success. Your story is the glue that holds everything together.

Similarly, understanding your own story from the perspective of how your core identity has influenced you can provide insights that are like an elixir for understanding your current and future path. *When you know it, you can utilise it.*

PIECE TOGETHER THE JIGSAW PUZZLE

Reflect on how you got to be where you are, where you are going and the key turning points along the way, armed with the knowledge you now have about your core identity. You will find lots of evidence giving you clues; trying to steer you towards your authentic purpose.

The exercise below will help to highlight the strengths of your core identity and you will gain an appreciation of how its power can be utilised for you to live authentically while being guided towards your unique purpose.

CORE INSIGHT ACTION

CRAFTING YOUR STORY

When my clients first start coaching, I ask them to complete a short biography as part of their introductory questionnaire. This provides important insights that inform the sessions. Golden nuggets of clues emerge from their story, that enables me to reveal connections that were not previously considered by the client.

Think of your story as a mini biography of how you got to be where you are today, keeping in mind, your key turning points, highlights and how you overcame various challenges. What were your significant influences? Think about what you are most proud of, your hopes for the future and include any major disappointments.

Focus on *who you were* in your life's journey to date. What parts of your personality, talents, values and guiding beliefs were operating? What was motivating you?

Practical exercise

Consider

- Who was I as a child and as an adult?
- What informed the key decisions that I made both positively and/or negatively?
- What memorable moments stand out, and why?
- What were my inner motivations and goals?
- What was I most proud of?
- What were my major disappointments, and why?
- Who was I in previous roles?
- What is the glue that holds my story together?

Review and put the pieces together

- What common threads can I see running through my story?
- How does my core identity illustrate continuity, despite the otherwise disparate connections?
- How did I utilise my attributes to my advantage?
- How does my story inform who I am now?

- What parts of my core identity did I use consistently well in the past?
- How do these insights point me in the right direction?
- How have I felt when using aspects of my core identity?

Highlight your inner motivations

Remember, keep your focus grounded in who you are and what motivates you, rather than what you have done. Concentrate on the learning from your *self-discovery* and use it to deepen your understanding of your core identity and how it works in practice: how you benefit when you are being authentic.

An example: I have a preference for introversion which enables me to be an excellent observer and listener and can easily understand different people's perspectives. People feel comfortable around me and rely on me to manage conflicts because they are confident that I take a balanced approach.

"OUR WHOLE SPIRITUAL TRANSFORMATION BRINGS US TO THE POINT WHERE WE REALISE THAT IN OUR OWN BEING, WE ARE ENOUGH."

RAM DASS

Part Four

TAKE ACTION

"Knowledge is power: You hear it all the time but knowledge is not power. It's only potential power. It only becomes power when we apply it and use it."

JIM KWIK

Chapter 24

YOUR PERSONAL BRAND AND MISSION: ZERO IN ON YOUR TARGET

"YOUR BRAND IS WHAT PEOPLE SAY ABOUT YOU WHEN YOU ARE NOT IN THE ROOM."

JEFF BEZOS

PART 1
CLARIFY YOUR PERSONAL BRAND

Whether you are aware of it or not, your personal brand is always on show. People get a measure of you by your actions and behaviour and whatever information you put out there for public consumption.

If you don't control the narrative of the story of who you are, you leave it up for interpretation. Like it or not, someone is always observing you, particularly online and what they find can have major implications for your personal or professional life. Linkedin, the world's largest professional online network, is just one example; your profile on its platform could potentially be viewed by 930 million people across 200 countries.

What are you known for right now? Does it reflect the new learning you have gained about your core identity? Does it convey the richness and abundance inside that was hidden behind your mask?

WHAT IS A PERSONAL BRAND?

Your personal brand is the combination of your unique attributes; your personality, values, strengths, skills, experience and passions. In short, the public expression of your core identity!

A successful personal brand is an authentic brand, which has its basis in who you genuinely are right now and can't be forced. There is a consistent message that dovetails with your story and highlights your unique value and is visible to your network and beyond.

Everything you do either builds your brand or weakens it, so it's important to take control of your brand and ensure that it reflects and honest and positive picture of yourself that doesn't compromise your values and what is important to you. Think of it as your personal accountability to live authentically.

Personal branding is an ingredient to your personal and professional success. It helps you to set and work towards your goals with clarity, ensuring that the unique essence of you permeates everything that you do. It provides a steer that enables you to work towards your purpose in a powerful and honest way.

> "TOO MANY PEOPLE OVERVALUE WHAT THEY ARE NOT AND UNDERVALUE WHAT THEY ARE."
>
> **MALCOLM FORBES**

Inauthentic personal brands are the equivalent of living a façade. The focus is on personal marketing, image building, selling and packaging outward appearances whether true or not.

It's hard work trying to be something that you're not and overtime you will only slip up in the process. The media is filled with inauthentic brands of celebrities, influencers and even companies whose image and reputation have been blown apart through scandals, slipups or public meltdowns.

Golf's golden boy, Tiger Woods was on top of the world in 2009, until his serial cheating was revealed. His respectable family man image crumbled along with his career and multiple sponsorship deals. Had he not colluded with and been rewarded for purporting this false persona, his descent from grace at the time may not have been so harsh.

Nicknamed *The Voice*, singer Whitney Houston gained mainstream appeal for many years with the *good girl* image cultivated for her by her mentor and record company. When the inauthentic personal brand began to disintegrate, disbelieving onlookers blamed her husband Bobby Brown for being the bad influence on the *good girl of pop*. It was many years and documentaries later that the truth was revealed. Houston was never the good girl that was presented to the world and as her life unravelled, it was clear she was no longer willing or able to play ball with her fake persona.

The current "cancel culture" is so unforgiving for any misstep, it's no wonder people are more afraid than ever to show who they really are and seek to fit into an acceptable mould. But honesty is the only way, the truth and reality always find a way of seeping out!

"I'M DIFFERENT, MY VOICE IS DIFFERENT, WHO I AM IS DIFFERENT."

VIOLA DAVIS

Conversely, actress Viola Davis is both refreshing and challenging in her openness and authenticity. Her determination to find a place to "shine her light", a light which is different from the Hollywood status quo has shifted paradigms in her industry as well as with those around the world.

In her autobiography *Finding Me*, Davis describes how her refusal to mould herself into "the same palette as her white counterparts" or become a "black female version of a white ideal" enabled her to bring her very own uniqueness and depth of talent and experience to her roles. Many of these roles have been critically acclaimed; Davis was the first African American actor to win the triple crown of Oscar, Tony and Emmy awards for acting and is the most-nominated Black actress of all time.

Davis chose not to fit in an be moulded, but instead channelled her personal power into being true to herself. As a result, her unique talents and life experiences have shone through in her work. It has also changed the narrative for many who can follow her example in whatever walk of life they are in. There is power in your uniqueness.

Finding Me, is searingly honest and vulnerable in its strength to draw the reader in like a force field that creates a supernatural connection, enabling readers to both identify and be inspired by her story.

TO UNDERSTAND SOMEONE IS TO KNOW THEIR STORY

An authentic personal brand reflects your true character. It is built on your dreams, purpose, values, uniqueness, genius, passion, specialisation, characteristics and favourite activities. An honest and holistic personal brand is strong, distinctive, meaningful and memorable. *Remember there is ONLY one of you*!

According to Brian Tracy: "One of the greatest claims is that people can say you're always the same on the outside as you are on the inside." This is not only a great boast, but it increases your inner peace, energy and fulfilment.

Your personal authentic brand communicates your value to the world. It's easier to maintain and won't become a burden. You build credibility and trust and stand out from the crowd. It helps people to build a connection with you and grows your network. You can capitalise on your strengths and convey your mission in life.

> "The keys to brand success are self-definition, transparency, authenticity and accountability."
>
> **SIMON MAINWARING**

Practical exercise

CORE INSIGHT ACTION

DEFINE YOUR PERSONAL BRAND

Now you have done the work to reveal your core identity and you have a better understanding of your story, it's time to clarify your personal brand. Think of it as an exercise in getting clear about who you are, what you stand for and how you present yourself to the world. Your *genuine* public face!

To recap, your personal brand is your *core identity* mixed with *your story, character, mission* and *purpose*. You can capitalise on your personal attributes and strengths here. What will you choose to showcase? And why?

- What makes you unique?
- What are your strengths?
- What do you want to be known for?
- What is your personal, career or business vision?
- Why is it important to you?
- What is your consistent message?
- How will you incorporate these into your current activities and online presence?
- What will you do more of?
- What will you do less of?
- Make a note of your answers in your journal.

DÉJÀ VU EXERCISE

Five years from now, looking back, how would you want someone to describe you? What do you want them to say about the kind of person you were and what you were known for? What words would they use? What is the most important word?

YOUR ONLINE AUDIT

Clean up and nurture your online presence

Now you are clear about your personal brand. It's time for an online audit. Do a quick google search of your name and see what comes up. How closely does the information reflect your personal brand? Edit and update your information to ensure there is a consistent message of who you are; your unique value and what you want to be known for.

Be truly authentic: produce good content on social media. And when you tell your story, stay true to who you are and what you believe in. Check your privacy settings and make sure all the information you post is aligned with your personal brand and available to your target audience.

People are always screening you online. Your personal brand can generate opportunities for advancement. It's your calling card, so focus on what makes you memorable.

> "Too many companies want their brands to reflect some idealised, perfected image of themselves. As a consequence, their brands acquire no texture, no character and no public trust."
>
> **RICHARD BRANSON**

PART 2
UNCOVER AND CRAFT YOUR MISSION

Bravo on making it this far, you're almost there!

Part three of this book has focused on the discovery of your core identity. If you have diligently completed all the exercises and taken time to reflect on your learning you will be very close if not already arrived at discovering your purpose, or at the very least, your ladder is now leaning against the right wall.

You've taken off your mask, shifted some paradigms and the inner conflict is no longer growing muscles from its previous daily workouts.

You will be fully aware of your core identity and noticing the benefits of living authentically, with confidence to express your true self. You understand your strengths and talents, what motivates and energises you, your impact on others and how to honour your top values.

Unexplored desires that were bubbling away under the surface may now seem possible. You now appreciate how the attributes within you can achieve what previously seemed like a dream. You understand more of your story and what's possible. You are more courageous; the inner confidence is real.

You've reflected on the importance of purpose and not wasting the time you have left. Now you are positioned in the right direction *baggage free*, it's time to move closer to your purpose by crafting your mission statement.

When Stephen Covey wrote *The 7 Habits of Highly Effective People in 1989*, he suggested individuals create their own mission statement as part of his second habit: begin with the end in mind. Over 30 years later, personal mission statements, sometimes called purpose statements, are widely used by successful people.

Think of your mission as the broad outcome of your life. When you know the kind of footprint you want to leave on this earth after your journey here is done, you are well on your way to defining your life as having purpose and a mission.

Your mission consists of the central motivating aims of your life, the reasons you get up in the morning. It can guide life decisions, influence behaviour, shape goals, offer a sense of direction and create meaning.

Now you are aware of your core identity, writing your mission statement is the opportunity to think about how you will *honour your uniqueness and talents* in the world and remain personally accountable.

We all have talents and abilities that are God-given to be used for the benefit of others in some way. For example, you may have the ability to sing beautifully. You are fulfilled when performing in your gift and other people are entertained by the beauty of your vocal prowess. Your mission is to exercise the talent which you most delight to use, shaped by your values and guiding beliefs in the sphere of life that speaks most to your heart.

We detect, rather than invent our missions in life. Take one step at a time, even when you don't see where it is leading (the end destination), rely on your core identity and stay in tune with honouring who you are. It will guide you. According to Covey: "Each of us has an internal monitor or sense that gives is an awareness of our own uniqueness and the singular contributions that we can make." That's your core identity!

The process of writing a mission statement is as important as the mission statement itself. It forces you to think through your priorities deeply and carefully and align your behaviour with your guiding beliefs. Your sense of mission that is highly motivating will be evident to you and those around you as you're not just reacting to whatever happens around you.

Personal mission statements vary, there is no set template. Some focus on a particular theme or guiding purpose for their life, while others focus on the values and beliefs that will guide their purpose. But all have some sense of the broad outcome of their mission, and focus on the end goal.

Here are a few examples from public figures:

Amanda Steinberg

To use my gifts of intelligence, charisma, and serial optimism to cultivate the self-worth and net-worth of women around the world. (Financial expert, entrepreneur, human rights activist and founder of DailyWorth).

Oprah Winfrey

To be a teacher. And to be known for inspiring my students to be more than they thought they could be.

Mahatma Gandhi

I shall not fear anyone on Earth. I shall fear only God. I shall not bear ill will toward anyone. I shall not submit to injustice from anyone. I shall conquer untruth by truth. And in resisting untruth, I shall put up with all suffering.

You can see from these simple statements how their work in various spheres of life dovetails with their personal mission statements.

CORE INSIGHT ACTION

WRITE YOUR MISSION STATEMENT

Practical exercise

To help you get started, consider your previous insights and reflect on the questions below:

- How have the pieces of your core identity come together?
- What did you learn from the consistent messages in your story?
- What did you find when you saw your passions up close?
- What strengths of your personality do you most want to utilise?
- What talents and abilities do you most delight to use?

For additional focus, I have adapted an exercise from Richard Bolles, author of career guide *What Colour is your Parachute*? Bolles believed that: “God’s will is written in our members” first in the talents He has lodged there and then in His guidance for our heart as to which talents give us the greatest pleasure from its exercise.

There are nine spheres of life. Most individuals will find one or perhaps two on which to focus their energy and mission. Read through the following spheres and pick out the one that appeals most to you.

THE NINE KINGDOMS OF MISSION AND PURPOSE:
What sphere of life do you want to make better?

1 The Senses When you have finished your life here on Earth, do you want there to be more beauty in the world, because you were here? If so, what kind of beauty captivates you? Is it art, music, flowers, photography, painting, crafts, clothing, jewellery, or what? If this is your main purpose in life, then write one paragraph about it.

2 The Body Do you want there to be more wholeness, fitness, or health in the world, more binding up of the body’s wounds and strength, more feeding of the hungry, and clothing of the poor, because you were here? What issue in particular?

3 Our Possessions Do you want there to be better stewardship of what we possess, as individuals, as a community, as a nation? If so, in what areas of human life in particular?

4 The Will or Conscience Do you want there to be more morality, more justice, more righteousness, more honesty in the world, because you were here? In what areas of human life and in what geographical area?

5 The Heart Do you want there to be more love and compassion in the world, because you were here? Love or compassion for whom? Or for what?

6 Entertainment Do you want there to be more lightening of people’s loads, more giving them perspective, more helping them to forget their cares for a spell, do you want there to be more laughter in the world and joy, because you were here? If so, what particular kind of entertainment do you want to contribute to the world?

7 The Earth Is this planet, your major concern? Do you want there to be better protection of this fragile planet, more exploration (not exploitation) of the world or the universe, more dealing with its problems and its energy, because you were here? Which problems or challenges in particular, draw your heart and soul?

8 The Spirit Do you want there to be more spirituality in the world, more faith, more compassion, more forgiveness, more love for God and the human family in all its diversity, because you were here? If so, with what ages, people, or with what parts of human life?

9 The Mind Do you want there to be more knowledge, truth, or clarity in the world, because you were here? In what areas?

REFLECTION & ACTION

Which one in particular draws you to it the most? Think about how your attributes chime with the sphere you have chosen that most inspires you; your personality, top core values, passions, strengths and natural abilities, and your guiding beliefs. Where do you most want to lend your brain, your energies, your skills and gifts, your life, to serve while you are here on this Earth? **Write a paragraph about it.**

The following mission statement is from Toni's career change case study in chapter eighteen. After completing the above exercise and others relating to her core identity, she identified most with the **sphere of the body** and crafted the following mission statement:

My mission in life is to help people lead an active and healthy life so they're able to live longer, delay any health issues and in the process become more body confident. I'd like to focus on 12–18-year-olds as they'll already be taking part in some kind of physical activity at school.

I've included my mission. I identified with the **sphere of the mind.**

My mission is to help people free themselves to be who they really are so they can fulfil their divine purpose on this Earth and be all that God has created them to be, while experiencing the joy and peace of inner acceptance.

Now take some time to write your mission statement. With the knowledge and insights you've gained, you will be able to draft a statement that is authentic and meaningful to you. It may take a few attempts to fine tune it, but it's well worth the effort. Think of it as the lamp guiding you along a dark road where you would otherwise not see the path ahead.

Remember your mission statement will be:

- A tool for making difficult decisions
- A framework for how you want to live your life and express your life mission
- A beacon to those around you about who you really are
- A declaration that motivates and inspires you to stay the course
- A statement of your values and life priorities.

"THE PURPOSE OF LIFE IS A LIFE OF PURPOSE."

ROBERT BYRNE

Chapter 25

GOALS: A GOAL WITHOUT A PLAN IS JUST A WISH

"There is no hope of success for the person who does not have a central purpose, or definite goal at which to aim."

NAPOLEON HILL

Now you are aware of the central motivating aims of your life (mission) and what strengths you will capitalise on from your personal brand it's time to turn these aims into action by setting your goals.

Personal goals can be described as the personal aspirations or objectives a person creates to focus on and achieve. Setting goals is the first step to turning the invisible into the visible. According to *Think and Grow Rich* author Napoleon Hill: "First comes thought; then organisation of that thought, into ideas and plans; then transformation of those plans into reality. The beginning, as you will observe, is in your imagination."

Life is filled with goals; whether you are a goal-oriented person or not, you just can't get away from them. There are short, medium and long-term goals, big goals and small goals, goals that take you out of your comfort zone and those that are part of your daily routine.

CONSIDER THE WEEKLY GROCERY SHOP

Scenario 1:

You go grocery shopping. There has been no preparation for this task, you are unsure of what has actually run out and needs to be replaced. You have no meal plan for the week and you have not prepared a list. When you get to the store you spend more time browsing and succumbing to offers and items that you've just decided you need because they're in front of you. You end up spending much more than was necessary and most of what you purchase remains unused and thrown away.

Scenario 2:

You create a list before you go shopping, taking into account your needs for the week. You have budgeted for precisely what you need. When shopping you are less likely to get side-tracked and spend unnecessary money on what you think you need just because it's in front of you. You will spend no time, or a minimal amount of time browsing. You're efficient because the purpose of your goal was well defined: buy a specific number of items within a specific budget.

The difference between the two is that the second option was a well-defined goal with a plan and a specific outcome. Buy specific grocery items for the week according to the meal plan with a budget of xxxx amount. This approach is an effective use of time and money and minimises waste.

A goal driven life enables you to do more and achieve more with the resources that you have. It's like throwing your dart and hitting the bullseye, rather than a "scatter gun approach" of just aiming in the vicinity of the dart board and hoping that when you throw your dart it will land somewhere on the board. Numerous attempts later, you still haven't landed anywhere near your target.

Everyone is busy being busy, but this doesn't mean it's achieving meaningful goals. Many people work hard but don't seem to get anywhere worthwhile. They haven't spent enough time thinking about and planning what they truly want out of life and haven't set well formed goals. The most beneficial goals are the ones linked to your mission and purpose in life.

GOALS GIVE YOU FOCUS

In coaching there is an exercise called red car and blue car. The coach asks the client to look out of the window for one minute and count the number of red cars that drive by. The client completes the task successfully. The coach then asks the client to tell them how many blue cars also drove past within the same period of time. The client had no idea because their focus was only on counting the red cars.

This is a good illustration to highlight how you become razor sharp when you are focused on a particular intention. You can only act pre-emptively on what you are focused on. You will start noticing things you didn't before which can assist you with your mission. Now you know where you are headed, fewer opportunities will be missed. Having well-formed written goals enables you to eliminate unwanted and unhelpful information and activities that can lead you off course.

THE IMPORTANCE OF WRITTEN GOALS

In my coach training I was told of a study on goals by Yale University which found only three percent of the graduating class had specific written goals for their futures. Twenty years later that three percent were found to be earning 10 times more than the 97% that had no clear written goals. After searching diligently to find the original study it was nothing more than an urban myth, but a very convincing one nevertheless.

What I could substantiate though was recent research by Gail Matthews, a psychology professor at Dominican University in California who did a study on goal setting with 267 participants. Matthews found that you are 42% more likely to achieve your goals just by writing them down.

While goals begin with a vision for the future. It's unlikely to be achieved without a plan:

A dream written down with a date becomes a goal.

A goal broken down into steps becomes a plan.

A plan backed by action makes your dreams come true.

The act of setting written goals forces you to contemplate what you truly want out of life. It gives you long-term vision and short-term motivation. It focuses your acquisition of knowledge and helps you to organise your time and resources so that you can make the most of your life.

Even if you can't see the full picture in technicolour right now, follow the direction that your new learning has taken you.

There is a wealth of information online about how to set impactful or SMART goals[33] which is very useful. However, I define well-formed goals as more than being SMART; they are goals that dovetail and agree with your core identity. They match your top values, agree with your passions and motivations, play to your top strengths and natural talents and marry with your personality. They are authentic and enable you to breathe, even when challenging; fun and enjoyment are there.

I believe one of the reasons most New Year's resolutions don't materialise is because they are mostly aspirational goals that are not linked to your *core identity* or your *true mission* in life. Around 25% of people abandon their New Year's resolutions after one week and 60% of people abandon them within six months. The average person makes the same New Year's resolution 10 separate times without success.

THINK BIG AND TAKE SMALL INCREMENTAL STEPS

A good way to think of setting goals that encapsulate your mission and core identity is to *begin with the end in mind.* Based on your mission statement, create your "big picture" of when you have achieved your mission or are fully operating and living within your purpose. Think 10 years ahead or more; identify the large-scale goals that you want to achieve then work backwards. What would need to happen in the first year, second year and so on to achieve the end result. From there you can set journey goals for the first month, six months, a year and so on.

Then turn your journey goals into the smaller and smaller targets that you must meet to reach your lifetime mission goals. This becomes your plan. From here you create daily "to do lists" of things you should do to fulfil your journey goals and over time you will systematically achieve your mission goals one step at a time.

Breaking the goal into smaller journey goals also enables you to avoid feeling overwhelmed or even panicked. Your journey goals are achievable and within your circle of influence and control. The more you achieve, the greater your circle of influence becomes and the closer you will be to fulfilling your purpose.

CELEBRATE YOUR SMALL VICTORIES

Lots of small incremental steps go towards achieving a much bigger goal. Take care not to be so driven to achieve your end goal, that you have not taken any time to enjoy the highlights along the journey it took to get there. The end goal may seem like an anti-climax if you haven't taken time to celebrate the small victories, and learn from the obstacles you've navigated. Both are there to teach you more about yourself.

I can personally relate to this. As I have learned to be much kinder to myself, I've appreciated the journey much more. When particular journey goals are reached, I always observe it with some act of kindness to myself. This could be going to see a matinee at the theatre or celebrating with friends. These moments enable me to show gratitude and reflect on the learning and journey to date. It can also provide inspiration and the motivation to continue on.

Journaling is a great way to chart your progress. As you look back and reflect there will be so much learning from your journey. Afterall, we live life forwards and understand it backwards. Hindsight is 20-20 vision.

If you are not yet persuaded on the benefits of writing your personal goals, here is a recap:

- When you precisely know what you want to achieve, you will know where you have to concentrate your efforts. You'll also quickly spot the distractions that can so easily lead you astray
- It will force you to clarify what you want
- It will motivate you to take action
- It will provide a filter for other opportunities
- It will help you overcome resistance
- It will enable you to see and celebrate your progress.

"We have to be braver than we think we can be, because God is constantly calling us to be more than we are."

MADELINE L'ENGLE

STEP OUT OF YOUR COMFORT ZONE

Don't play safe; come out of your comfort zone. Set challenging BUT achievable goals. You can step out and be more than you are right now. Now you have a vision of something bigger, don't let the knocks, fears and "what ifs" of life leave you in the comfort zone: it may be easy, familiar and safe, but nothing new or exciting rarely happens there either. Growth does not happen there. Nothing of any consequence happens there.

The truth is, in your comfort zone you operate on very little of your true potential; potential that is just waiting to be ignited and nurtured by new challenges and experiences. You *are* much more than where you are right now, but *only you* can decide to step out and venture into unchartered waters to see the possibilities that await you.

Stretch zone is the optimal place for achieving goals. To utilise your potential and fulfil your unique purpose in life, you will often be in *stretch*. This is where you are entering into unchartered territory, but have the resources you need to accomplish the task at hand. Think of an elastic band. It is only useful when it is used in its capacity to stretch and hold multiple objects together. But if stretched too far or too fast it will snap and not be fit for its purpose.

When you are in stretch, you challenge yourself with activities or interactions that are unfamiliar. For instance, you may solo travel abroad for the first time or learn a new activity or skill. In the stretch zone, you do not feel panicked and overwhelmed, but are able to step up to the challenge. You are motivated and even excited at the prospect of experiencing or learning something new and receiving the reward that's waiting on the other side of unchartered waters.

And when you accomplish things, your self-esteem and skill set increases and you become more persistent in your endeavours.

On a recent hiking trip, I got talking to a mother and daughter in the group. They explained their first hiking trip was like a "baptism of fire". They were generally not fit as they didn't do regular exercise, so they picked a hiking event they believed was for beginners. They ended up on an 18-kilometre hike on Devils Dyke in the South Downs. At many points along the way, particularly at the steep inclines, they thought about quitting as they believed that it was not humanly possible for them to complete the four-hour trek. But with much persuasion and encouragement they reached the top and were rewarded with amazing views of the landscape beneath them. The ascent was challenging and bordering on alarm as their bodies along with their minds had a "physical and mental shock", and took a while to catch up to the reality of the situation they felt partially unprepared for.

After the summit, the descent they said was "easy". Although they spent the next three days physically stiff and generally aching, they described the confidence and motivation the experience gave them to take on other tasks in their life with gusto. If they could climb Devil's Dyke, they could do anything!

In reality, they were in stretch. Had they known it was a moderate climb and not for beginners, they probably wouldn't have booked it. However, both mother and daughter achieved something they didn't believe they were capable of. Because it was unfamiliar and a bit daunting their minds took a while to catch up and accept this new endeavour was indeed possible. But stepping out of their comfort zone and accepting the challenge boosted their positive mindset and ability to succeed in other areas.

DON'T SNAP YOUR ELASTIC BAND – STRETCH DON'T PANIC

While failing to challenge yourself leads to stagnation, be careful not to become overloaded with pressure. This leads to panic and your performance and chances of success will be on a steep decline.

For example, what would be your chances of success if you were asked to do a presentation to 500 people in a week's time when you'd never attempted public speaking before or even written a presentation? PANIC.

CHALLENGE YOURSELF

I try new things outside of my comfort zone to challenge myself and I pay attention to the internal feedback it gives me. I've not been one for doing physical pursuits where I feel I don't have control at any given time. At primary school I would even do a risk assessment to consider swinging from the playground monkey bars. The thought of "letting go" and my feet being that high above the ground was all the deterrent I needed. As I mentioned previously, I left the cave in Wales "by any means necessary!"

But with this in mind I set myself a challenge to partake in the various waterpark slides and activities while on holiday abroad. There was a ride called the Tsunami which I decided to try with a friend. It was as the name suggested and the most feared ride in the park. A quick Google search just now informs me that people have been knocked unconscious on this ride. I remember ascending the steps with my knees trembling and my heart beating fast. In my mind, being pushed down from that high platform was like taking a massive step into the unknown where I could not control the outcome. I screamed so loud for the duration of the ride I could be heard throughout the two-acre site. When I landed on "terra firma" a college friend I hadn't seen for almost thirty years found me and said: "I recognised you by your voice!"

Taking on new challenges and overcoming fears can do wonders for your confidence and ability to step out and achieve things you may not immediately believe are possible. By taking on that particular personal challenge, I was no longer a bystander in an environment designed for fun and enjoyment. But it gave me much more too. The experience of "feeling the fear and doing it anyway" which fuelled my belief in my ability to achieve greater challenges within my purpose.

Challenge yourself regularly, you can start taking small steps with moderate challenge. For example, joining a new club, signing up for voice lessons, taking a community art class or anything else that is new and intriguing for you. Consider things that relate to your core identity and are within your purpose and mission.

Begin to dream again, remove the fog from your vision and fan the flames that ignite the passion within you that has been dimmed in your comfort zone.

Set some goals, make a plan and take small steps every day towards your goals. The difference between you and someone who is driving forward in their potential, is that they believe that they can and have taken action.

Be brave, take the journey to being *more than you are right now* and see how much more there is for you to discover and achieve.

Today is the beginning of the rest of your life, what direction will you choose?

"FEAR GUIDES THE RESTRICTION OF OUR AMBITION. YOU DO NOT HAVE TO BE SCARED; BE AUDACIOUS, BE AMBITIOUS. YOUR LIFE CAN BE WILDER THAN YOUR WILDEST DREAM."

ARSÈNE WENGER

Chapter 26

BLIND SPOTS

Thank you for taking on the challenge of swapping your straight jacket for a bespoke suit. As you look forward to the rest of your life, I hope your vista now looks beautiful, cleared of the haze and smog that previously blurred your view. There is now a custom-made landscape ahead, tailored to you.

Writing this book has also been a process of continuous personal growth for myself. I too had several epiphanies and I'd like to share one of them with you.

Just before my birthday in 2020, I had a dream about my first love that caused me some concern. From then on, he remained on my mind. I decided to read a series of letters from him that I'd kept, they were more than 30 years old. In all those years I had never revisited them, I had just neatly filed them away.

Well, I was not prepared for what happened. I spent the entire night until sunrise reading those letters. When I finished, I wept.

For the first time I realised that there was someone back then who knew me. He could see me; REALLY see me and loved me unconditionally. He saw me, before I could truly see myself. I had then what some can only dream about. Yet, at the time I didn't see it fully for what is actually was. *I knew* he loved me and I believed that I loved him, as far as I understood love to be at the time. However, I was not able to receive the depth of his love back then, as I had not accepted myself, I didn't even know myself.

To truly *know yourself and accept yourself, is to love yourself.* From that place you can receive the love of others. When you do not know who you are or are not accepting of who you really are, it's impossible to receive genuine love and connection.

Philosopher Ralph Waldo Emmerson said: "Most of the shadows of this life are caused by standing in one's own sunshine." This was certainly the case for me back then. But those shadows that cause blind spots are obliterated the more we become our authentic selves.

Seeing myself through the eyes of someone who loved me unconditionally just as I was, gave me a brand-new set of eyes and a new perspective. A paradigm shift took place.

As I revaluated that time in my life, I realised that my inner filters had dismissed the depth of his love as not real. The limiting beliefs I held then told me that "it's just talk, all men say this to make you feel good but they don't really mean it". When I look back at the same situation now, I recognise that his love was genuine and sincere. However, it could not fully penetrate my inner filters and reach my heart.

At that young age, I had no reference point. I had not experienced this kind of love from my parents. In particular, my father did not model this type of love towards me. We often gravitate subconsciously to what is familiar and what we know. In addition, I did not love myself unconditionally, I didn't even know who I was.

When I then re-examined a few subsequent relationships, I realised that in them I'd gravitated to what I knew; less affection, less acceptance and connection. But I did this as though sleepwalking. I can only look back now in hindsight to identify the cause and my ensuing behaviour.

When I simultaneously grieved that loss and embraced those realisations, I experienced his love again as though it was a living thing, breathing new life into me. From my current perspective of understanding and accepting myself – living out of the truest form of my core identity – I received, felt and accepted that love, which was utterly affirming. It was energising and created joy within me. I experienced an inner validation of the *teenage Suzanne* that I'd never known previously.

I got out of the way and *my sunshine* was able to beam at 1000 watts!

This belated gift has had an overwhelmingly positive effect on my most meaningful relationships.

It took a long journey into myself to swap my straight jacket for my bespoke suit. But what a worthwhile journey of exploration and transformation it was. So much more now makes sense, as the pieces of my jigsaw puzzle have come together.

For example, the Psalm: "I praise you because I am fearfully and wonderfully made; your works are wonderful I know that full well... Thank you for making me so wonderfully complex!" I always used to struggle with embracing the meaning of this Psalm because I couldn't relate to it. When I was in conflict with myself and hadn't yet discovered my core identity, I did not feel completely happy with the way I was. As I mentioned in chapter nine, I'd struggled with not feeling good enough, or being enough.

Now I understand who I really am, I can honestly say I appreciate the way God made me. I really am fearfully and wonderfully made. God made me just right; the way I think, my personality, skills, talents, motivations and idiosyncrasies are perfectly suited to my purpose here on Earth. I am wholly fulfilled when I express the truest form of my core identity. I am the round peg in the round hole!

Love is powerful and life giving. The more you accept your true self, the more open you will be to experience the depths of love from others. I hope you will fall in love with the person you have discovered on this journey as you exhale in your comfortable bespoke suit.

"BEAUTY BEGINS THE MOMENT YOU DECIDE TO BE YOURSELF."

COCO CHANEL

WHO AM I?

Who am I beneath the gloss and façade?
Behind the status and the smile
Who am I?
When all is stripped away?
The layers of possessions
The public face

Who am I, if not for a day, a mother, a wife, sister and friend?
Who would I be, without the chorus of worries that plague me?

Who can I be?
If I could break free of childhood demons that paralyse me
From fully moving on to live without limitations of a childhood long gone

Who would I be?
If healed from the heartache and betrayal, living with the enemy
Who could be if I fully step outside the box of expectations imposed on me?

Who am I then?
Thank God *I now know*, and have embraced my future road
I have broken free and see the divine path for my destiny
Now I know myself and embrace the gifts that I possess
No longer bound by inner fears and mindless cares
I see my light and live right there
Thank you, Lord, I've found ME.

[*15 November 2022*]

WHO AM I?

Swap Your Straight Jacket for a Bespoke Suit

CORE INSIGHT TRANSFORMATION PROGRAMME

Connect with Suzanne to unlock your core identity and free yourself to be who you really are.

Have you enjoyed this book and want to delve deeper? Work with Suzanne for a personalised approach to your transformation journey.

- Banish imposter syndrome, take off your mask and connect with who you really are.
- Create alignment with what you truly want.
- Eliminate stress, burnout and inner conflict.
- Gain the confidence to live out of the truest expression of yourself.
- Delve into your unique purpose.
- Fine tune your bespoke road map to success.

The six-month programme includes:

- 1-2-1 coaching sessions with Suzanne for a deep dive into your personal transformation process.
- A structured workbook with tried and tested tools and techniques from the core identity model to guide you into your *bespoke suit.*

Email: info@suzannesimmonslewis.com to register for this programme.

WWW.SUZANNESIMMONSLEWIS.COM

RESOURCES

FREE PERSONALITY TESTS

https://www.16personalities.com/free-personality-test
https://www.personalitydata.org
https://www.humanmetrics.com/personality/test
[Active at time of publishing]

RECOMMENDED READING

Eat that Frog (2013) Brain Tracy
Goals (2003) Brain Tracy
Finding Me, (2022) Viola Davis
Living your Best Life (2001) Laura Berman Fortgang
The Five Love Languages (2004) Gary Chapman
The 7 Habits of Highly Effective People (2004) Stephen Covey
What Colour is Your Parachute (2013) Richard N Bolles
Who Moved My Cheese? (1998) Dr Spencer Johnson

PDF DOWNLOADS AND OTHER RESOURCES

Visit **www.suzannesimmonslewis.com** for PDF versions of the detailed practical exercises from this book and other useful resources.

REFERENCES

Books

The Best of Bits and Pieces, Chicken Soup for the Woman's Soul (1996). Jack Canfield et al
The Body Keeps Score (2015) Bessel van der Kolk
Co Active Coaching, 2nd edition, (2007) Laura Whitworth et al
Do Yourself a Favour… Forgive (2012) Joyce Meyer
Emotional Unavailability; Recognising It, Avoiding It and Understanding Its Trap. (1997) Bryn C Collins
Finding Me, (2022) Viola Davis
The Games People Play (1964) Eric Berne

The Gifts of Imperfection: Let go of who you think you're supposed to be and embrace who you are. (2010) Brené Brown
Goals (2003) Brain Tracy
Holy Bible
Identity, Your Passport to Success, (2012) Steadman Graham
Knowing your Why, The Key to Unlocking Your Full Potential (2016) Dr Jeffery A Williams
Living Your Best Life (2001) Laura Berman Fortgang
Man's Search for Meaning (2004) Viktor Frankl
My American Journey (2003) Colin Powell
Seeing What Others Don't (2017) Gary Klein
The 7 Habits of Highly Effective People (2004) Stephen Covey
What Colour is your Parachute (2013) Richard N Bolles

Articles

Don't keep saying yes, why you need to stop being so nice, Antonia Hoyle, The Telegraph (19.9.2015)
People pleaser and losing out on love, George Hartwell M.Sc, healmylife.com
A physicist explains how Simone Biles' signature flip basically defies gravity, Yasmin Tayag Inverse.com (17.08 2017)
Are you a people pleaser or just kind? Darlene Lancer (14.1.2020) medium.com
Louise Redknapp on living apart from Jamie and why she still loves him, Louise Gannon (7.10.2017) telegraph.co.uk
Mehrabian's communication theory: verbal, non-verbal, body language, businessballs.com
The deadly consequences of unforgiveness, Lorie Johnson (22.6.2015) CBN News
Finding peace through forgiveness, Edward-Elmhurst Health (21.12.2017) eehealth.org
You are the average of the five people you spend the most time with, Maarten van Doorn (20.06.2018) medium.com

Mindsets – what they are and why they matter, Gary Klein Ph.D (1.5.2006) psychologytoday.com
Social acceptance and rejection: the sweet and the bitter, Nathan DeWall and Brad J Bushman (12.08.2011) *Current Directions in Psychological Science*, psychologicalscience.org
What great listeners actually do, Jack Zenger and Jospeh Folkman: (14.7.2016) hbr.com
How to express yourself clearly and get your needs met, Tracy Seed (08.03.2019) tracyseed.com
Bitterness makes the heart grow sicker, Monika Merkes, (11.9.2011) theconversation.com
What breaking the 4-minute mile taught us about the limits of conventional thinking, Bill Taylor (9.3.2018) hbr.com
What is gratitude and why is it so important? Courtney E Ackerman MA. (28.2.2017) positivepsychology.com
Why meditate? Deepak Chopra (5.3.2017) deepakchopra.com
Why is influence so important, Dr Karen Keller, kellerinstitute.com
Culture and Self-Expression, Heejung S. Kim, Deborah Ko (2007) University of California Santa Barbara, Psychology Press
Social relationships and health: A flashpoint for health policy, Debra Umberson and Jennifer Karas Montez (4.8.2011) Journal of Health and Social Behaviour Study
Self-concept and interpersonal communication, Prabhakararao Sampthirao (April - June, 2016), The International Journal of Indian Psychology
Social rejection shares somatosensory representations with physical pain, Ethan Krossa, Marc G. Bermana et al (28.03.2011) pnas.org
Why rejection hurts so much and what to do about it, Guy Winch (8.12.2015) ideas.ted.com
The temptation of self-rejection and the promise of self-acceptance. Maury Joseph PsyD (18.9.2017) www.goodtherapy.org
Peak experiences in psychology, Kendra Cherry (26.11.2022) verywellmind.com

Jamal Edwards, music entrepreneur and YouTube star, dies aged 31, Alexa Philips (21.2.2022) news.sky.com
How Jamal Edwards became teenage millionaire after mum Brenda's selfless sacrifice, Kyle O'Sullivan (25.4.2022) mirror.co.uk
What is personality? Kendra Cherry (7.11.2022) verywellmind.com
https://en.wikipedia.org/wiki/Nonviolent_Communication
https://en.wikipedia.org/wiki/Identity_formation
https://www.dominican.edu/sites/default/files/2020-02/gailmatthews-harvard-goals-researchsummary.pdf
https://www.truity.com/myers-briggs/about-myers-briggs-personality-typing
https://www.16personalities.com/articles/our-theory
https://dwayne-fields.com/dwaynes-story/

Broadcasts

Dolly Parton: The Queen of Country (2016) Channel 5
Jane Fonda in Five Acts – (2018) HBO
Miss Americana, (2020) Netflix
Talking Pictures: Orson Welles (2013) BBC
Teddy Pendergrass: If You Don't Know Me (2019) Showtime

Definitions

https://en.wikipedia.org/wiki/Second_wind
https://www.merriam-webster.com/dictionary/forgive
https://www.apa.org/topics/personality
https://en.wikipedia.org/wiki/Peak_experience

NOTES

[1]Oxford Living Dictionaries
[2]Cambridge Dictionary
[3]The Free Dictionary
[4]James D. Fearon Department of Political Science, Stanford University. What is Identity (as we now use the word)?
[5]Stephen Covey popularized the term *paradigm*, which comes from the Greek root paradigma, meaning a pattern, model, or representation of something. Our paradigms are the perceptions, frames of reference, worldviews, value systems, or lenses through which we see everyone and everything, including ourselves. They add meaning, true or false, to the world around us, and affect the way we interpret what we see and experience, and how we interact and relate with others. www.franklincoveysuriname.com/check-your-paradigms-2
[6]An alter ego means an alternate self, which is believed to be distinct from a person's normal or true original personality
[7]Neill, J.T. (2004). Nature vs Nurture in Intelligence. wilderdom.com
[8]Self-image is how you perceive yourself, based on your experiences and aspirations. Self-image is not a FACT but a mental picture you have composed of the conclusions you have reached about yourself.
[9]Jack Canfield et al, The Best of Bits and Pieces, Chicken Soup for the Woman's Soul, P.61, (1996).
[10]The circle of *influence* is where proactive people concentrate their efforts. They focus on issues and concerns that they can influence. Their positive energy expands and magnifies, which causes their circle of influence to grow.
[11]Laura Whitworth et al, Co Active Coaching, 2nd edition, p.31 (2007)
[12]Brain Tracy, Goals. P.41, (2003)
[13]Apart from a one sibling who attended my primary school for her final two years.
[14]Amos 3:3, Holy Bible
[15]Pearson, J., & Nelson, P. (2000). An introduction to human communication: understanding and sharing (p. 6). Boston, MA: McGraw-Hill.
[16]The Win/lose paradigm makes everything a competition, making it seem that one person's success must come at the expense of someone else's success.
[17]Stephen Covey's 4th Habit. Think Win/Win
Win/win is a frame of mind and heart that constantly seeks mutual benefit in all human interaction. Agreements and solutions are mutually beneficial and satisfying. It takes a cooperative rather than competitive position. Most people think in terms of strong or weak, win or lose, good cop bad cop, a perception that is based on power and position, rather than on principle. Win/win is based on the principle that there is plenty for everybody and one

person's success is not achieved at the expense or exclusion of the success of others. 7 Habits of Highly Effective People. P.207, Stephen Covey (2004)
[18]When two people with a Lose/Lose paradigm encounter each other, their attitudes can result in nobody winning. With such a mindset, an individual may be willing to take the hit to ensure the other person loses. *If can't win, neither can you!*
[19]Bryn C Collins (1997) Emotional Unavailability
[20]Joyce Meyer (2012) Do Yourself a Favour... Forgive, P.53
[21]http://theconversation.com/bitterness-makes-the-heart-grow-sicker-2832
[22]https://www.newworldencyclopedia.org/entry/Forgiveness
[23]https://www.hopehealstherapy.com/why-rejection-hurts-ways-to-cope-with-rejection
[24]The temptation of self-rejection and the promise of self-acceptance. Maury Joseph PsyD (18.9.2017) www.goodtherapy.org
[25]In general, a vision board helps to clarify and maintain focus on your aspirations. It can be used as an effective vehicle for discovery in your journey towards achieving your dreams and goals.
[26]Dr Myles Munroe, Preparing for Kingdom Experience and expansion (2006)
[27]Psychological Flow captures the positive mental state of being completely absorbed, focused, and involved in your activities at a certain point in time, as well as deriving enjoyment from being engaged in that activity. Perhaps the Flow state, colloquially termed being 'in the zone', is best described by one of the participants interviewed in the earliest stages of 'Flow research' (Csikszentmihalyi and Csikszentmihalyi, 1988: 195): https://positivepsychology.com/what-is-flowo
[28]https://en.wikipedia.org/wiki/Second_wind
[29]Vitiligo is a long-term condition where pale white patches develop on the skin. It's caused by the lack of melanin, which is the pigment in skin.
[30]https://www.verywellmind.com/what-is-personality-2795416
[31]https://www.truity.com/myers-briggs/about-myers-briggs-personality-typing
[32]Privette, G. Defining moments of self-actualization: Peak performance and peak experience, in K. J. Schneider, J. F. T. Bugental, and J. F. Pierson (Eds.). The Handbook of Humanistic Psychology, 161-180; 2001.
[33]A SMART goal is used to guide goal setting. SMART is an acronym that stands for **S**pecific, **M**easurable, **A**chievable, **R**ealistic, and **T**imely. Therefore, a SMART goal incorporates all of these criteria to help focus your efforts and increase the chances of achieving your goal.

INDEX

INDEX continued

ABOUT THE AUTHOR

Suzanne Simmons-Lewis MA, BA Hons, is a qualified executive and personal performance coach with more than two decades' experience in journalism and communications strategy. She delivers a holistic and integrated approach to achieving personal, career and business success through bespoke coaching programmes and consultancy services.

Suzanne works primarily with ambitious, high performing women using her signature Core Identity Model to enable her clients to swap their metaphorical "straight jacket" for a bespoke suit. This helps them to connect with who they really are and create alignment with what they genuinely want. This process is essential as it helps to eliminate stress, burnout, and inner conflict, allowing women to gain the insight and confidence they need to reinvent themselves with intent and step into their unique purpose.

Suzanne's uses warmth, humour, storytelling, spirituality, intuition and creativity in supporting clients to accomplish sustainable, authentic transformation.

CONNECT WITH SUZANNE

Website www.suzannesimmonslewis.com
Email info@suzannesimmonslewis.com
Facebook Suzanne Simmons-Lewis Consultancy
Linkedin Suzanne Simmons-Lewis

Printed in Great Britain
by Amazon

29041896R00195